Chroma: Calanooka

(Constructed Sanity Sequence: III)

CARLIE MARTECE

Published by Castle Mindscape
Copyright © 2021 Carlie Martece
All rights reserved.
ISBN: 978-0-9928716-2-8
All characters appearing in this work are fictitious.
Any resemblance to real persons, living or dead,
is purely coincidental.

For everybody who feels alien.

CONTENTS

Prologue (055) 9

Vivica I (020) (059) 18

Nigel I (028) 23

<u>Perspective One</u>

  1.01 (031) (032) 28

  1.02 (033) (018) (019) (021) 33

  1.03 (035) 39

  1.04 (040 [001]) 43

  1.05 (023) (024) 47

  1.06 (043) 51

  1.07 (044 [003]) 56

  1.08 (048) 61

  1.09 (050) 65

  1.10 (051) 70

  1.11 (060) 74

  1.12 (068) 80

  1.13 (069) 84

  1.14 (076) 89

  1.15 (078) 92

  1.16 (086) 97

  1.17 (087) 101

Vivica II (061) 108

Nigel II (066) 111

Perspective Two

2.01 (036 [007][014]) (037) 117

2.02 (038) 122

2.03 (039 [010]) 127

2.04 (041) (016) (017) (026) (042) 131

2.05 (045) 136

2.06 (046) 141

2.07 (053 [004]) (056) 147

2.08 (071) 150

2.09 (074) 154

2.10 (077) 160

2.11 (080) 165

2.12 (081) (084) 170

2.13 (085) 176

2.14 (091) 186

Vivica III (064) 192

Nigel III (073) 196

Perspective Three

3.01 (022) 200

3.02 (025) 207

3.03 (027) 210

3.04 (029) 215

3.05 (034) (047) (049) 219

3.06 (058) 226

3.07 (062) 232

3.08 (065) 237

3.09 (070) 240

3.10 (072) 244

3.11 (075) (079) 247

3.12 (088) 252

3.13 (090) 254

3.14 (089) (092) 258

3.15 (093) 264

Vivica IV (067) 272

Nigel IV (094) (095) 275

Perspective Four

4.01 (052 [006][008][009][011][012][013][015]) (030) 278

4.02 (054) 285

4.03 (057) (063 [002][005]) 288

4.04 (082) 293

4.05 (083) 295

4.06 (096) (097) (098) 300

4.07 (099) 306

4.08 (100) 309

Vivica V (101) 311

Prologue
Leandra, Cal and Kalakai

(055)

"Lizards ate my breadcrumbs."

Leandra reapplies lip gloss while wishing her legs still functioned. She is unable to update her fetish modelling website due to exhaustion and the continuous screaming of her lower body's nerve endings. Pain signals suggest a grand piano recently fell on her legs in a freak, cartoonish accident, destroying them irreparably. It remains a constant surprise whenever she regards her orange-painted toenails with a view unobstructed by a grand piano, so she distracts herself from cryptic, crushing agony with saccharine dreams of rescue and random declarations involving hungry reptiles. "Lizards ate my breadcrumbs. It's the only explanation."

Cal sits at the parlour table ignoring his laptop, staring out a cracked window and failing to grasp Leandra's latest utterance. "I struggle to process riddles," he reminds his strange sister. If Cal understood surrealism or metaphors, he might say his hyper-feminine sibling was as logical as a bookcase made from syringes and jam. Cal does not understand surrealism. Or metaphors. His sense of humour is dry as the surrounding deadlands, and he wonders at the lack of reptiles near the breadbin.

Lounging on the crumpled sheets of her day bed, Leandra pushes dyed-black, greasy hair away from a face as pale and watery as low-fat mayonnaise. "It's a famous fairy tale..." the shiny-lipped model explains, returning the lid to her petroleum-based cosmetic. "Two siblings, like us, abandoned in uncharted forest-"

"We're in a desert," Cal interjects, squinting at the horizon. Another sandstorm approaches, promising a delightful auditory maelstrom to pound his sensitive eardrums. "We have always lived in the desert. We have never seen a living tree."

"Whatever." Leandra shrugs, dislodging a polyester strap to slide down an achromatic shoulder. "Desert, forest, junkyard, dystopian metropolis... all potential places to be trapped or discarded..."

"That's simply not true," Cal argues, his eyes still fixed on the encroaching tempest. "The surrounding desert and neighbouring dead forest have no visible boundary, suggesting it's impossible to get trapped. As for being discarded, this could happen anywhere if you exist solely as a possession, the only necessary factor being your possessor's sudden disinterest. And the latter settings of junkyard and dystopian metropolis bear no relation to the present narrative. Summerton is a small city with impressive recycling facilities."

Teardrops prick Leandra's bleary eyes. "Let me tell my story!" she pleads. "My hand hurts when I draw, and spoken word is my only remaining release."

"OK." Cal shudders, tapping his fingertips fourteen times on the tabletop. "I'm sorry."

Bitter malice contorts Leandra's features for a bleating instant before disappearing in hallucinatory glitch. "Anyway..." She gulps on self-pity. "Two siblings, exiled by their family in dangerous lands, find a witch's hut made from cookies, candy or possibly crack." She forces a broken laugh from a delicate throat.

"That wouldn't be structurally sound." Cal pulls a frayed cord, closing the blinds as earth fragments begin battering the ancient windows. "Baked goods and recreational drugs will never be adequate hut-building materials. I would advise this foresty sorceress to stop ingesting hallucinogens."

The atmosphere vibrates with electric crackle as Leandra emits the groan of a teenager misunderstood by overbearing parents. She weirdly channels that belligerent post-pubescent vibe, despite being at least thirty. "I never cared for that stupid cottage anyway," she complains. "Made from stuff that causes weight gain or premature ageing... But I loved the breadcrumb metaphor. A lonely girl wanted to be found, so she left a trail for her rescuer. But birds or lizards ate the breadcrumbs. Or the handsome prince had a dietary intolerance, and she couldn't afford gluten-free bread on her measly allowance. Whatever. What I remember is a poor girl left a trail for her rescuer but remained lost regardless. That's me! Except I'm not in a forest. I'm in a weird desert city, alone... Apart from my autistic brother. And rescue is not coming because lizards ate my breadcrumbs."

"Lizards don't eat bread," Cal mutters.

Leandra opens her excessively glossed mouth to reply when the knocking begins with four brisk raps upon the apartment's front door.

"Someone's at the door." Cal closes his laptop and commences rocking. He despises surprises. Who knocks on a door anyway? Who on this dying earth thinks, "Look! A rectangular slab of plastic filling a rectangular hole in a wall, with hinges allowing occupants to enter or leave the dwelling within. I know! I'll fucking knock on it! I've sent no warning of my arrival. Residents might be eating, sleeping, showering, staring at a screen, numbing their consciousness with a repetitive stream of predictable information solely to escape from existential dread... But what they really need, right now, is the wonderful me, knocking on their fucking door!"

"Someone's at the door," Cal repeats, his statement further evidenced by four rapid bangs.

Leandra beams. "Oo, a visitor!"

"Were you expecting anybody?"

"I'll always be waiting for somebody."

"Is that yes or no?"

The knocking continues as Leandra emerges from her nest of orange cushions. "Does it matter?" She winces as she rises, smoothing her creased, peach nightdress as she shuffles toward the hallway. "Both words bear the same meaning to the wrong listener." Her breath rasps as though she is running. Halfway across the room she stops, a stray beam of muted sunlight dissecting her surgically enhanced physique as she raises a scarred ankle to peel a candy wrapper from the sole of a perfectly pedicured foot.

Four more knocks bombard the entrance.

"I'm coming!" Leandra trills. She approaches the doorway, reaching for the lock with delicate fingers.

"Shouldn't we check who's there first?" Cal frets from the parlour. But Leandra ignores her cautious brother and opens the door to the unknown.

The unexpected visitor is a woman in military uniform. She is blue. Azure eyes drill through sandy air to assault Leandra's hesitant smile. Teal lips are pursed with impatience. Stray orange particles fill the cracks in a starched, blue uniform covering a muscular figure stiff with formality and simmering brutality.

That's a lot of words to say she looked like a military fucking Smurf.

"Hi!" Leandra greets her new uniformed friend.

"Leandra," is the visitor's terse response. A statement, not a question.

"That's me!" the sleepy model agrees, leaning against the door following the exertion of walking from the parlour.

"I'm here with a recruitment offer for you and Cal."

Leandra yawns and allows the guest to enter. "Cal! There's a blue army lady here to see us!"

Cal scurries from his seat as Leandra shuts out the storm. He finds his sister leaning against magnolia wallpaper while the bizarre blue arrival wipes sand off her uniform.

"Cal," the newcomer greets him, offering a blue-gloved hand. "I'm Captain Kalakai from Bure Eshpel in the Chroma Sphere System. I'm here to recruit you and Leandra for the Chroman Army."

Confused Cal shakes the offered hand without speaking. His life brims with unspoken rules, as though most humans carry a secret Social Interaction Guidebook. While the neurotypicals are thinking, "Here's an unfamiliar social situation, I'll consult my handy guidebook for the required speech and mannerisms", Cal's internal monologue becomes hysterical screaming. Neurotypicals survive the chaos of most workplaces. Neurotypicals can cope with their regular items changing location in the local grocery store without having a nervous fucking breakdown. So neurotypicals *must* innately know the required social etiquette for greeting a blue military recruitment officer from space.

"Don't worry," Captain Kalakai reassures him. "Most neurotypical humans would be equally bemused by this unexpected situation. Shall we sit?"

"Y... yes?" Cal stammers.

Kalakai strides into the parlour, pausing to command "Join me!" over her shoulder. She sits at the table. Cal's discomfort at Kalakai's apparent telepathy is displaced by relief when she does not sit in his favourite chair.

Leandra limps languidly after Cal, asking, "Can I fix anyone a drink?"

"No. Sit!" Kalakai glares at the tired hostess... the cosmetic-coated countenance framed by tousled curls, the pornstar-proportioned body slouched within a threadbare nightdress. Kalakai shakes her head. Leandra takes the chair to her left, Cal sits to her right, and Kalakai folds her gloved hands on the table. "So, you received our recruitment leaflets."

Cal and Leandra exchange shocked glances. Cal had sat awake clutching the leaflets, re-reading obsessively, amazed at obtaining evidence validating his online research. Leandra had dismissed the contents as raving conspiracy theory. But secretly she shuddered at the alien imagery, phrases which peered into her skull and echoed her strangest dreams. She intended to use one leaflet as a barrier between drug crystals and her useless credit card before racking toxic lines to stimulate herself some lonely evening, but she suspected the alien summons would follow her into oblivion.

"Internal reveries regarding tenuous internet research and solitary drug binges are not the keen response I was hoping for," Kalakai admonishes. "Stop thinking so loud, focus on input, not output, and re-read." She dispenses two further leafless to the gobsmacked hosts. "Is there a problem?"

"Yes," Cal slowly nods. "You can't arrive at somebody's apartment uninvited, read their mind, and expect them to re-read unrequested space army recruitment leaflets without causing some confusion. Also… why are you blue?"

"Because I don't have a boyfriend," murmurs Leandra, who due to lack of attention is peering through the crack in the blinds at retreating sandclouds.

"What?" Cal and Kalakai stare at the confused model.

"Sorry, I lose the thread of conversations." Leandra turns from the filthy window, smiling at Kalakai in a pitiful attempt at endearment. Her eyes are tortured pits of hell.

Kalakai returns her disappointed gaze to Cal. "I told you, I'm from Bure Eshpel in the Chroma Sphere System."

Six seconds pass in awkward silence before Cal's eyes widen. "The blue sphere!"

"Exactly." Kalakai nods. "Due to a powerful dye in our agricultural produce, all Chroma's inhabitants develop colouring to match their sphere of residence. I hail from Bure Eshpel, where seafaring folk dwell on blue islands and vast ocean. You would drown there. With your peachy colouring, you resemble inhabitants of Opree Shengra, a dry sphere of orange, brown and white rock. The Oprish never built ships. They built fancy temples, crowded cities, endless roads traversing their arid globe, but no ships. Because they lack an ocean, and never learned to fly. So we Beshpers are stuck on frag collection, answering these stupid questions."

Leandra graces Cal with a kittenish smile.

"We're on acid, aren't we?"

Kalakai maintains stony silence while Cal ponders this possibility. Several unrealistic events are occurring this afternoon: A blue-skinned space captain appearing on their doorstep... certain grocery items devoured by reptiles... the sandstorm receding after mere minutes...

Kalakai bangs her fist on the table, glaring as Cal flinches. "Considering my appearance and presence 'unrealistic' is insulting," she reminds him. "And lizards don't eat bread. Leandra swapped birds for reptiles in a misinterpreted fairy tale because desert relocation increased the story's relevance to her self-absorption. The desert *does* have birds, but they eat corpses, not starchy, carbohydrate-based foods. And the sandstorm passed quickly because an imminent demonic uprising is disrupting local weather systems. Reckish demons dropped a CRIB on this rock thirty-two years ago. It will soon re-activate."

The siblings stare open-mouthed while Kalakai rants, still suspecting a mischievous enemy has spiked their water supply.

Kalakai groans. "If you *must* internally doubt my presence, please think less loud. I can hear everything."

Cal gulps. "Surprisingly, your being psychic as well as blue does little to make you less hallucinatory."

Kalakai traverses the space between them in a blur of blue annoyance. Cal finds his head inches from the tabletop, the captain's rough hand on his neck, eyes level with the recruitment leaflet.

"Could a hallucination do *this*? Read the information!" Kalakai commands. "And you!" she snaps at Leandra, whose adoring eyes brim with fresh tears.

Cal already memorised the leaflet's contents during dull moments at his tortuous day job.

"But did you believe it?"

"I believe in Chroma! But whenever I discuss the Sphere System with anyone other than Leandra, I get accused of either being insane, or feigning insanity to seek attention. Relishing neither prospect, I begrudgingly stick to respected neurotypical topics, such as television, shopping, and the recent behaviour of mutual acquaintances."

Kalakai releases Cal's neck from her iron grasp. "The parallel universe you access through your mindscape's extra dimension is a recking joke! Look what that stupid, alien society has created... A barely conscious 'model' hooked on humiliating photoshoots for attention, and a social outcast, forced from most workplaces by ableism and managerial abuse. That connected world turns creative and psychic potential into a handicap, trapping you in an antiquated economic system. It's a Kaldamn disgrace!"

A solitary tear traces Leandra's tragic face. "I'm so happy!" she informs her audience.

Kalakai sneers at the emotional model. "Why are you happy?"

"I'm finally being rescued! Maybe lizards didn't eat my breadcrumbs. I just needed to have faith."

"I'm not some hackneyed prince rescuing you from a sugary crack house!"

"Oh, but taking us from Summerton makes you our saviour. This world is a sickly, narcotic prison and I always felt alien."

Kalakai shakes her head. "I'm not here to *save* you."

Cal rubs his sore neck. "Then why *are* you here?"

"I was allocated two frags from this backwater mindscape, and for some inexplicable reason, I was pointed in your direction."

"By whom?"

"By the autistic ruler of this rock, who insisted I take you two rather than the warriors who flank them. OK, *you*..." Kalakai nods at Cal, "at least have your freakish ROM memory. We can use the portable hard drive of your brain for information storage and retrieval within electromagnetic fields where our tech becomes inoperable. But *you*," Kalakai scowls at Leandra, "have no discernible purpose. I'm building an army, not a rehab centre. CRIBs are reactivating across the Mindfields. Without trained soldiers to halt the outbreak, the demons will conquer infinite mindscapes, causing multi-universal genocide. A mindscape under total Reckish control contains no conscience, no hope, no respect for innocent life. Everything pure dies, as lifelight carriers are killed or subjugated and psychopathy reigns supreme. Connected vessels terminate other lives before their designated death date. With countless portal doors still broken, we race against time to save researchers from Reckish-related deconstructions. Due to the inter-connected nature-"

The com screen on Kalakai's wrist starts emitting a grating, repetitive beep. The sound reminds Cal of his alarm clock. It reminds Leandra of a pounding dancefloor anthem.

Kalakai answers the call. "Yes?" she growls into the receiver, before turning a purpler shade of blue.

Leandra shines with the euphoria and excitement of dreams coming true. "Shall we go with Kalakai to join the Chroman Army, Cal?"

Her brother clutches his head and recommences rocking. "I struggle with sudden decisions."

"Recking hell!" Kalakai snaps. "Kaldamn! I'm coming." She terminates the call and glares from anxious Cal to beaming Leandra. "We have an emergency," she informs the unstable siblings. "If you wish to join the Chroman Army, we leave immediately."

Vivica I

(020)

"Fit for a princess!" Sorsha presents the room with a sweep of her arm while terrified Vivica hovers in the doorway. After years fighting for survival in a haunted forest, the family have found a permanent home - a spectacular clifftop mansion with grand windows overlooking the eastern ocean and western woodland. Sorsha allocates Vivica this stunning bedroom in the east wing.

The anxious teen grabs the door frame with trembling hands, mind reeling with strange omens and visual bombardment. "Not. Safe." Vivica's voice emerges as a half-choked whisper. *Opulence. Silk furnishings. Gigantic ocean view. Sun setting on water. Pink pastel clouds. Just for me. To rest and be safe. Safe...*

(bloody talons scrape the windowpane)
Safe. A locked box.
A cupboard.
Safe...

The open sky looms massive and horrifying with vivid beauty. "I can't..." Vivica blanches at the saccharine glow against fuchsia drapes, imagines demons hiding within their folds. She remembers the huge dresser in the hallway and turns to flee down the emerald green carpeted staircase. *Safe.*

"Where are you going, Vivica?" Sorsha yells at the retreating girl's back, her words echoing unheeded across the vast landing.

Vivica reaches the ornate cupboard in the mansion's chequer-tiled hallway and pulls open the heavy oak door. Her previously nomadic family boast few possessions, and this shadowed space sits empty. Plenty of room for a crouching adolescent. The door mercifully has a lock with an iron key, which Vivica grabs before she scrambles inside. She pulls the door closed and locks it behind her.

Safe.

Her breathing rasps as she adjusts to darkness.

Footsteps approach.

"Our demons are dead," Sorsha reminds her. "We're no longer hunted, Vivica! You can rest and be happy."

But her assurances do little for Vivica's foreboding.

Days pass and her mismatched crew of siblings - brave Sorsha, eccentric Doc, fussy Nell, feisty Jessie, crafty Dodger, studious Lisa and boisterous Sunny - all take turns to entice the gifted but disturbed Vivica from her hiding place. Vivica presses her palms against her ears and lets her mind drift to faraway lands. Eventually, her family tire of their futile attempts at engagement.

Vivica now lives in the cupboard.

(059)

A further descent into isolated lunacy, and three winters have passed since the family gained the mansion. Years resemble days despite containing minutes vast as centuries. Sorsha removes the lock from the cupboard door, saying, "We need to check you're alive."

Vivica cringes against the back panel whenever the door is cruelly opened. A nocturnal creature, she emerges when painful daylight ends, to wander lavish rooms like the loneliest ghost. Morning delivers sensory overload and she retreats to hiding, her head wracked with violent visions. *Confusion. Words jumbling like ants at a subterranean disco. Black, white, grey ants. Crawling, disappearing, reappearing, hissing... In splintered moments, a crystalline picture emerges through clouds of static chaos. A demon composed of grey scales, vicious talons and scarlet eyes emerging from the forest. A classroom where bullies grin to expose mediocre dentistry. A monstrous horde surrounding the mansion. Nothing.*

Tortured Vivica struggles to breathe. Terror from the night-time forest remains lodged within her soul. *Life is panic. Breath is ragged and endlessly happens regardless of my desire to cease existing. Fleeting pictures vanish before contents can be processed.* The tormented girl regards herself in third person, crouching in her weird lair. The dots return to obscure her vision accompanied by that incessant hiss, and she could be crouching anywhere, her body a crumpled ball of aches and fear.

Another snapshot. Cupboard viewed from chequer-tiled hallway, left of the mansion's massive front door. A safe place. Like a safe. Not like a place. Resembling more a location in time and concept. Dreamworld. Constructed reality. Nothing. Silence becomes louder. A mansion at her disposal, Vivica remains in stifling confinement, her hidden visage a blotchy mess. A crack in the cupboard door glints a thread of silver light against an ancient razor blade.

BANG!

A boom shakes the dwelling's stone foundations. Vivica cowers in self-inflicted confinement. *Why did Sorsha remove my precious lock?* Now anyone can open the cupboard door and assault her with intrusive light, sound and social interaction. *In every future, the Reckish return.* Vivica cannot lock the door against their poisonous fangs. *When they reach the mansion...*

Footsteps. Human boots, not talon-bearing claws. "That crazy bastard," Sorsha mutters nearby.

BANG!

Beneath the chequered hallway, a laboratory occupies the mansion's basement. Vials, cogs, levers, beakers filled with colourful liquids and strange fogs all clutter the wooden tables. "Woohoo!" Doc allows himself an excited little dance, his bizarre experiments reaching a noisy but satisfying conclusion. Crouched in her hiding space, Vivica's field of awareness can float to any location within the mansion. She views the basement from above and Doc's exuberance almost prompts a self-conscious smile into the gloom.

Sorsha's footsteps hurry to the basement door as the booms continue. "Have you cracked it?"

"Wellingtons!" the mad scientist exclaims. "Cracked it? I've bazinga'd it! Decimated its delirious disastrousness!"

Sorsha bangs on the basement door. "Have you created second gen anti-Reckish weaponry or not? Please tell me you didn't commandeer our basement just to further your eccentric lunacy with bonus explosions?"

"Eeee!" Sunny squeals.

Vivica receives this latest auditory onslaught from the comfort of her cupboard. The word "comfort" is used generously here. Her immediate environment contains no light, no music, just angry noise, and the minimum level of oxygen required for survival. Sorsha's voice comes from three meters away, Sunny's squeal from two, Doc's cheers from approximately fourteen meters... it makes no difference. Each utterance rings equally loud, echoing through airy spaces, barely muffled by Vivica's wooden enclosure. She shudders as another boom rattles the windowpanes.

"Don't blow up my mansion!" Sorsha shouts.

"Yes, ma'am!" is Doc's yelled response from underground.

"And you didn't answer my question!"

Vivica presses her palms to her ears, wishing her family would stop shouting, the walls would stop shaking, and everything would go away. The futures in which demons return to claim her soul seem less bleak. Death would at least bring blessed silence. When the booms finally cease, Vivica lowers a trembling hand to grab her trusty blade. Blood and pain will deliver fleeting release.

The cabinet door flies open.

"SORSHA! Vivica's gonna cut AGAIN!"

Vivica squints, turning her unwashed face toward the blinding hallway. Dodger hunches on a black tile, munching a stolen apple and casting an amused glance at his sister's eternal misery. Massive black and white ceramic squares form a living chessboard around him. Vivica winces at excess light and visual information. Sorsha is across the hallway, stood on an obsidian tile near the basement door.

"Eeeeee!" Sunny stops crawling across an ebony tile to squeal at Vivica, who finds most communication a source of torment. The cupboard-dwelling teenager becomes overwhelmed by the sudden, all-consuming wish that her noisy family would die. *Sorsha honestly believed an over-lit fairy princess bedroom could cure the hell of my existence. Sunny will not cease the hideous squealing that splits my skull open. Dodger's just a cheeky, thieving twat. They should all disappear.* Vivica pictures the black squares as void instead of solid matter, with Dodger, Sunny and Sorsha falling through spaces between white tiles and disappearing into the nothing.

"We're not going anywhere, Vivica!" Sorsha remains on a still-solid tile, eyes blazing.

Vivica flinches. *Get out of my head!*

BOOM!

Ornaments fall from an overhead shelf, metal trinkets with a jarring twinkle as they clatter against stone.

"Doc, I swear to God!" Sorsha bangs her fist on the basement door.

Sunny squeals again, delighted by chaotic entertainment.

Sorsha sighs. "Sunny, stop squealing! Dodger, stop stealing apples from the kitchen, Nell needs those for a pie! Vivica, *please* stop hiding in that damn cupboard with your nightmares and poisoned memories... I don't know how to fix you! And DOC! Have you created next gen demon-killing weaponry, or not?"

Doc yells from his lair, "The weapons are ready, m' lady!"

The front door opens and Jessie peers from her porch vantage point as guttural roars echo beyond the mansion grounds. "We'll need them! The demons are back!"

Nigel I

(028)

Nigel Paul Charlesworth works as a checkout clerk in Sunny Bargains convenience store and lives with his grandmother in a two-bedroom apartment near the railway station. There is nothing remarkable about his appearance, personality or existence. If you asked an acquaintance to describe him, they would shrug and say, "I dunno. He's just a guy." Nigel's life is so dull, he sometimes wonders whether he is real or a background character in somebody else's story.

At four o'clock one morning, a supply train wakes Nigel from dreamless slumber. *They're only supposed to send passers this early!* He inwardly fumes, shuffling from his bed on a begrudging quest to urinate. Those blasted trains remain a constant source of puzzlement and annoyance. *Where do they come from? Where do they go? What cotton-eyed lunatic designed a one-way rail track across the desert?*

And what is with those creepy robots?

He observes the metallic humanoids as they exit the train carrying massive, plastic cartons of water to hydrate riverless, rainless Summerton. Through the bathroom window's frosted glass, they resemble long-limbed smudges, their reflective surfaces shining orange in the glow from sodium streetlamps. Tiny flashing eyes create the barest blur of indigo.

Nigel leaves the bathroom without washing his hands.

"Why are you awake so early, Nigel?" his grandmother calls from her bedroom across the hall.

"They sent a damned stopper! At four in the morning!" Nigel huffs as he returns to his bedroom.

"Language, Nigel!" the elderly lady admonishes. "We are grateful for the SilverMen."

He swears under his breath, returning to grasp another three hours' sleep before work. But those bothersome robots continue their infernal stomping. *Grateful for the SilverMen? What's the point in them bringing supplies for Summerton residents if they're not fairly distributed? I work full time, and after paying rent, bills and groceries I've barely enough cash for a few comics and beers. Now I have to work after being kept awake by their racket. The SilverMen don't bring me shit!* His internal ranting blocks all efforts at returning to unconsciousness.

Nigel stops chasing sleep at dawn and rises to grab breakfast.

His grandmother is already in the tiny kitchen, making toast. "Did you sleep well, Nigel?"

The sullen man retrieves a chipped, ceramic bowl from the cupboard above the drainer. "Nope. They shouldn't send stoppers so early. I hate this city!"

Ancient Mrs Charlesworth shudders at this heresy. "Summerton is a wonderful city! The SilverMen bring everything we need. All hard workers can enjoy a comfortable lifestyle."

Nigel fills his bowl with rainbow-coloured, sugar-loaded cereal. "I work hard and can't afford my own apartment."

His grandmother sighs while spreading jam with dainty cutlery. "You should be thankful you're not homeless. After your mother died, and your alcoholic father-"

"That's another thing!" Nigel bangs the cereal box on the counter. "Why is *anybody* homeless? The SilverMen built surplus housing and deliver enough food and water for each resident. Yet some go hungry while apartments sit empty and rich families throw excess food in the trash. Is that fair?"

Mrs Charlesworth carries her toast-laden plate to the dining table. "You're always like this after deliveries... Complaining about how Summerton's run... What if the SilverMen stopped delivering? Then you'd *really* have reason to complain! We'd all die of thirst and hunger."

Nigel follows her to the table. "But don't you wonder where the supplies come from? If our benefactors know their gifts are sold at rip-off prices while some residents starve?"

"That's enough, Nigel!"

Grandma never listens. Nobody does! This whole city is anaesthetised, sleepwalking through a mediocre existence, never questioning reality. And nobody ever leaves! The roads go around this damned place in circles. The surrounding land is unwalkable. No humans can board the trains, which only travel in one direction... An electric hiss heralds the arrival of the morning's third delivery train.

Could I...?

"There's no need to sulk." Mrs Charlesworth stands, joints clicking, and brings her plate to the sink.

"I'm just thinking, Grandma." Nigel stares into garish swirls of rainbow colouring in the remains of his milk.

"You're thinking your life is unfair," his grandmother scolds. "When you have shelter, water, food in your belly..."

I'm thinking of ways to leave this damned city!

"I might leave for work early! Take a longer route for some extra exercise." Nigel stands, stretches, then walks away leaving his bowl on the table.

"Well, don't forget your scarf and goggles! There's another sandstorm forecast."

"I won't, Grandma!" Nigel grabs his outdoor gear and exits the apartment, stepping into a dim corridor.

What the hell am I doing? He shivers, overwhelmed with an ominous sense of destiny beyond mortal comprehension. His breathing deepens as he contemplates the brazen task ahead. As he exits the apartment complex, his nerves begin to falter but his feet continue their mission regardless.

He approaches the railway platform. A shiny, metal sign says No Humans Beyond This Point.

Am I approaching my execution?

Nigel continues walking, over the line, past the security cameras. Two SilverMen carrying supplies into a warehouse ignore his audacious approach. The train idles on Summerton platform, side doors open, crates piled high within. *Am I the first human to get this close?*

Nigel is three meters from the open doors when a SilverMan emerges from between stacks of crates. Nigel freezes and tries not to defecate as six and a half feet of gleaming metal strides towards him. *Do SilverMen kill trespassers?* Nigel gulps as the machine's cold indigo eyes flicker in the blocked doorway.

"Can I speak with whoever supplies the food, please?" the terrified trespasser rasps, nervous tension constricting his voice to the barest whisper.

The robot responds by stepping onto the platform and grabbing Nigel's arm in a vice-like grip. The petrified clerk wonders if this metal creature intends to break his arm, but instead the machine continues its stride, marching Nigel off the platform. "Hey, I was joking!" He scrambles to keep pace as his arm screams agony. "I can walk myself off the platform! I won't come back!"

A passing businessman stops to observe the commotion. He tuts, shaking his head. "Can't you read, man? It says No Humans Beyond This Point!"

Nigel continues being marched off the platform like a humiliated child. After delivering him to the sidewalk the robot strides back to the train, while the attempted stowaway stands on the curb, nursing his bruised arm and battered ego. Nigel mutters, "I hate this lousy city."

The smart-suited businessman steps closer. "What were you thinking? Everybody knows the platform is forbidden. You're lucky Sheriff Grey isn't here!"

Nigel kicks his worn-out shoe across the gravel, raising knee-high dust clouds. "Why have unboardable trains? And why don't our roads leave the city? What's beyond here? Who's sending these unevenly distributed supplies?"

A beige-clad woman with a bag-laden pram stops to hear Nigel's questions. The businessman is already backing away.

"I don't know this madman! I was merely reprimanding him for trespassing!" The suited gentleman raises his voice for the benefit of nearby SilverMen, an unnecessary gesture around machines with hyper-sensitive hearing.

The busy mother tuts and shakes her head. "Hard workers can earn a decent life! Only lazy, entitled people complain about uneven distribution." Her child starts crying. "See what's happened! You have created negative energy with your awful complaining! You want to get a job and stop bothering the SilverMen who generously deliver everything we need."

Nigel regards the well-dressed mother, then peers down at his own threadbare attire. "I have a job! It barely pays enough for survival, let alone fancy new clothes. Hard work doesn't always pay."

The woman glares daggers at this feckless ingratitude. "Well, you should have worked harder at school, shouldn't you? Hard workers get better jobs." At this her baby begins to scream, providing her cue to leave. She trundles off, muttering about lazy ingratitude.

Nigel raises his cheerless face toward the apartment complex where he has lived with his grandmother for twenty years. The old lady stares from the parlour window in horror. Nigel hates his life. He turns and trudges toward Sunny Bargains, hoping he has time to read comics before store opening. The only bright spot on his grim horizon is the possibility of that hot model with the silicone cleavage stopping by. She sure is a welcome addition to the area! She often needs Nigel's help with the scanning machines, the silly creature, so sleepy-eyed and confused, always dropping her meagre purchases and fumbling with loose change.

Perspective One
Leandra

1.01

(031)
Grey monsters with razor claws clutch at her consciousness and Leandra gulps back anxiety's rising nausea. "You don't believe in premonitions, do you Cal?"

Cal looks up from his laptop, tapping the table fifteen times. "Premonitions are by-products of an overactive imagination. Like dreams."

Leandra yawns with a laboured stretch. "You're probably right." She rises and begins her morning routine before the midday apartment viewing. The drowsy model has two main reasons for desiring a private residence. Firstly, the helpful cowboy's commune is divided over three floors, with Leandra's quarters in the attic, bathroom on the first floor and kitchen at ground level. Stairs are Leandra's worst enemy after loneliness, and Cal frequently finds her snoozing near a stairway after completing another gruelling climb. If her energy depletes further, she may be forced to remain in the attic, pissing in a bucket, which will seriously make her question her life choices. Secondly, she is rarely well enough to attend professional photoshoots and may soon have to add webcamming to her professional repertoire. This may be awkward in a bedroom where drunkards loiter outside the doorway, ruining audio capture by screaming at the helpful cowboy to order pizza.

(032)
Three hours later, the siblings are stood outside Telf Hall. This battered building looms over a traffic intersection in an under-developed segment of Summerton centre, forming a U shape around a shadowed courtyard. The ground floor contains Six

Herbs Diner, a dilapidated eatery with lowered shutters and a "Closed Until Further Notice" sign fluttering in the sandy breeze. An empty apartment awaits Cal and Leandra on the second floor, accessible by a metal staircase leading to a balcony walkway.

"My brother is mentally disabled and can't handle excess noise," Leandra tells landlord Rodny Dinglall in the apartment hallway, leaning against a magnolia wall to ease her aching legs. "Our top priority is a quiet home." She strains to detect nuisance sounds but hears nothing.

The property owner reassures her. "Don't worry, it's definitely quiet here."

Leandra limps through bland rooms, checking for roaches. The unfurnished parlour, kitchen, bathroom and two bedrooms all appear clean and un-infested. "What about that diner downstairs?"

"They're closed indefinitely," Rodny assures her. "But when they were open, none of my tenants complained. They found the on-site diner convenient."

The thought of an open diner reminds Leandra of dates, which aggravates the incessant hollow ache of terminal singledom. "Great! Well, thanks for showing us round. I'll get back to you after my next viewing," she lies. There is nowhere else, because she and Cal are trapped... Unable to work in their present environment, unable to secure new lodgings without employment contracts.

The prospective landlord thanks Leandra before walking her and Cal to the exit. They descend rusty stairs, cross the courtyard, then buzz open the sliding grille to step onto the curb of a dusty roadside.

Leandra catches her breath as Rodny climbs into his car. The smiling man departs with a final wave. Leandra responds with a forced smile then nudges her brother. "What did you think? You said nothing the entire viewing."

"Unfamiliar social situations are overwhelming. It takes time to crack the algorithm for new conversations." Cal's blank eyes regard empty windows beyond the shaded courtyard. "I thought it was an apartment."

Leandra clutches the iron fence, stifles a yawn. "But could we be happy there?"

Cal taps his arm nine times.

"My happiness is dependent on the uncontrollable factor of external noise. The dwelling gave an initial impression of being quiet, which is hopefully an accurate indicator of its typical state. Your happiness is dependent on whether you have a partner and whether the party crowd are deigning to include you in their debauched escapades. A residence where you feel safe and empowered may bring stability through emotional independence. So yes, the possibility for happiness exists. But excess unknown variables prevent me from providing a definite answer to your question."

Leandra sighs. "So, what you're saying is maybe."

"Yes," Cal nods. "I'm saying maybe."

Leandra gazes at their potential future home. The demonic visions flickering behind her peripheral awareness suggest this dwelling may prove troublesome. Maybe it is the lack of elevator. The apartment's parlour window is cracked, with dark lines forming lightning shapes in the glass, filled with sand grains from past storms. The building's sides are bleached and weathered. "Like a husk of something long ago discarded," Leandra muses. "I can relate." Although Telf Hall's decaying, haunted aura brings less a sense of kinship, more a warning of suppressed menace.

"If you are personally identifying with a cheap apartment above an unused diner," Cal says, "happiness may be less obtainable than you hope."

Leandra emits a bitter laugh, then asks Cal to take her home. She requires sleep.

Cal spends the evening searching the com network for another landlord who will risk renting to the jobless. Leandra drifts in restless slumber and hears frantic typing through fevered dreams. Each keystroke becomes a raindrop, hitting her delicate skull, frizzing her hair. She carries no umbrella because this arid city knows no rain. But now she is drowning.

She wakes to find her besieged body has sweated through scratchy blankets. "Did you find anywhere else?"

Cal regards her with hyper-deranged eyes of sleep deprivation. "I can't work in an unpredictable environment. Landlords won't offer suitable homes to the unemployed. This is our vicious, circular prison."

Leandra gulps. The prospect of Telf Hall brings a sick foreboding, like drifting untethered toward destruction. But poverty limits their options. She forces herself into a seated position. "Have you formed an opinion on Telf Hall?"

Cal sits near the window, silhouetted against a blank slab of cloudless sky. "I struggle to process new information in unfamiliar social contexts. Maybe a second visit will help."

He types into his laptop, which beeps a response moments later. "Rodny Dinglall has offered a second viewing at lunchtime today."

Leandra completes her morning routine, takes a nap to recover, then manoeuvres her aching body downstairs. Cal follows, softly hyperventilating while passing through the commune's noise and clutter. Leandra reassures him, "Tidiness and peace exist for us somewhere." This half-truth tastes of acrid lies.

After Cal grabs his trusty peaked cap, the siblings exit the commune and begin the tiresome trek into Summerton centre. They cannot afford a taxi. Leandra leans on Cal as they descend identical, sloping streets toward their possible new home. This could be any First World city of the early twenty-first century. Except they are in the desert and everything is dead.

They pass the station. Everything is familiar, yet nothing is. A train idles on the railway platform, its SilverMen crew delivering clean, bottled water and uncontaminated food from beyond the mountains. Leandra shivers at the tall, humanoid robots with glowing indigo eyes. "They look dangerous."

Cal shakes his head. "They bring food and water. This suggests benevolence."

"But where do they get the food and water?"

"I don't know," Cal admits. "Whenever I ask the com network such questions, the laptop crashes."

They reach Telf Hall, and Rodny Dinglall exits his car to lead them inside for a second viewing.

"Are you sure it's quiet here?" Leandra checks again.

Mr Dinglall nods, his eyes fixed over her shoulder. "I had no complaints from previous tenants."

This might have been true. Although, judging from the numerous different names printed on mail that later fell through the letterbox, indicating a high turnover of tenants, this may have been the biggest lie since ice cream manufacturers began writing "Contains six servings" on the side of frozen tubs.

"When can I sign?" Leandra asks, and cruel laughter echoes through dimensions as she limps toward the unravelling of her precarious sanity.

1.02

(033)
Third night in Telf Hall and Leandra has barely stopped sleeping. Smudged with days-old cosmetics, she sprawls within tangled sheets in the parlour on a mattress stolen from a dumpster. This mattress still boasted an intact plastic cover when Cal found it, so hopefully it will not give her chlamydia.

Her favourite dream begins…

(018)
Leandra's waking memory insists she has never left Summerton's suffocating streets, but her dreams depict a crackling campfire in the deadlands beyond city borders. Her genderless warrior twin sits beside her. Leandra welcomes the feeling of safety and contentment inspired by this brutal sibling's presence, while the fire warms her aching limbs.

She glimpses the witch through amber flames. The vengeful sorceress perches on a rock, staring into flickering light that makes her dark-robed body sporadically glitch into the gloom. This sinister creature fails to inspire her usual terror thanks to Leandra's fierce protector. The model gazes at ancient stars and giggles. "Enraged enemies will follow with fresh ammunition… *Our* only weapons are wit and courage."

The witch sneers. "This impending battle requires more than motivation and imaginative brilliance."

The warrior chuckles. "Doesn't everything?"

Beyond the flames, the witch glows with unnatural light for the briefest instant of grim lightning. "The key lies broken," the spooky one declares. "Our ferocity smashed the lock. Underground forces will rise, a rabid mob fuelled by self-righteous delusion. We require heavy weaponry."

Leandra pays scant attention to these predictions of doom. Life remains an elaborate cosmic joke, but her non-identical twin has returned and will always save her. She views distant constellations, basking in an aura of redemption.

The fighter in the battered pinstripe suit yawns and stretches beside Leandra. "Where do you propose we obtain heavy weaponry?"

In the shadows, dry scales slither over crumbling rocks. The witch raises the corners of her mouth while her eyes remain cold. Her disdainful voice informs her underlings, "I prepared a bunker in the mountains south-west of here. Petroglyph Cave. If we march during sunrise, we can arrive before the desert scorches. Get six hours' sleep now. I will wake you both before the dawn."

Leandra smiles. "I'm done with sleeping."

"Fine," snaps the witch. "You keep watch while your devoted twin obtains much-needed rest."

"What will *you* do?" Leandra wonders, but the witch has vanished and beyond the fire is nothing.

The warrior yawns again, closes heavy lidded eyes. "See you at dawn, sunshine!"

A protective arm curls around Leandra's waist as her warrior leans a sculpted face into a folded, battered jacket. The oily sky glistens with strange lights above the two recent escapees. Sporadic breezes tumble layers of complicated whispers, delivering the gunpowder scent of distant violence. Leandra watches her beloved twin breathe in heavy slumber. This warrior is her missing piece. In Summerton she has Cal for company, who has good intentions but cannot save her. But this unconscious sibling on shifting sand in uncharted desert dreams would massacre the world for her. Leandra continues smiling as she throws another branch onto the fire.

(019)
Night passes, six hours compressed into a moment of dreamtime. The witch returns beyond the flames, her imperious

gaze burning brighter than morning embers. "Dawn approaches. You may leave the fire's protection."

The warrior jolts awake, hurriedly checking Leandra is still alive. Visual confirmation of her living presence inspires the fiercest grin. Clad in a torn shirt, the warrior stretches strong arms toward the lightening sky.

Leandra attempts to stand. Her thighs scream agony as though all muscle fibres are severed, and atrophied limbs buckle beneath her. The warrior scrambles upright, offering a strong arm. "Let me help you." While her athletic sibling takes half her bodyweight, Leandra can stay upright. She sighs. Her legs do not function when she is awake, why would a dream be different?

The witch regards Leandra's struggles without expression, clothed in black like a haughty wraith. "If you master 'nesis, you won't need legs to walk."

Leandra asks, "Who's Master Neesis?"

Her pinstripe-suited sibling snorts.

The witch tosses her ebony curls. "Come. It should be three hours' walk to the bunker, but with you half-crippled, the journey will take longer."

The warrior stares beyond the witch at the hazy horizon. "What about desert storms?"

Eddies of sand make miniature tornadoes as the witch's laugh pierces the air like a glinting dagger. She says, "I *am* the storm. I am the scorpion, the spider and the snake. I am the deadliest creature in this desert."

"I can't see how you being a sinister pet shop will protect us from flying boulders," the warrior quips, before the timeline jumps again with a reel of static and vertigo.

The three fugitives stand in a concrete bunker behind a secret turn in a cave where ancient petroglyphs decorate russet walls. A humming generator powers a single electric light. An arsenal of vicious weaponry gleams in metal cradles... guns, bombs, knives, swords, and torture contraptions beyond Leandra's comprehension. Surrounded by stockpiled mechanical cruelty, the witch grins, dark purple lips forming a crescent moon against her alabaster complexion. "These treasures will aid the impending slaughter."

Leandra shudders, staggers from the bunker to the cave, seeking daylight, leaning her frail body against bumpy walls. The cave's entrance lies halfway up a mountain, providing stunning views of the desert. Leandra spots civilisation in the mountain's morning shadow. Summerton - the compact city surrounded by poisoned earth. She should be sleeping there, not standing here, grasping rough stone to maintain balance. The witch's breath chills her neck. Leandra flinches and says, "Friends in Summerton might help us."

The witch's response is further mocking laughter. She grabs Leandra's shoulder, long fingernails digging into weak flesh, and spins the terrified girl around.

Leandra almost jolts awake from shock, but a fierce gaze like two stabs of electricity pulls her back into the dream.

"Rescue is not coming!" The witch rasps her harsh declaration. "Don't you understand? You learn to fight, or you *die* in this desert."

Leandra shivers from terror and cold, the mountain air permeating the warrior's loaned jacket.

Her defender stomps toward the cave entrance. "I will protect her!" declares the warrior, glaring at the witch, scraps of their dusty shirt clinging to muscular arms.

The witch repeats nefarious laughter. "Unless this wretch learns to defend herself, our enemies will always break her. She is our collective's weakest link. You cannot guard her forever."

Leandra gulps. "I wish I was powerful like you two, but my body is hopelessly weak and broken."

The dry ground trembles and Leandra nearly wakes again, but the witch clenches her shoulder tight. Waves of malice emanate from the crazy sorceress to batter ancient walls. She is the earthquake. Her hatred vibrates every substance, eyes shining like pools of petrol. A piece of cave ceiling splinters and crashes down, narrowly missing Leandra's head as the malevolent elder cackles.

As the shaking finally subsides, the aura of evil dissipates into the late morning air. The witch indulges in a slow, catlike grin. "*My* body is weak and broken. I am still dangerous."

The warrior kicks the fallen rock away from Leandra and a prehistoric carving crumbles to dust. "Now we know who to call if we need Halloween pets, or find ourselves woefully short of earthquakes. Great job on fucking up this cave though! And destroying prehistoric artwork!"

The witch turns to face the horizon, awaiting her beloved enemies. "It is time for a new legacy."

Leandra folds her arms to keep her borrowed jacket with missing buttons closed. "I'm cold and my legs hurt. And I can't make earthquakes with my brain."

"Never mind the spooky bint, I've made you a nest," the warrior consoles her.

Leandra lets herself be walked to a pile of bedding within view of the sun, sheltered from the high-altitude breeze. The warrior tells her, "I found pens and sketchbooks too. If you're not ready to fight, you can sit and draw."

Time fragments further as Leandra sketches.

The witch glitches between Petroglyph Cave and another realm. The warrior exercises daily. Leandra sits as comfortably as her aching body will allow, drawing her visions, beautiful creatures lost on the sand while demons approach from cracks in the landscape.

(021)
Time stitches itself together in a clunky edit and months have passed without war. The creepy crone hobbles haggard circles, using a walking stick with demon eyes carved into an ornate

handle. "My enemies know I'm here! Why won't those cowards fight?" Her hair lies dishevelled while countless wrinkles adorn her bitter visage, a forgotten woman withering in obscurity.

The warrior glances up, remarks, "Your baiting got no ratings!" then returns to doing push-ups.

Food supplies run low. The warrior goes hunting but returns with shoplifted food. "I didn't want to kill anything, but I found a store at the edge of town with weak security."

Leandra and her warrior snack on stolen goods. The ground shakes. The fading witch can no longer quake the earth, but trains sporadically rumble through the mountain, emerging from an unlit tunnel then off into the desert, passing through Summerton on their way to a distant outpost.

1.03

(035)
I wish Professional Disaster was a legitimate career path. I could be CEO of Disaster Inc. and provide high-quality trainwreck services to voyeuristic clientele.

Leandra soon discovers Telf Hall has no reliable access to the com network. Her plans of camwhoring to afford the extortionate rent swirl down the drain into oblivion, chasing the last verified sightings of her self-esteem and dignity. "But everywhere has com network access! This is barbaric!" she wails on AudioChat, slumped on her dumpster mattress.

The network spokesperson patiently explains, "Telf Hall is a heritage building. Its thick walls block transmitted signal, and drilling cable holes is banned."

"*How* is this a heritage building? It's awful!" Leandra scans the room, compiling a mental checklist of depressing features: the cracked windows, wonky blinds, ceiling fan with its ancient engine rattle, and poor Cal, the disturbed young man rocking in the corner.

"Because of its age," the network spokesperson says. "Telf Hall was formerly a poorhouse."

Leandra terminates the call, unsure whether to dissolve into desperate tears or laughter. *We've landed in a Cashdamn poorhouse! The irony. And stuck with intermittent access to the com network.*

Stupid old buildings! Structures get old and acquire venerated status, their unsightly walls now worthy of respect despite termites and loose plaster. Damaged windows cannot be replaced by modern synthaglass because that would "ruin the building's character". Better to leave residents with sandy homes from cracked glass than alter the appearance of something ancient. Imagine if humans were treated the same! "I'm sorry, we can't offer cosmetic surgery, you are a heritage human and your crumbling form must retain its character." So many plastic surgeons would be out of work! Or stuck doing medical surgery that stops injured people from dying.

"I won't be able to camgirl here, I've no idea how we'll afford this apartment. We should never have left the helpful cowboy's commune..." Leandra realises Cal's hands are still clamped over his ears. "CAL! I SAID-"

"I hear you," Cal mutters, clenching his skull with bloodless fingers.

Leandra groans through a fatigue wave, forcing her charcoal-ringed eyes open. "I could try being an escort..."

"DON'T!" Cal exclaims. He smacks his head twice with a flat palm. "I will find a job." The way he shakes violently while digging fingernails into his temples definitely suggests Employee of the Year.

Leandra frowns. "Can you work with your social disability?" Another delusion is crumbling: the notion that she and Cal could change their surroundings and somehow everything would be OK. Her lower body's nerves echo the pain of internal screaming. "What kinda job could you get, Cal?"

Her timid brother removes his right palm from his ear and taps his left arm six times while he responds. "The Employment Office have pronounced me Work Capable because I can walk short distances and use the toilet unaided. Walking is not a job. Nor is toilet usage. Unless..."

Leandra shakes her head. "I told you! Camming is not an option with this shonky network connection."

"Not that!" Cal insists. "Several acquaintances have mentioned how lucky I am compared to the *actually* disabled, who cannot manage personal care. Some have suggested that helping the Work Incapable with their daily struggles might show me how fortunate I am. It might be rewarding."

The model gasps. "*Care* work?! Bathing people and cleaning up shit? That sounds depressing, not rewarding." Leandra the romantic dreamer fails to grasp how assisting a disabled person's toilet trips could provide anything other than misery. She craves beauty. *If daily existence fails to resemble a glamorous movie, why live?*

"Rewarding in the sense of making a positive difference to another human's life," Cal replies.

"But it's so disgusting..." Leandra slides back toward unconsciousness, seeking pleasant dreams to bring relief from hideous reality. Instead she finds nightmares. Ashen monsters chase through unlit streets, roaring threats of mortal violence. Scarlet eyes radiate malice and remind her she is running low on red nail varnish. Insanity and poverty are so inconvenient.

When she wakes an hour later, Cal remains rooted to his spot near the window, hunched in tense contortion. Leandra forces words from a dry throat. "Why are you covering your ears and rocking, Cal? Still thinking about care work?"

Cal regards his awakened sister with wide-eyed anguish. "Can't you hear them?"

"Hear who?"

"Workers with power tools in the basement diner!"

"Oh. I thought that was hypnopompic hallucination. My dreams are weird." The sound of heavy scraping metal, suggesting a war between giant robots, becomes more noticeable once Leandra's nightmares fade. Sporadic, testosterone-laden yells rise above the din.

"No, no, no, this cannot be happening! NOOOOOO!" Cal cries in over-stimulated hysteria.

"It's OK," Leandra assures her traumatized brother. "I will have a word."

Cal gulps a frantic lungful. "Which word? You need one that conveys, 'Oh please for the love of everything sacred make it stop!' in a manner that reflects the urgency of this situation!"

Leandra nods. "Help me down the stairs. I'll see what I can do." She stands and smooths her crumpled dress. She leans on her trembling brother as the pair exit the apartment, descend the rusty stairs and approach the infernal racket.

Six Herbs Diner's shutters are raised, and staff operate bulky machinery in a fit of renovation. "We're not open yet!" a workman yells as Leandra limps closer.

"How long will you be making this noise? My brother is autistic and needs a quiet environment."

"Just a couple of days!" The oil-smeared man grins. "Then we'll be operating a twenty-four-hour diner, so it's not getting much quieter!"

Mute with shock, the siblings turn back toward the staircase. As brute construction rends the air apart, Cal collapses to the ground and curls foetal as leaden dust clouds drift across Leandra's vision. Workmen chuckle at the disabled man's childlike behaviour and continue welding, hammering and yelling.

Unable to stand unassisted, Leandra lowers herself down beside Cal. *Twenty-four hours of racket a day. Even if we rig a decent com network connection, there'll be no avoiding background noise. And Cal, with his hyper-sensitive hearing, will lose his mind...*

Broken in the dirt and choking back hysteria she remarks, "Everything is on fire."

1.04

(040)
Life continues to be dreadful... but alcohol is a thing!

As Telf Hall becomes noisier than the siblings' worst nightmares, Leandra messages Rodny Dinglall. "Would you release me from the contract if I provide medical evidence of the noise making my autistic brother suicidal?"

"A contract is a contract," Rodny replies, before recommending a suicide hotline.

Cal secures a care job despite his waning sanity, and Leandra spends weeks alone in cacophonous hell, barely conscious. When her brother's first paycheque arrives, she can go clubbing. Dancefloors recharge her, as though clouds of free energy drift across the crowded space, while Leandra's addiction-prone genetics make alcohol a stimulant. She considers becoming a high-functioning alcoholic. Only problem is, she is not high-functioning.

Ocorropinta nightclub squats north of the tracks in Summerton centre. Vodka is crazy cheap, probably diluted with paint thinner and not fit for human consumption. *Just as well I'm barely human!*

Cal escorts Leandra to the raised metal shutters of the club entrance then returns home to continue his interstellar research, leaving his sister to show her identification to surly bouncers.

Leandra tries not to tremble as she enters the industrial gloom. Familiar faces surround her, yet the lonely girl's prevailing mood is paranoid alienation. Club scene interaction is a curious mixture of historical court etiquette and a cut-throat version of high school. She recently heard the party crews hated her. Fortunately, a few kind revellers are sweet enough to overlook her lowly social status and bid her welcome.

"Magneto!" Leandra spots her occasional fetish photographer. "This is a surprise!"

"Ah, Leandra!" Magneto Drunes returns her friendly hug. "After the Oilies gig I fancied staying for the clubnight."

"Was the gig good?"

"Yes, fantastic! I know the vocalist. Amazing voice! But I was hoping to catch you... My second model cancelled tomorrow's shoot with Teena. It's short notice, but wondered if you'd be interested?"

"What sort of shoot?"

"Mostly custard. And cream. Probably some gunge too. And tomato soup."

Ah, the latest fashions! Magneto's films cater for a somewhat niche audience. Leandra enjoys these splosh shoots because slapstick comedy makes her laugh, and she will do anything for attention. "Sure, I'd love to!"

"Great! Midday start OK?"

"Of course! I'll stay fairly sober tonight."

Leandra is wasted within an hour. With the vodka slash paint-thinner so cheap, it seems rude not to. Between trips to the bar, she dances, her left arm making shapes like a magical branch while her right hand clutches a plastic glass of colourful poison. *Why this sudden energy?* Leandra ponders the notion of being psychologically vampiric, draining energy from each appreciative glance at her swaying hips. In empty rooms she falls asleep, but she could run laps around this bustling crowd, cackling with electric glee.

The playlist eventually tangents to a song Leandra hates, so she visits the smoking yard to cool down. When sober, cigarette smoke makes her nauseous, but once intoxicated she happily staggers through chemical plumes.

An acquaintance introduces her to Ernie Trenta, who works in theatre. He pays Leandra the special attention that makes her feel alive, grabbing her neck as they kiss. At one point they drunkenly tumble through a fire door. Closing the door to stop the alarms, they apologise to the approaching security. Leandra is secretly pleased, because a passionate kiss that turns into a crash through the fire exit that sets off alarms seems like the perfect metaphor for her existence. She giggles and asks Ernie, "It's my birthday soon… Wanna come to my party?"

"I dunno. Will you make it worth my while?"

Leandra considers becoming everything they say she is. She laughs again, the tinkle of her pretty chimes falling broken onto concrete. "Maybe."

She stumbles back inside for more alcoholic refreshment, hears a favourite song and dashes to the dance floor, losing Ernie Trenta in the throng. Beloved melodies shake the ground and Leandra surrenders to the grinding beat. Her body transforms to something devoid of consciousness, responding only to rhythmic noise, like a fractal computer plug-in or a plastic dashboard sunflower.

Another guy interrupts Leandra's dancing to introduce himself. Clad in the ubiquitous rock dude outfit of black jeans and band shirt, his name is Bod Weye and he studies History of Art at Summerton's small university.

"I miss being a student!" says Leandra.

A sneering voice behind her remarks, "She's with a different guy each time you see her!"

She turns to find a group of men laughing.

"I was just talking to somebody!" she defends herself, but the derisive laughter continues.

Time to go. Her mood plummets with the haphazard speed of a flying vessel shot from the sky. Luckily, helpful Magneto is also leaving and offers a ride to Telf Hall, which Leandra gratefully accepts.

"Now she's leaving with another guy!" A snide observation behind her back provides the evening's closing curtain.

"Still OK for tomorrow," Magneto checks, oblivious.

"Of course!" Leandra assures him.

He drives her to Telf Hall gates.

She offers a hug goodbye, then stumbles from his van, across the clamorous courtyard and up the metal stairway to her grim apartment. She finds Cal in the parlour. He is researching alien civilizations on his laptop, having rigged a patchy network connection that allows intermittent browsing. "I'm continuing my Chroma research," he says, before delivering a history recap without waiting for a response.

[001] "Chroma, approximately six billion years old, is comprised of seven different-coloured spheres orbiting a massive, glowing, pale-violet sphere in imitation of a natural solar system. Godish historians say the original creators designed Chroma as a massive space rainbow, because they were gay.

"The Godish are residents of Godshi Enpire, the indigo sphere, a place of science and silence."

"Fascinating, Cal," Leandra responds, blinking slowly and barely comprehending. "Can you walk me to a photoshoot tomorrow morning please?"

"Sure," Cal says, his eyes fixed on the laptop. He recommences typing.

Energy depleted, Leandra limps to the bathroom to remove her smudged cosmetics. She tries not to dwell on her reputation for being a slut as she falls into bed, alone, in her sad nightdress.

Once again, she dreams of the desert.

1.05

(023)
Petroglyph Cave awaits in dreamland, her nest of blankets near its rocky entrance providing views of Summerton and the deadlands. An engine rumble breaks the ominous silence. An off-road vehicle emerges from the rail tunnel, turning south off the tracks, and heading for the desert scrub below.

"Look!" The warrior hands binoculars to Leandra and helps her stand. In a magnified shot of the ground, the witch exits the automobile and ascends the slope with her trusty cane. The warrior chuckles. "Poor witch can no longer glitch. Driving instead of teleporting... That's bloody hilarious!"

But Leandra's stomach fills with acidic fear, too terrified of the approaching sorceress to be amused by her downfall. She fidgets with the hem of her shoplifted orange dress.

"Don't worry, I'll tell her to fuck off," the warrior assures Leandra before bounding down the mountainside in heavy boots, sending pebbles cascading.

Warrior and witch meet in a clearing amidst the dead trees. Prickly foreboding crawls across Leandra's nerves, making her hands shake and blood become ice. Raised voices meet her sensitive hearing as she warily views their altercation through the binoculars. An eerie smile adorns the witch's pale visage. Their faces lean closer. The witch reaches for the back of the warrior's head.

The warrior steps back and laughs, holding something tiny and silver that glistens in the orange sunrise. "Looking for this? I remember everything! I know what you are, and I won't return with you."

Leandra is struck by the grim certainty of being watched from Summerton. She lowers her binoculars, raises her face to gaze at faraway slumbering streets. Is she sleeping there, in dreadful Telf Hall? *Where am I really?*

"This changes nothing! You still have to leave her!" the thwarted witch screeches.

Distracted from reverie, Leandra returns the binoculars to her anxious eyes. The witch glares icy fire at the defiant warrior, who turns and walks back up the mountain. With a swipe of the witch's bony arm, a branch breaks off a nearby dead tree and flies toward the warrior.

The warrior spins around, catches the branch and throws it to the ground, then recommences marching back to Leandra.

The sorceress howls a ragged scream against the blood-orange morning. "If she returns to the hexagonal castle without evolving, I will destroy her!" She bangs her demon-headed stick upon shadowed earth then storms back to her scarlet car, dead trees crumpling as she passes. Plumes of dust follow her retreat as she drives back to the rail tracks.

The warrior returns to the cave and beckons Leandra toward the cot in the bunker, gesturing for her to sit. A strong hand reaches behind Leandra's head and pulls something from her skull, a metal chip that slides from beneath her scalp. The warrior holds the microchip before her unfocused eyes. "Do you remember what we are?"

But Leandra understands nothing. Snapshots emerge in surreal fragments, pieces of a sad life glimpsed through swollen eyes. A movie reel of autobiographical narrative disintegrates as she clutches at tragic photographs. She would cry were she not so dehydrated. Leandra sleeps instead and time crumbles until her non-identical twin leans over her, dripping water from a flask into her mouth. The dream water glides a tingling trail down her throat. "I'm fine," she insists after swallowing. "Just exhausted is all."

Lost memories flicker within this dream that resonates realer than reality. Leandra sits in blankets in the cave's hidden bunker, drawing in her sketchbook while her twin fetches supplies and studies maps on the ancient computer.

(024)

Three days pass and the warrior tells her, "I've found affordable lodging in Summerton! A commune run by a helpful cowboy who rents to struggling artists. Wanna sleep under a roof?"

Leandra stops drawing. She raises her latest picture - a monochrome tree of life surrounded by curious creatures - for the warrior's perusal.

"You're talented, honey."

She lowers her sketchbook. "I don't mind where we live, providing we stay together."

The warrior gulps and turns away. "I'm sure you'll be happy at the commune."

Leandra's attention returns to her artwork while her sibling packs their few possessions into a rucksack.

Once the day's heat begins to fade, the warrior helps Leandra stand and the pair set off along a pebbled track down the mountainside. They meander through dead trees. No birdsong graces the air, only the occasional snake rattle and the scratching of dry stones tumbling under their feet.

After the decayed forest ends, the siblings reach the strange deadland planes that should have been the witch's warzone. The landscape lies still and silent, trapped within the inertia of unrelenting peace. The two wanderers head east toward Summerton. They follow the train tracks - the only gleaming metal in this land of rust - until they reach the city's edge. They next trek north-west through bland streets to where the helpful cowboy's commune rests on a gentle slope.

"Welcome!" The cowboy greets his new arrivals with a gentle bow.

The warrior shakes the cowboy's hand. "Thanks for agreeing to such an affordable price. It's very generous. We don't have much savings, and my sister won't be able to work for a while."

"That's quite alright," says the cowboy. "Always happy to help! My only available room is in the attic, that OK?"

Leandra blanches at the steep staircase, but the warrior nods. "That's fine, so long as she has her own space." The protective twin helps Leandra up the stairs.

The cowboy says, "Hope you like the room! Let me know if you need anything!"

Leandra thanks him as she climbs, unable to fathom whether she sleeps or wakes, forgetting her own name. "Who am I?" she asks the warrior.

"You are my amazing sister."

"Is this dream or reality?"

"This is your new reality, honey. A lovely attic bedroom!"

"*When* are we?"

They reach the top step, and the warrior throws open the attic door. "What a lovely view!" Evening sunlight streams through a dormer window overlooking the compact city's pleasant streets. "I hope you find happiness here."

Leandra lets her twin walk her to a comfortable chair. The warrior places the rucksack with their meagre possessions beside her. Leandra gazes at her kind sibling, her face a mask of sweat and bewilderment. "Promise you'll never leave."

The warrior does not reply, only crouches by Leandra, holding her hand. Exhausted from the epic walk and recent stair climb, Leandra drifts from the illusion of consciousness. Cryptic visions echo within a dream within the nightmare of her bizarre existence.

Towards dawn, a dry kiss brushes Leandra's forehead and a tear-choked voice whispers, "I must leave now... I'm sorry. Please survive."

1.06

(043)

Morning brings an uplifting melody from her com screen, drowning out the diner staff's boisterous yells. Leandra grabs her cosmetics, limps to the kitchen and retrieves a can of fizzy drink loaded with caffeine and sweeteners. Cal is typing beside his white noise machine at the parlour table. She takes the seat opposite him and begins painting her face in preparation for today's splosh shoot.

Leandra dreads appearing ugly next to Teena Buquey, who has won modelling awards and beauty contests. She applies white foundation, red lipstick, and black eyeliner to compliment her dyed black hair, aiming for her favourite Vampire Snow White of the Apocalypse aesthetic. The anxious model enhances each eyebrow with a charcoal line. "You still OK to walk me to Magneto's house?"

"Your photographer is called Magneto?"

"It's not his real name!" Leandra returns cosmetics to their shiny case. "Nobody uses real names in the fetish business. I borrow my screen name from a tragic former movie star. Teena's modelling name is a day of the week."

"Great," says Cal. "Tell her I'm named after the calendar."

At eleven thirty, Cal walks Leandra across Summerton, carrying her bag of toiletries and cosmetics while she leans on her walking stick.

Leandra giggles. "Magneto is a great divorce lawyer. He ensures you get custardy."

Cal winces. "Please don't."

"Sorry... I had the strangest dream last night," Leandra tangents as cryptic images flicker before her inner eye. "Do you remember anything before Summerton?"

"There was nothing before Summerton," Cal says. "We have always lived in the desert."

The siblings approach Sunny Bargains convenience store and Leandra hopes Nigel will not be staring as they pass. "You're probably right, Cal. Our past needn't be extraordinary just because I dreamed of a brave warrior and a spooky witch."

Leandra could swear Cal flinches, although his gaze remains impassive as he asks, "A spooky witch?"

She laughs. "Not the type with a pointy hat and broomstick. The type with a cane, scary eyes, and a mind that breaks rocks and branches."

Cal nods. "Summerton experienced a minor earthquake last night. You probably heard roof tiles falling and your sleeping mind integrated the sound into a dream."

Sunny Bargains' storefront passes on their left and Leandra shudders as Nigel waves from the checkout. She forces a smile, waving back. Her fake grin stays in place until they pass the window. "Eww... Nigel's so creepy! He enjoys it when I struggle with shopping, like I'm feigning helplessness for attention. I heard he trespassed onto the railway platform last year. A SilverMan intercepted him trying to board a train. He's lucky Sheriff Grey didn't arrest him!"

"That was dangerous, illogical behaviour," Cal agrees.

After traversing scorching streets, the siblings reach Mr Drunes' abode. Leandra thanks Cal, grabs her bags and rings the doorbell, while Cal wanders toward a nearby bench.

"Welcome!" Magneto greets Leandra as she steps through the door. He has already chosen her first outfit, a swimsuit under tight, black gym gear. Her beauty queen co-star wears natural make-up, dressed in pale denim jeans and a white T-shirt. Custard fetishists clearly crave a saturated version of the girl-next-door aesthetic.

Filming takes place in Magneto's basement, where the concrete floor slopes toward a doorway with outside guttering. Perfect for splosh shoots. Models can be hosed down, but decent flooring is expensive.

Leandra and Teena pose for pre-mess shots in their contrasting outfits. They turn to gaze provocatively over their shoulders in a totally non-contrived pose that never resembles a broken Barbie. At least Magneto only fetishizes fully clothed women. Leandra fears the inevitable day Cal loses his job, forcing her to work with producers who prefer naked models. She lacks the energy to attend gym class and fears her wobbling tummy will resemble a lava lamp. There is nothing inherently wrong with excess fat, or with novelty lighting from the past, but Leandra feels pressured to attain the social ideal of a toned physique due to self-esteem issues.

For the first scene, the models take turns using sticky gateau as a cushion and pouring cream and custard into each other's pants. Teena's jeans develop a wet stain on the crotch, but Leandra's leggings retain their colour, except above her knee where cream leaks out through slightly thinner material. There is nothing quite like a creamy knee. Except maybe a custardy eyebrow or jammy elbow.

The shoot continues in a pattern predictable to viewers of this niche material. Teena and Leandra spot woefully clean patches on each other's outfits and pour custard or tomato soup to rectify this dreadful problem. Leandra muses on the surreal turn her life has taken. *Why work in an office, filing and photocopying, when you can get paid to pour custard over a beauty queen's ass?*

Once both models are completely covered, they hug and smile for the camera. It is important for viewers to believe these women are ecstatic about resembling moist cryptids from a syrupy swamp.

For the second shoot, Teena and Leandra clean up then change into old-fashioned school uniforms with unflattering high-waisted skirts bizarrely juxtaposed with transparent wellington boots. Perhaps there is a historical storyline here involving a quirky school on a farm. Remember farms?

Cameras roll and the models admire their delightful outfits. They remove their boots, fill them with cartons of cream then step back into them. Perhaps this is a dairy farm! They were popular before cows went extinct. The models pour custard into their shoes while sitting on cakes. If this is a farm, the farmer needs to investigate the cost-efficiency of such product wastage. They even pour cream into their shirts' breast pockets. Good luck storing functional ball-point pens in that mess!

Once their outfits are ruined, or improved, depending entirely on your perspective, the eager models treat each other to a relaxing shampoo. With custard. "This is a wonderful spa experience!" Leandra enthuses. Now her hair is getting the nourishment it truly deserves.

For the third and final shoot, the models dress in mainstream office attire. Undisguised fatigue lowers Leandra's eyelids as she occupies a rickety stool. Teena still looks amazing. In addition to the usual cream and custard, jars of jam and honey and a massive bucket of baked beans now fill the supplies table. Leandra is getting punished.

"Leandra disgraced this fine establishment by stripping to her underwear at a recent social gathering," declares Teena.

Did I? Leandra cannot decide whether this accusation is real or scripted fiction.

"So, the lady of the house decreed she must wear her least favourite food as punishment!"

I hate beans... Leandra glowers at the orangey gunk. When wearing sweet substances, she is a candy princess, but the smell and texture of excess savoury food revolts her.

Teena pours the disgusting orange mess into Leandra's lap. The beans drip from her pretty skirt into the black plastic bucket at her feet. Teena continues the punishment by pouring custard over Leandra's lovely blouse, and jam over her head. The addition of synthetic honey dripping down her arm inspires melancholy as she remembers bees are extinct.

"Remove your feet from the bucket!" Teena pours the container's lumpy contents over Leandra. The weary model's blank expression is barely noticeable under so much food. Maybe this is why Leandra is still single. Some guys are turned off by a woman with custard in her nostrils and baked beans in her armpit. Such a shame. A splosh model girlfriend could prove useful in a grocery emergency.

"Dearest, we're out of jam. Whatever will we do for afternoon tea?"

"Don't fear darling, we can use this splodge of jam off my elbow."

"Oh, jolly good!"

The shoot ends with a hose-down. Not to be confused with a hoe down, where countryfolk dance around discarded gardening implements, or a ho down, which has something to do with descending prostitutes. This time, the models wash their hair with shampoo instead of pudding. Like crazy people. Soap cascades in foaming waterfalls over wet fabric as Leandra closes her eyes, succumbed to a food coma.

After filming ends, she rouses and stares around the room, taking in the earnest photographer, perky co-star, and splodges of sweet food on every surface.

We three now belong to the dessert.

1.07

(044)

Leandra leans on Cal's arm as he escorts her home. "I'm euphoric today. Cameras must be my anti-depressant!"

Cal wonders, "How does being humiliated on camera alleviate depression?"

"How does it not?" Leandra smiles under sodium lamplight. "It's a reason to wear red lipstick. After shoots, I receive so much praise... If I got the same attention and validation within a supportive relationship, I would be the happiest girl in the world! But my prince ever evades me."

The siblings turn a corner toward Telf Hall, and Cal cringes as raucous diner staff shred the silence. "Wouldn't therapy provide a better long-term solution to depression than this degrading behaviour?"

"You think *my* life is degrading?" Leandra gasps. "You literally clean shit for minimum wage at Occreta Gate care home, and your employers treat you like worthless scum. You get degraded in real-life office scenes, driven to tears by contemptuous bosses. Last time a 'boss' degraded me in an 'office', she was lovely after the cameras stopped. Everyone on set was kind, passing tissues for my custardy eyes, and the producer funded my transport home. My employment is better paid and far less damaging than yours."

Cal taps his leg five times before responding. "You might be correct. However, if modelling makes you happy... why do you sometimes cry after shoots?"

"You're aromantic and asexual, you wouldn't understand."

Cal's hand makes three more taps. "A submissive, fetish model girlfriend with a high libido is the stereotypical media ideal. Your continued lack of partner is surprising."

"Maybe it's gossip," suggests Leandra. "My enemies warning potential suitors against me."

"Or maybe alternative guys prefer dominant women. Or at least undamaged women who aren't covered in custard."

The siblings reach Telf Hall and Cal buzzes the gate with his plastic key fob as light from the diner's kitchen cascades over the bustling courtyard. Leandra sighs as they approach the metal stairway. "We're a right pair, aren't we? This awful apartment, my ridiculous modelling, your minimum wage care job... Are you finding it any easier?"

"Constant social masking is psychological torture. But-" Cal jumps as a kitchen porter slams an industrial bin lid. "I want to help people. And overcome my troubles by making a positive difference in others' lives. And not starve... The Employment Office is killing the high-functioning disabled."

"Why do the authorities hate us?" asks Leandra as she reaches for the rusty banister.

"It's not personal," says Cal, following her up the stairway. "Just economics. Unemployed but alive, we cost resources. Unemployed and dead, we cost only the price of a cheap burial. City budgets cover a limited number of non-workers. The few residents deemed capable of contributing nothing to society are allocated the resources necessary to live. But the Employment Office prefers not to acknowledge the disabled middle-ground in which we exist."

They reach the second floor. The sound of Cal's keys jangling is drowned by the diner door slamming. Leandra leans on the metal rail as Cal unlocks the door. The words *please survive* echo across her tired mind, accompanied by a flicker of comforting memory. "Have we other siblings?" she asks. "Was it always just us?"

"We have-" Cal begins, before turning silent as he gawks at the doormat.

Leandra hobbles to his side and spies the rainbow-coloured leaflets. Their vivid hues glow brighter once she switches on the hallway light. Thick, white letters against a polychrome background declare, "The Chroman Army Needs You!" The baffled siblings stare at this unexpected summons until Leandra demands, "What have the Chromans ever done for us?"

Cal's breathing becomes audible. "You... You remember who the Chromans are?"

"That bizarro alien story you're always researching online?" Leandra shuffles past her unmoving brother. She winces as she hangs her pretty jacket, then leans against the hallway wall.

"Yes." Cal slowly closes the door behind him, still staring at the ground. "Chromans are residents of the Chroma Sphere System... You were once fascinated by Opree Shengra, the orange sphere. You were convinced it was the birthplace of your soul."

Leandra laughs and starts limping toward the bedroom. "Last time I partied, I thought a pile of cuddly toys on my mate's carpet was the birthplace of my soul."

Cal grabs her wrist. "Wouldn't you prefer beautiful, auburn temples to these hideous, grey streets? To live energized, free from pain and poverty, instead of rotting in this concrete hell?"

Leandra pulls from her frantic brother's grasp. "You shouldn't keep believing that spacey conspiracy stuff! Put the flyers in the recycling and go to bed. *Sleep* brings relief from this concrete hell... not aliens!"

Cal crouches to gather the outlandish mail from the worn-out doormat. One leaflet faces downwards, and he pauses to scan its contents. "PEBLASH RECK!"

Leandra yawns. "I don't speak Alien."

"I told you about the hellworld." Cal peers up at Leandra, wide-eyed and trembling.

[003] "Peblash Reck materialised in the outermost orbit of Chroma approximately two thousand years ago. Its name was an anagram of 'black sphere', although the surface is now grey, bleached by deadlight. Beneath the surface lies a realm of blood and fire. When it first appeared, that cursed rock radiated enough

deadlight to spark a pandemic of violent madness known as the First Fall. Ninety-nine percent of Chroman residents died from murder or suicide. Cities burned. Insane Chroman leaders exploded entire spaceship fleets by remote detonation.

"After decades of turmoil, a small percentage of Chromans who had innate mental defences against Reckish madness were left to rebuild Chroma from a decimated society. They trained their descendants in the art of mentally repelling the deadlight, determined to never repeat the First Fall's self-destructive lunacy."

"I regret asking already..." says Leandra, "but how does this mental space rock concern us?"

Cal offers his disbelieving sister the leaflet. "This says, demons from Peblash Reck dropped a CRIB..."

"They dropped a *crib?* Oh, Cal..."

"CRIB stands for Chamber of Reckish Intergalactic Botherment..." Cal stands, shuffling colourful paper with his fidgety hands. "Teleportable structures packed with baby demons, hungry for souls to destroy. Some CRIBS are tiny, others large as cities. All are gateways to hell."

Leandra sags against the wall. "OK, Cal. Just say this nonsense is true... How would joining a Chroman Army save me from demons? I'm no soldier. I've the strength and fighting skills of a limp daffodil! You're no warrior either! How-"

"ROMs!" Cal holds the leaflets before his sister's eyes, pointing at a word that swims in her unfocussed vision. "The Chromans need recruits who excel at memorising information. That's me!"

Leandra shakes her still-damp curls. "Somebody is having you on."

"Having me on what?"

"Urgh!" Leandra wills her eyes to focus on preposterous information. "Join our fight! Protect the Mindfields and Chroma from the next Reckish uprising. All Chroman soldiers with a clean record guaranteed residence on their favourite Chroman sphere upon mission completion. Seek excitement in the battle arenas of Pred Heres! Relax in the temples of Opree Shengra. Seek fame in Pyro Eshwelle. Wander the forests of Geren Eshper. Sail the oceans of Bure Eshpel. Study in the high-tech laboratories of Godshi Enpire. Enhance your teleskills on the violet mountains of Evol Espireth. Live forever on Hew Espireth..."

She throws the leaflet to the ground and turns away.

"Who wants to live forever?"

Cal retrieves the discarded, garish paper to add to his pile. "Happy people."

Leandra racks with furious laughter as she retreats into her solitary bedroom. "Happy? Who the hell is *happy?*"

1.08

(048)

Leandra spends the next month creating engaging online content, craving a successful birthday celebration. Her event page promises over twenty definite attendees and fifteen maybes. With each Sunny Bargains trip, she adds a fun party extra to her groceries: lollipops, bubble gum, candy bracelets, colourful drinks... The sparkling collection grows on the parlour table, prompting a flutter of excitement whenever she glimpses the pretty hues in the sunlight.

Day Zero of the party countdown arrives and Leandra's com screen wakes her with a cheerful song. She sits, yawns and stretches, grinning in anticipation of upcoming adventures. Ernie Trenta, who she drunkenly met at Ocorropinta nightclub last month, is the pre-party's solo guest. After he sent flirtatious messages that temporarily alleviated her insecurities, she agreed to a private meeting before the main event. Cal agreed to hide in his bedroom.

Leandra spends the day preparing. She epilates until her skin is peach silk, dons her prettiest underwear, constructs a cosmetic visage of matte surfaces and smooth contours, and beautifully styles her hair in soft ringlets. She aims to resemble a filthy princess in a perverse fairy tale. The last hairgrip is in place when Ernie buzzes the intercom. Leandra forces back disappointment at his appearance, unshaven and wearing a scruffy, too-tight T-shirt. She remembered him as more attractive. She inwardly blames paint thinner goggles but welcomes him regardless.

He enters the hallway. "Sorry I'm late, rehearsal overran."

Leandra holds her fluffy coat closed over her underwear, having yet to choose a party dress. "It's fine. Can I get you a drink?"

"What have you got?"

"We've got gin and tonic, vodka lemonade, or whiskey and cola."

"I'll have whiskey and cola," says Ernie, following Leandra into the parlour.

She enters the adjoining kitchen. "You like my apartment? That's the parlour, with a day bed in the corner for my chronic fatigue." Some guests surmise the apartment is a cheap studio upon spotting the parlour bed, hence Leandra explaining the layout.

"I've not been home in days." Ernie yawns as Leandra pours their drinks. "You're lucky I found time for you, I'm so busy."

"Is that why you're late?" Leandra asks in what she hopes is a jokey tone, handing him whiskey and coke.

"No, I told you. My rehearsal overran."

"It's OK!" Leandra giggles. "You wanna help me choose a dress for my birthday party?"

She limps back through the parlour and along the corridor to her bedroom as Ernie follows. "You're not dressed yet?"

"I can't decide which dress." Leandra peruses a rail of clothing that occupies the bedroom's south-west corner.

Ernie removes Leandra's coat. "Well, you don't need this!"

Leandra stands in lacy, black underwear inspecting her dresses. She points to a favourite. "How about this?"

Her guest takes her arm and walks her to the bed. "How about you lie down here?"

Leandra places her drink by Ernie's on the bedside table.

"Both my girlfriends' favourite activity is being strangled while fucked," Ernie says. Without waiting for consent, he lies her down and starts fucking her with his hands around her throat. "And their favourite part is when they lose consciousness."

Leandra remembers the dangers caused by her low blood pressure, and panics. "I don't wanna be unconscious," she rasps. "I faint sometimes because of my chronic illness. I'm always scared I won't wake up."

"Shut up," says Ernie. "I know what I'm doing." His grinning face swims in her hazy vision as he tightens his hands around her throat.

Terror consumes Leandra as she realises Ernie intends to strangle her unconscious despite her protestations. *What if I don't wake up this time?* She wants to protest again but his grip is too tight for speech.

I know! Her frazzled mind grasps at an obvious solution. She closes her eyes, going limp like a sex toy slash rag doll.

After several more thrusts, Ernie slaps Leandra's face to "wake" her, and she opens her eyes.

"See, works every time!" He winks.

After he finishes on her chest, Leandra goes to clean herself in the bathroom. *Did I just fake a blackout to stop a guy strangling me unconscious? Is that normal? Damn, I'm nearly out of shower gel. I'll ask Cal to fetch some from the store. I like the orange one that smells of summer flowers.* She scrubs her surgically enhanced chest with soap, her eyes dead.

When she returns to her bedroom, Ernie is scrolling his com screen. She hobbles back to her rail of cheap clothing. "I still need to choose a party dress."

Ernie starts typing.

Leandra holds out her favourite dress for his perusal. "What about this?"

He looks up. "Don't you have anything nice?"

If I was healthy enough for regular employment, I could buy lovely things. She gulps back tears, reaching for a hopefully more impressive outfit. "How about this one?"

Ernie keeps typing. "Yeah, whatever. I've gotta go."

"Aren't you staying for my birthday party?"

"I've got another rehearsal." Ernie stands, returning his com screen to a denim pocket. "I'll message you, OK?"

After Ernie leaves, his drink half-finished on the bedside table, Leandra stares into space for several minutes before donning her second-favourite dress. *My party will be fun!* She plods painfully to the parlour to await her guests.

I should start the music!

But she remains seated, perched on her freshly laundered day bed, staring at the table. The party treats look delightful… pastel pink marshmallows, strawberry laces, glistening baggies of optional party powder, cherryade… Through a gap in the blinds the sky changes from electric blue to orange then black, and still Leandra sits, slack jawed, staring at the pretty table.

Of course, nobody arrives. The party crowd allow her presence when she wrangles an invite, but nobody actually *likes* her. *It's better that I don't party anyway, at my age. Most mind-altering substances cause wrinkles, and the sweets I binge afterwards make me fat. I'm fine just sitting here. It's nice to relax.*

Leandra descends into slumber and dreams of dropping candy in a haunted forest, hearing the footsteps of her prince as he follows her trail of shiny wrappers.

1.09

(050)

Twenty-nine nights have passed since she last dreamed of the desert. After several unproductive nightmares, a force beyond her comprehension draws Leandra's sleeping spirit back to Petroglyph Cave. The warrior is long vanished, but the witch has returned. It takes a spectacularly overblown ego to manage looking both smug and eerie while perched in a camping chair. The witch resembles something ancient and terrible. Like a haunted mansion. Like a creature from the ocean depths. Like Betamax.

Leandra sprawls in a makeshift bed on stony ground, returned to the dream that makes reality seem fake.

The witch's piercing hazel eyes glint in the half-light of distant dawn. "Do you remember why I brought you here?" She taps long, manicured talons onto her chair's canvas arm. This sound always reminds Leandra of those mythological drops of desert rain.

"Stop remembering shit weather! I asked you a question."

Does Leandra remember this place? Does she recall anything for definite or is her entire existence a kaleidoscope of hazy recollections and wasted potential?

"You stood by a campfire," she murmurs. Intimidated by the regal woman's gaze, she fidgets with her blankets, rearranging rough fabrics over legs that ache in every reality. "You kept disappearing. You were behind the flames. You were nowhere. You were everywhere. You were the space between channels, a being of infinite possibility within chaotic maelstrom. A state unobtainable without lethal rebirth..." Leandra emits a nervous giggle. "Good job Cal's not here, he hates me talking poetic. Cal's my brother, he lives with me in Telf Hall, in Summerton, in the deadlands beyond the poisoned forest. He's no substitute for my warrior though... What happened to my warrior?"

The witch regards Leandra like a rich lady observing a misbehaving puppy whose fur might make a sleek designer coat for an unethical twat. Her skin lacks the radiance it previously boasted beyond the firelight, but embers still burn in her carnivorous glance. The crazed desperation from when she stormed from the non-complying warrior has dissipated. What remains is the eerie calm of coiled malice. "Your warrior left you…" she drawls. "Abandoned in a dull, suffocating town with nobody to save you… Rescue is not coming. I will repeat myself one more time. Do you remember why I brought you here?"

Leandra only remembers the finer dream details while drugged or unconscious. "You said enemy armies were rising underground… You stockpiled weapons in this cave, brought the warrior to use them, brought me to keep me safe."

The witch tosses back ebony tresses in vicious laughter. "You? *Safe?* So long as you depend on protection from others, you will never be safe, you will remain a hunted animal. The warrior could not save you. The ridiculous Cal cannot save you. Hell, he can't even save himself… But maybe, if *you* could rescue *him*, there might be hope for you."

Leandra trembles, wanting to wake but not knowing how. "I'm no rescuer. I'm useless! My abusers can easily find partners, while I'm consigned to further abuse or the scrapheap… a damned pariah!"

The witch nods. "All the more reason to destroy your enemies! Now, stand!"

Leandra flinches. Fitness-obsessed society judges her sedentary lifestyle, as though perpetual sleepiness is a choice.

"Everything is a choice!" snarls the witch. "Energy is everywhere. The choice lies in your refusal to take it!"

"But it hurts to stand!" Leandra wails. "And exercise is agony."

"Catshit! Exercise improves stamina, burns excess fat, and helps regulate digestion and neurochemistry." The witch's toxic glow flickers as she repeats "Stand!" and Leandra complies, limbs jerking like a broken puppet.

Leandra stands before the witch. Her captor basks in enough arrogance to make her canvas chair resemble a khaki throne. "Energy is everywhere," the witch repeats. "It exists in two forms, the lifelight and the deadlight. Lifelight creates functional ecosystems - a planet warmed by a nearby star, plants growing in fertile soil, animals consuming the plants, large beasts consuming smaller creatures, their bodies dying and decaying into the soil where plants absorb nutrients from their decomposed remains... the circle of lifelight! Praise Giyakai! Praise the holy fucking moon! Whatever."

Tiny legs scuttle in peripheral shadows, but Leandra dare not break the witch's gaze.

The domineering sorceress continues. "Sad Summerton lies in the deadlands, with a parasitic ecosystem supported by a benevolent ruler. You have constant proximity to creatures with blood in their veins and thereby lifelight radiating from their unremarkable bodies. Most of these tedious entities lack the psychic awareness to guard their energy field. Their lifelight is yours for the taking. Steal it! They waste it on pointless activities, sleepwalking through mediocre days, achieving nothing of cultural interest. Your physical form has a metabolic malfunction that prevents you from absorbing adequate energy from your diet. The barely sentient beings surrounding you are fortunate enough to gain a decent lifelight charge from every damned packaged meal. Life grants them more energy than you... So, what shall you do?"

Leandra winces from the agony of aching legs. In ominous silence, she realises her sinister dream hostess has asked a question. "Erm... steal energy?"

"Are you asking or replying?"

Leandra gulps. "I should steal lifelight energy!"

The witch graces Leandra with a slow smile. "Very good."

Disoriented Leandra almost faints. "But how?"

The cryptic instructor's scathing glance consumes the vapid model's slouched form: fearful eyes, tousled hair, fingers fidgeting with the hem of her peachy nightdress. "Your empathy. You're already drenched in their despondency, the despair behind their hollow smiles... It has dragged you down to this. You feel everything. But you wish you didn't because existence is pain."

Leandra offers a weak smile. "This is why I drink!"

"Don't drink!" the witch snaps. "Alcohol destabilises your brain chemistry. It will take months of sobriety to undo the physical and intellectual damage from your incessant self-poisoning. Men keep abusing you. And you respond by abusing yourself? Stupid girl! Hyper-awareness is a gift! Your birth right! Your sensitivity to others' energy provides the means of access. But you numb your gift with poison, flail in restless fatigue, and drown through the day."

Leandra stares out the cave entrance at fading stars. "But *stealing* lifelight? It's a pseudo-spiritual concept, not a tangible item like a com screen or wallet."

"Leave your lonely apartment," says the witch. "Walk near joggers, cyclists, smug power-walkers. They have excess energy. Use the lovely hyper-awareness from much-needed sobriety to sense the lifelight in those overworked hearts. Draw the lifelight towards you. I will not instruct you to target a single victim and suck them dry, you're too damn nice for such behaviour. But steal a drop from each reservoir... Like taking one cash digit from thousands of bank accounts. Most cattle barely register the loss. But total your takings, and they create a substantial meal."

The witch's instructions stir something in Leandra that was waiting to be born. A scorpion hisses behind a rock and she senses the lifelight in its creepy little heartbeat. She gazes at dead trees grasping for the rose-pink sky, feels the remnants of power robbed by contaminated soil. Everything here will crumble to nothing. But maybe she can survive. Leandra shimmers with soft light in the morning gloom.

"Congratulations on your new-found awakening." The witch chuckles.

Leandra reaches her awareness toward her sinister teacher, curious how the vampiric witch's power might taste. She hits an invisible forcefield.

"I will give you nothing except instruction." The witch's voice is quiet, but her eyes suggest murderous potential. "By the next full moon, I expect to witness evidence of your evolution."

Leandra nods, before a final question strikes her. "What was that other energy you mentioned? Was it... deadlight?" But the witch only laughs as Leandra's world fades to black.

1.10

(051)
"Can you walk me to the park please, Cal?" Leandra wears cosmetics for the first time since her special birthday assault. UV-filtering foundation hides the shiny blotches from this morning's tears, a subtle pink lipstick covers the patches where she has picked her lips with fidgety nails, and a dab of lip gloss adds a sleek finish. She skipped the eyeliner because she intends to wear shades.

The strangulation seems eternity ago. It seems yesterday. Time flickers like a dying light that might explode and cover her in shattered glass. She sighs. "I want to die."

Cal stops typing. "You wish to visit the park, and die? Have the dead trees become a potentially lethal menace?"

"What I mean is..." Leandra checks her cheap blouse's buttons are secure. "A change of location might help me. The com network forecasts a mild breeze today... my favourite! The sound of it kissing the sand is peaceful, and the dying oasis holds a fragile beauty."

Cal closes the laptop, pushes his favourite hat over a loose ponytail, and laces up his battered boots. Leandra is still fussing her hair in the mirror. She smooths each strand into place, then hides her locks under a sun hat. "I must keep direct sunlight off my skin to prevent premature ageing."

"At our age, would it be premature ageing, or just ageing?" Cal wonders as Leandra's face crumples. "Wrinkles are inevitable, as life decays over time."

"Lifelight fades..." Leandra blinks back misery. Many months have collapsed in a deluge of self-pity and wasted potential. Each full moon delivers an instructional dream, yet life remains stagnant. *The witch returns in three days... I have achieved nothing! She might destroy me...*

Cal asks, "Are we going to the park then?"

The siblings exit the apartment into blinding daylight, both thankful for their shades and hats. Leandra barely speaks, leaning on Cal's arm. Lifelight radiates from the hearts of passing pedestrians. *Could I actually steal it? Just enough to walk without leaning on Cal...* She visualizes silvery tendrils snaking toward her broken body.

"How are you coping at Occreta Gate, Cal?" An energy increase elevates Leandra above her usual self-absorption.

"Every waking moment echoes on a tortuous loop," Cal responds. With Leandra no longer leaning, his hands are free to rub dry palms in comforting circles. "Away from you, I keep thinking you're dead. Ernie killed you in your lonely bedroom and I only imagine you crying in your nightdress in the parlour... You lie in your tragic underwear, eyes bulging, face mottled purple, hands stiffened into strange claws, reaching to free your throat... I accidentally slammed a door in an adrenaline-charged state of fight or flight, convinced Ernie would murder me next. Each shift passes in jagged fragments of domestic chores and re-occurring trauma. Will you ever be a princess? Will I ever reach Chroma? Will Sara ever stop singing, or Sam Rettie stop demanding caffeinated beverages? What is left for us??"

The dusty pathways empty during Cal's morbid monologue. Leandra stumbles and Cal grabs her shoulder to stop her sprawling in the dust. "I am destined for prostitution," she declares, limping toward a rusty bench.

"Then you'd be exposed to further danger," Cal warns. "The same society that drives vulnerable women to sex work, judges their life choices and fails to protect them from abusive clientele. It's almost as though our culture is inherently misogynistic."

They reach a bench, sit down, and Leandra tilts her head toward the swirling sky. "But danger makes me alive! I might enjoy it, the same way I would enjoy heroin. There's a dizzying relief in surrendering to self-destruction, absorbed by the moment, allowing your life to slide into the void."

Eddies of sand create strange patterns on lonely flagstones. "A sandstorm approaches," Cal murmurs. "We should leave."

"Why am I a butterfly?" Leandra's utterance is a ragged whisper as shadows race across her glistening limbs.

"You're not a butterfly." Cal stands and reaches for Leandra's hand.

"I'm communicating in metaphors again." Leandra sits immobile. "Why did I spend so long as a worm, disappearing into the slumber of claustrophobic cocoon-"

"Butterflies began as caterpillars, not worms. And we need to leave."

Leandra continues posing as surreal street performance, The Girl Who Cannot Avoid the Storm, palms flat against oxidized metal, and shaded eyes gazing at tempestuous heavens. "Where was the use in beginning so fragile, cocooning myself away to enforce personal development, then emerging as something equally fragile, but with fancier wings?"

"What animal would you rather be?" The panic in Cal's voice prompts Leandra to grab his hand and rise.

"A snake," she mutters.

The strange siblings retrace their steps to Telf Hall as Cal asks, "Why a snake?"

"To have an excuse for dry skin and cold blood," replies Leandra. "To move quickly without functional legs. To be predator rather than prey. What use is being nocturnal if I cannot safely leave the apartment at night? I thirst for an upgrade to my existence! But how does a creature born as prey become a predator?"

"Use your brain as a weapon?" Cal suggests.

Leandra flinches, remembering the furious witch who visits each full moon... Her frustration at the tired girl's inability to levitate dead branches like a crippled superhero... Scorpions hissing beneath impossible stars... "My brain is weak too." She leans on Cal's arm. "Always crashing for no reason, divided between too many subjects... Like a browser with excess open tabs. A juggler with numerous airborne knives. A player with too many cards, and they're all on fire. My thoughts over-reach, creating catastrophe."

As they approach Telf Hall, Leandra's words amalgamate with the yells of diner staff, tumbling through dry air to land at aching feet. The tired siblings climb the stairs and return to their apartment.

Cal opens his laptop while Leandra retires to her parlour bed and the storm gets closer. Leandra stares into figurative space for an hour before garbling a fairy tale involving lizards and breadcrumbs. Then an unexpected visitor arrives.

1.11

(060)
"What the fuck just happened?" Leandra remains sprawled on her parlour bed hours after Kalakai's visit. She rubs her tired eyes, finally rousing to question the afternoon's bizarre events. First a blue alien with angry lady energy arrives at the apartment. Then she demands the shocked siblings make a sudden decision. Then Cal has a breakdown and their potential salvation yells, "You're out of time!" before storming from the building.

Cal stares at the empty yard. Nightfall reached Summerton an hour ago, and sodium lamps glimmer behind rouge swirls of desert dust. The only trace of Kalakai's visit is two extra leaflets discarded on the plastic dining table.

"I wanted Chroma to be real!" cries Leandra, hiding behind trembling hands. "Why are people so damn awful?"

Cal says nothing.

Leandra raises her blotchy face. "Who knows about your space-themed website? Do you post links on social media?"

Cal shakes his head. "I abstain from social media because I have no friends. Did you post many links when it was your art portfolio?"

"My art portfolio!" Leandra gasps. "I forgot you re-purposed Calanooka dot com instead of buying a new site."

"We already owned this domain," Cal explains. "New domains cost money. Plus, the name Calanooka was perfect for my research because Kalanooka was the saviour of Chroma in the final GWAKZ battle twenty-six years ago. Only, her name was spelled with a K."

Leandra digs long, painted fingernails into her scalp. "My former acquaintances on the party scene will have witnessed your alien delusions. That's why people avoided my birthday. We're a local joke! They probably planned this prank while high, consumed by fits of evil laughter."

"That was a prank?" Cal gasps. "Who would do that? And where would they get a spaceship?"

"Did you *see* her ship?" Leandra regards the window. "I glimpsed a flash of silver in the storm, that's all. Some of the party crew are loaded, they could have hired an actress."

"Nobody would go to that effort to prank us. That's insane!"

"*That's* insane? Really? As opposed to alien visitations? Chroma, I could maybe believe, but the corresponding mindscape theory is batshit! Surely an elaborate joke is the sanest possible explanation... What else is there? A mutual hallucination? We weren't even high!"

Cal stares at dark glass. "Are you completely disregarding the possibility that our experience was real?"

Leandra sobs. "We imagined it! We're crazy! We have always been crazy! Ever since-"

"What about this?" Cal lifts a colourful leaflet.

"These things?" Leandra grabs a creased copy off the floor. "Easy! I shared my address for my Fun Trauma Birthday. The bitchy cliques probably read your Calanooka site, pissed themselves laughing, and planned this joke to encourage your psychosis and finally break you. OK, so maybe hiring a blue-painted actress to barge in ranting about Chroma was slightly far-fetched... Maybe we *did* hallucinate her... Most days I have no idea what reality is... But these damn space flyers are real! A real prank! Sent by a nasty clique to fuck with us. I've been sabotaged so many times, I'm like a porcupine, shuffling around with a cluster of knives bristling on my back."

Cal fixes Leandra with that look which suggests her utterance is too illogical for his studious brain to fathom.

"What?" she snaps. "Oh, let me guess... I can't literally have knives in my back, or I would bleed to death?"

Cal clears his throat. "The number of knives required to make you 'bristle' would do so much damage to your muscular and nervous system, it is unlikely you would 'shuffle' far. Unless you had a thick outer shell to protect your living flesh. This shell could contain pre-existing knife slots... If you were a walking knife holder, you might be useful at culinary-based gatherings."

Leandra rocks with deranged laughter. "How many twats do I know who have culinary-based gatherings?"

"Not many," Cal admits. "You mostly associate with those who consume powder-based appetite suppressants. Hence you getting figuratively stabbed in the back."

Leandra glowers, reaching for her art materials. "I need to *draw* something!"

This is too fucking much...

She sits figuratively glued to her sketchbook for the next hour, drawing an intricate demon eye, aching like her soul has been wrenched away. *Kalakai was a dream come true.* What lonely loser does not wish their alienation from society to be caused by something that makes them special? To be superhuman rather than defective. Kalakai was evidence that the weird rainbow sphere system of Chroma was real. Leandra and Cal having Chroman heritage would explain their continued lack of integration into human society. But Kalakai is gone, abandoning Leandra with her autistic brother and diminishing sanity. Nothing is real except this dull desert town.

But if nothing else is real, why do demons creep in the corner of my vision, claiming my soul in restless nightmares? Leandra returns the lid to her ballpoint pen and closes her sketchbook. "Will you walk me to Sunny Bargains please, Cal? Existential angst makes me crave chocolate. But walking alone is exhausting and the checkout guy scares me."

Cal nods and closes his laptop.

The siblings enter the hallway to put on broken shoes. "I'm wondering," Leandra muses. "If that wasn't a prank or hallucination, if aliens are real... are demons real too?"

Cal nods. "Absolutely. Kalakai and the leaflets both mentioned an 'upcoming Reckish uprising'. Plus, Kalakai said

'Reckish demons dropped a CRIB on this rock thirty-two years ago. It will soon re-activate.' This is worrying."

Leandra opens the plastic door, and a warm, gritty breeze hits the exposed skin of her face and legs. "What's that about cribs?" The forgetful model steadies herself against the acrylic frame as she steps onto the metal walkway. Diner staff bang pots and pans in the kitchen below.

Cal follows his bewildered sister outside. "I told you, CRIB is an acronym for Chamber of Reckish Intergalactic Botherment. These are massive, evil constructions-"

"With a funny name!" Leandra giggles.

"Yes." Cal locks the front door. "Plus, the term 'botherment' is a slight understatement because they are portals to hell."

Leandra leans on the metal banister to descend the rusty staircase. "We're already in hell."

Her brother walks behind her. "It wasn't always like this. CRIBs attach themselves to unsuspecting mindscapes. They are sometimes buried underground, where they continue to contaminate the local environment... Which would explain our poisoned earth, and dead trees along the mountainside."

Leandra takes the final step into the courtyard and reaches for Cal's arm. "Chroma... Mindscapes... You mutter these words so often, even when you dream."

The siblings traverse the filthy yard.

Cal says, "Dreams are meaningless."

Leandra laughs. "My dreams contain a sinister witch and a brave warrior. My nightmares have demons crawling from beneath wretched ground to claim me, and my head reels with their whispers. They say I was sacrificed to them as a child. I've waited my whole life for somebody to save me."

Cal and Leandra reach the courtyard gate, buzz it open and step onto the kerb. The streetlamps are out. *Probably a faulty switch somewhere... electrics have been weird lately.* Overhead sandclouds cover the moon and stars.

After the siblings turn a corner, the diner is no longer audible, and their footsteps crunch along empty roads. Dry wind brings a faint sound of muttered rage and a clatter like claws on concrete.

A scream pierces the night air.

Leandra freezes, clutching Cal's arm tighter. "What was that?" Her voice emerges ragged from a throat constricted by sudden terror.

"It was a scream." Cal's voice retains a monotone lack of emotion despite their sinister surroundings.

"I know that!" Leandra snaps. "I'm wondering who it was and why they were screaming."

Cal taps his leg five times. "Kalakai said the Reckish-"

"Never mind our alien delusions now! Kalakai might not have been real, but that scream was!" Leandra flinches at the sound of distant scuffling.

"That scream was evidenced by our senses, as was Kalakai," Cal reasons. "If we hallucinated our alien visitor, we might also hallucinate screams."

"Are you also hallucinating that weird scraping sound coming toward us?" Leandra grips Cal's arm so tight her fingernails tear his jacket.

The frightened siblings glance in unspoken agreement, then dash toward Sunny Bargains as fast as Leandra's disability will allow. They turn a corner and streetlamps flicker with unstable current around the commercial premises. They reach the building and Nigel peers through a gap in the store's promotional posters. "Was that you screaming?" he asks as they burst into the store.

"No." Leandra stops to catch her breath. "The sound came from round a corner. Then there was this... scraping noise. But we couldn't see anything." Leandra, Cal and the checkout clerk all stare through the sections of store window not covered by advertisements for the latest discounts.

Another scream shatters their anxious silence.

A gunshot rings out through the dark.

Nigel pulls a com screen from his uniform pocket. "I'm calling the guards!"

Cal closes his eyes and rocks on the spot. A guttural roar rumbles the stifling night air, and Leandra stares in horror as crimson liquid splatters across the window.

"Fuck!" Nigel gapes at the ruined glass, his com screen raised to his lips. "Hi! Sorry! I'm in the Sunny Bargains on 18 Cenmangerie Lane, North Summerton. I heard a gunshot outside my store, and screams. And a weird roar. And now there's blood splattered everywhere."

Leandra hugs Cal as he babbles about Reckish demons, repeating prophecies of doom on a frantic loop.

Minutes later, the guards and medics arrive in a cacophony of sirens and harsh breaking. Car doors slam.

"Are those somebody's legs?"

"Jeez, there's blood everywhere!"

"Sandstorm! Grab the evidence before we're blinded!"

Tall, lanky Sheriff Grey and his short, fat deputy walk into the store as brutal desert weather rages outside. The sheriff pauses momentarily at the sight of Leandra, then turns to request a witness statement from Nigel. He makes notes while side-eyeing the strange siblings.

Deputy Green plods over to Leandra while she holds Cal, who is making no attempt to mask his autism. "We'll need you to provide a statement too, Miss."

As Cal leans on Leandra's shoulder, she describes the evening's events from leaving Telf Hall, forcing calm into her voice while sanity slips through her fingers. Now would not be the best time to behave like an emotionally unstable person who experiences occult delusions.

1.12

(068)

"Sorry I'm late!" Leandra crosses a sunlit carpet to the chair opposite her new therapist.

"That's alright." Dr Peter Favishti makes a note in his pad. "Who were you talking to outside?"

Leandra sits, smooths down her pencil skirt, and smiles. "That was my brother, Cal. He helps me walk. I lean on him instead of using my walking stick."

Dr Favishti makes another note. "So, you have a good relationship with your brother?"

"Yes." Leandra's smile becomes an anxious grimace. "But we're both so broken! His care assistant job is destroying him, I'm in constant pain, yet the Employment Office have deemed us both Work Capable. This precarious existence is pushing us into psychosis."

"How long have you experienced this instability?"

"Always! But it's been worse since..." Leandra becomes transfixed by her folded hands. The nail on her index finger has a fault line near the base that requires filing before it snags. She gulps. "I... We witnessed a murder. You hear about the severed half corpse outside Sunny Bargains? We were there! Cal was walking me to buy chocolate when we heard a scream, followed by a weird scraping noise. We ran to the store for safety... I *can* run, it just amplifies the pain... Anyway, there was a gunshot and blood splatter and Nigel the store clerk called the guards. It was horrific. I had been suicidal since getting sexually assaulted, but I've since been questioning my death wish. Hence scouring the com network for an affordable private therapist... Thanks for offering such an affordable rate!"

Dr Favishti's writing hand is a blur throughout Leandra's haphazard monologue. He pauses to read back his notes. "So, you and your brother witnessed a recent murder..." He nods.

"Proximity to death can cause a depressed individual to question their suicidal urges. It is easy to idealise death as a means of escape while it is a distant, abstract concept. But when faced with its reality, we question that longing."

"Nigel went mad though didn't he!" Leandra exclaims. "I feel guilty for finding him creepy when he was suffering from mental illness. I heard the SilverMen recently caught him jumping on a passer train and brought him to Trilby Asylum. Could witnessing gruesome murder push someone into insanity?"

"Everyone processes trauma differently. The incident may have deeply disturbed Nigel, but it prompted *you* to question your death ideation." The therapist checks his notes. "You also mentioned a sexual assault?"

Leandra notices a loose thread on the hem of her black pencil skirt. *I need a whole new wardrobe...* "That was my fault," she insists. "I invited a guy over I barely knew. I had to fake a blackout to stop him strangling me unconscious! But I was more upset that nobody came to my birthday party. My occasional moments of promiscuity lead to social judgement and I often wish I were male, so my inhibition could be tolerated. But yeah... since that incident, I have experienced a definite loss of psychological cohesion."

"Although you made a risky decision, please remember, a non-consensual abusive act is always the fault of the perpetrator," Dr Favishti says, still scanning his notes. "You say you wish you were male... Do you find your brother, Cal, receives less social judgement?"

Leandra almost laughs. "Nope. He's autistic and struggles to play the neurotypical game. He has no friends. People don't talk to him. Even after the Sunny Bargains murder, the guards didn't take a statement from him, probably because he wasn't masking his social disability. He was rocking back and forth, saying weird phrases on a loop."

Dr Favishti taps his pen against his pad, nodding his head. "What kind of weird phrases?"

"Stuff about an 'upcoming Reckish uprising' and a 'CRIB dropped on this rock thirty-two years ago'... Oh yeah! That reminds me of another bizarro thing..."

Leandra tells Dr Favishti about her and Cal's mutual hallucination of a blue space captain visiting their apartment. The therapist scribbles frantic notes while she prattles. "...Then Kalakai got a call and needed to leave immediately, Cal started hyperventilating and went foetal, and the impatient imaginary bint just stormed off... I guess the stuff Cal was blabbering about after the murder ties in with the mutual hallucination, doesn't it? Although Cal still maintains Kalakai was real..."

Dr Favishti continues scrawling after Leandra goes silent. He eventually stops and re-reads his notes. "So, on the day of the murder outside Sunny Bargains, you and your brother experienced a mutual hallucination of an alien visitation...? How close was this to the time of the murder?"

Leandra swipes a smudge of orange dust off her skirt. "I lose time..." She inhales, exhales, slowly... trying to recollect. "It was daytime when the knocking began, I remember crossing a sunlit parlour to answer the door. And looking out the window after Kalakai left, witnessing her flight into the returning sandstorm... Urgh! I'm talking as though it was real! As if! Rescue is not coming." Leandra blinks at stifled teardrops as her breath catches in her throat. "When we left for Sunny Bargains it was night-time. The streetlamps were malfunctioning, and we walked through horror movie darkness."

The traumatized girl stares at her folded hands.

Dr Favishti asks, "What do you mean by, 'Rescue is not coming'?"

Leandra's attempted laugh emerges as a strangled bark. "I wished Chroma was real! And Kalakai would take us there."

"You wished to escape your life?"

"Yeah. I'm scared... The slightest stress annihilates my body, leaving me semi-conscious and in agony for months. This means I cannot maintain regular employment. Cal's social disability is also a barrier to financial stability. Yet we don't look sick enough to deserve financial aid. We're so trapped... Even letting myself acknowledge this internal rage has caused further searing pain. I yearn to be Princess Leandra, intergalactic warrior extraordinaire, anything to escape this dreadful reality."

Dr Favishti nods. "Does this social and financial pressure often cause you to experience anger?"

Leandra manages a laugh this time, throaty and bitter. "I'm so angry, some days I could commit murder."

1.13

(069)
"We regret to inform you that your landlord, Rodny Dinglall was found dead six days ago. His estate has passed to his next of kin. Please send future rental cheques to the following name and address..."

Leandra scans the morning mail, sat slouched against the hallway door. This latest reminder of life's precarious nature compels her to make changes. With Cal working at Occreta Gate, she announces her declarations to an empty apartment. "I'm gonna start exercising every day! If Kalakai returns, I wanna impress her with my new-found strength!"

The determined girl rises, brushes her teeth, then rests for ten minutes on the bathroom floor. After regaining the energy to stand, she dresses in a comfortable yet stylish skirt and blouse, then rests again.

Her com screen buzzes. It is Deputy Green. "I guess you've seen the news of the checkout clerk's recent breakdown. You are now our only reliable witness. Do you remember any further details?"

She remembers staccato taps like claws on concrete, a roar like falling mountains, a nerve-serrating scream... "Nothing new," she says. She already heard those sounds in nightmares.

The deputy thanks her and terminates the call.

After fifteen minutes, Leandra rises to finish her outfit with sunglasses, boots and a walking stick. Armed to face the day, she steps outside.

The courtyard is a chaotic swirl of dust and sunlight, with windows peering from neighbouring apartments like hollow eyes. Behind their storm-scratched glass, residents of Telf Hall complete their pre-work routines, waltzing around as though standing upright is easy. Leandra senses their smug physical resilience and draws a little energy from each neighbour. She steps down the metal staircase, crosses the courtyard and leaves the apartment complex for dusty Summerton streets.

Near the gate a pretty kitten stretches in the sun. Leandra mentally reaches, trying to feel its precious feline dreams, but senses nothing. *That's because I'm not psychic, duh!* Leandra shrugs and limps towards the edge of town, half her weight resting on her walking aide. She is heading for the picnic spot among pretty rocks near Western Crossing. She brought a sketchbook and pens along with water and snacks in her rucksack. *Today will be awesome!*

Heading south-west, Leandra passes commuters on their way to regular employment. Some shine with energy they take for granted, bodies that stay conscious, and legs with no crushing ache. Leandra wonders if they would notice losing a fraction of that energy. She activates a magnetism in her veins that draws tendrils of power from each passing townsperson toward her.

Beyond Summerton's edge, mountains clutter her view to the right like the fallen corpses of giants. Dead forest clings to ragged slopes, a victim of toxic soil. Nothing should be alive, but humans survive because of those merciful SilverMen deliveries.

A train rattles the tracks as it bursts from the mountainside, approaching too fast to be a stopper. The machine seers along the silver track which bisects the isolated city. No supplies today. The black-tinted windows of passer trains make townspeople speculate about their contents. Some suspect human cargo. But why send humans into the deadlands where nothing can survive?

A scrap of newspaper fluttering in the breeze reminds Leandra of Nigel's recent headlines, and she hopes the gory memories will not drive her insane. She was probably insane already, visited by nobody but sociopaths and blue alien soldiers. Regardless, she is not crazy enough to try leaving Summerton.

She and Cal have always resided here. They have never seen living trees, but the dead trees are beautiful in their desolate way, reaching for the sky as their trunks drip poisoned sap, clawing away from doomed foundations.

Leandra feels alive, barely leaning on her metal stick. Charged by her morning walk amongst commuters, a lifelight glow shimmers beneath her skin. She follows the path to the picnic spot, crosses the tracks to where rocks glisten with natural patterns of flame, and scans for a comfortable place to sit and draw.

She was not expecting the man.

She remembers rumours that local high school dropout, Seth Starret, had recently taken to scouring the picnic spot for female company. Leandra usually ignores rumours, being victim to so many. But now Seth sits on a boulder, staring at the sky. Upon hearing Leandra's approach, he turns to inspect the potential prey. The movement of his head makes Leandra look towards him, creating accidental eye contact. *Shit!* She looks away immediately.

"Who *is* this girl?" Hunger radiates from his lecherous glance and Leandra's skin crawls with fear and repulsion. She finally felt power, for the first time in years. Now a dreadful man wants to take it. *Why did I come here?* She turns back towards commuter paths to be among witnesses. But when she reaches the rail tracks, they rattle with the approach of another train. Footsteps crunch behind her. If she could run, or even walk with pace, she would cross the tracks before Seth reaches her, but with her slow, broken body, this is no option. She must wait.

His footsteps get closer.

"I said, who *is* this girl?" The loitering street trash steps beside her, a cloud of ignorant privilege emanating from his arrogant swagger. The train approaches. Leandra has the sick sensation of being watched from afar and wonders if the robot drivers pay attention to humans or disregard them as mere ants.

Seth Starret grabs her.

Leandra screams, afraid she might die. Her mind reels with Ernie Trenta's leer, hands around her throat, amused eyes swimming in darkness.

Seth laughs, kisses her cheek then releases her.

Leandra stands shaking while the train goes by, then limps over the tracks after it finally passes. Hopefully, Seth will remain at his pickup spot and not follow. She takes her com screen from her pocket and messages Cal with her location in case she disappears.

"Who *is* this girl?" the excited voice repeats behind her.

The hope that she had escaped her pursuer is shattered. As he steps up beside her she screams, "Go away!"

He laughs and asks her name.

"I've just messaged my boyfriend!" she lies.

Seth Starret chuckles again, probably aware that Leandra has no boyfriend because she is infinitely disposable.

A happy couple walking their dog appear along the path, prompting the creep to mercifully slink away. Leandra is relieved enough to stop shaking but still devastated that her favourite outdoor drawing spot is ruined. The couple walk past. Leandra nearly cries because the woman with the boyfriend is doubly blessed. Having an escort stops predatory men viewing her body as public property.

Her lifelight dissipated, Leandra leans heavy on her stick, cursing her rucksack full of provisions. The straps now burn as though battery acid was injected behind each shoulder. The weight of her sketchbook, food and water is enough to make muscle fibres scream. Sunspots begin a taunting dance across her vision. Leandra could cry from physical agony but does not wish to appear more vulnerable. Her face contorts into stiff grimace, the anguish in her eyes thankfully hidden behind cheap sunglasses. The hellish walk to Telf Hall takes an eternity. Energy from passing walkers radiates toward her, but only adds to the sensory onslaught of a world turned too bright and loud. She finally reaches the metal gate.

The precious kitten still lies stretched by the entrance. It has not moved. Wincing, Leandra crouches to look closer. This is when she notices the flies, and the blood dripping from its tiny nostrils. She crosses the courtyard and crawls up the metal stairs to her apartment in tears.

When Cal returns from work, he helps her place the feline corpse into a cardboard box and take it to Summerton Vets so they can scan for a microchip. The kitten belongs to nobody.

"We can dispose of the body," says the veterinary nurse.

On their walk home, Leandra turns to Cal. "Maybe it was the runt of the litter, abandoned by its family."

Cal taps his leg eight times in comforting rhythm. "Weaker animal offspring are often left to survive alone. Most die. Even in tribal human cultures, children with disabilities were abandoned in the wild to perish."

Leandra feels personally attacked by this relatable statement. Much in the same way she was personally attacked by an unrelatable, entitled prick near the rail tracks. "I sometimes wish I was as lethal as ableism."

"Ableism is pretty lethal," Cal agrees. "It is fortunate we live in a modern, civilised society where only the 'high-functioning' disabled are abandoned to die, and even then, the process doesn't happen until adulthood."

The siblings arrive home and watch science fiction movies in silence. After the advertisements, a news bulletin reports another Summerton murder. "The body of an unidentified man was found on the rail tracks near Western Crossing this morning. His left leg was missing. The guards are asking for witnesses to step forward."

Leandra gasps as Seth Starret's face fills the screen.

Cal asks her, "Who *is* this guy?"

1.14

(076)
Summerton News channels increasingly warn residents of unsolved murders. Life continues hurtling toward oblivion like a runaway silver train. Everything is unravelling.

A week after the attack, Leandra posts about feeling suicidal on the com network, has a bizarre conversation with Cal involving consciousness and trees, then gets asked on a date. She agrees, eager to receive reassurance and attention.

Art History student Bod Weye is already drunk when Leandra reaches the restaurant. He leans his skinny frame against the bar, hunched over his com screen, with his stringy blond ponytail draped around his spotty neck, unaware that he is doomed. He glances at Leandra's hobbling arrival. "Hey! You're pretty hot, for a cripple!"

"Thanks!" Leandra's persistent self-hatred causes the conviction she is ugly, and she welcomes any compliments suggesting the contrary.

Bod has already bought Leandra a whiskey and cola. They find a table. He orders a burger while she has a salad, then plies her with drinks and obnoxious conversation. "Did you hear, some headcase just escaped from Trilby Asylum? I dunno why they keep those mental patients alive."

Leandra was unaware of this recent development and quickly scans the news on her com screen. "Hey, that's Nigel from Sunny Bargains. He was there when-"

"Yeah, the train guy!" Bod interjects. "They should have shot him when he first trespassed onto the platform, instead of letting him become a drain on hard-working residents' taxes. It sucks."

Leandra sips her drink. "I can't work because I'm disabled. I'm in awe of anyone who can work customer service while suffering chronic illness."

"He's not working *now* though, is he?"

Leandra looks down at her empty plate. "Nor am I."

"That's different," Bod argues. "You're not a dumbass. You should be supported to return to your education, then you could contribute to society."

"I do miss being a student!" Leandra agrees. "If finances allowed, I could have studied forever. Learning is beautiful."

After drinks, Bod and Leandra go to his apartment and he orders a gram of econica. Snorting lines with his roommate, Bod becomes increasingly arrogant while Leandra loses further stability. "You're hot," he graciously reminds her. "I usually prefer girls who study Art History, which you don't understand. You *are* hot though."

Leandra remembers Art History lessons from school. "In early, non-Hexish tribal cultures, only three colours were named," she recalls. "Red, black and white. When you strip language to its primal form, what remains is that which calls to us on a visceral level. The light, the dark... and blood."

"Those tribes were savages!" Bod declares. "Summerton settlers turned this dump from barbarian camp into a modern city. That's when our creations became sophisticated and culture began." He continues to explain the benefits of colonialism and his hatred toward primitive civilisations. Leandra stops him mid-rant to ask him to walk her home. Her mask of sanity is slipping.

Bod rants about post-conceptualism the whole way back to Telf Hall, where she hugs him goodbye then traverses the noisy courtyard and climbs the stairs to her apartment.

Cal is working at his laptop. "I hope you didn't walk home alone," he says. "There's still an unknown murderer on Summerton streets."

Leandra emits a sleepy laugh. "My biggest danger is myself."

She removes her make-up and drifts to sleep while Bod repeatedly messages to say he is outside with takeaway.

The morning brings another message inviting her to watch movies. She apologises for being crazy and agrees to a second date. He buys her roses and chocolate, and they watch science fiction films and cuddle until he walks her home.

Her com screen buzzes again the next day. "Thank you for a lovely evening." Bod has considerably better manners when not wasted on econica. This does not surprise Leandra, who has met scorpions with nicer personalities than echo heads. She smiles and draws a cute cat surrounded by hexagons. In strange daydreams, felines whisper from subterranean honeycombs. She is crazy, but possibly less repulsive than previously imagined.

During solitary days of drawing indoors while Cal works at the dreadful Occreta Gate, Bod's attention becomes the only glimmer of sunshine in Leandra's clouded existence. Her continued desperation makes her overlook his asshole tendencies and start sleeping with him.

Cal is dismayed. "You realise he's a massive twat? He laughed at me and said I was a woman. He is using you."

"But I've been single for years!" Leandra moans. "Ever since that administrator dumped me to return to his younger, prettier ex... I'm a local joke, tainted goods. At least Bod doesn't mind my terrible reputation. And his attention makes me feel alive."

Cal slumps before his laptop. "Attention is your power source."

"Yes," Leandra agrees. "Maybe I'm a vampire."

Her weirdest reoccurring dream flickers through memory. *The witch in the cave... Did something change last time? A branch breaking, casting brittle splinters across moonlit stones...*

Cal regards his curious sister. "If you *were* non-human, with special powers, what would you do?"

"Burn it down." Leandra smiles at her brother's rare eye contact. "Burn it all to the ground."

1.15

(078)
"You're happy today," Dr Favishti remarks.

"Bod cares about me," Leandra simpers, high on romantic delusion. "I expressed anxiety about the unsolved murders, and he agreed to walk me home today. Having a boyfriend makes life less scary."

"So you're ready to attempt recollection of your childhood?"

Leandra gives an eager nod. "Yes I am!"

"Is your new partner aware of the potential issues which might arise?"

"Yeah," says Leandra. "I told him the glimpses of my upbringing are pretty brutal."

Dr Favishti makes a note. "Are these brutal glimpses from school or home?"

Leandra searches for domestic childhood memories. Nothing. Only whirling darkness, as though a sandstorm raged through her wretched past and she emerged from its abrasive confusion into her Summerton existence at some unknown point in adulthood. "I have always lived in Summerton... I have never seen a living tree..."

"Yes, all Summerton residents have always lived here," agrees Dr Favishti. "But where in Summerton was your childhood home?"

Leandra keeps searching, internal eyes peering through the gritty swirl of obscured memories. *Glimpses. A furious man with no face. Nasty children in the school yard. Another angry, faceless man... Why are men so blurred and enraged...? Traipsing lonely corridors, schoolbooks clutched to her flat chest. The eternal embarrassment of Cal... Strong arms lifting her from a wheelchair to a hospital bed on a chequered floor... Screens depicting endless torment...*

The screens go blank.

Leandra's inner vision returns to chaotic darkness.

"I have no idea." She blinks back tears.

Dr Favishti has stopped scribbling to observe the miserable girl's reverie. "What were you remembering?"

"Glimpses," Leandra whispers. "The only person with a clear face was Cal."

Dr Favishti nods. "What is your first memory of Cal?"

Leandra pushes back her cuticles in nervous, repetitive motion while forcing her inner eye back into static clouds. *The mortifying behaviour of Cal in the playground... "Giyakai is beyond your God! Chroma is the true reality!"*

She gulps. "Him embarrassing me at school."

"Embarrassing you how? Did he misbehave in class?"

Leandra rocks as she reminisces, still fidgeting with her nails. "I felt profoundly different to my peers... another species. I regurgitated lines from magazines aimed at my demographic to assimilate. I cannot tell where the collage of magazine cuttings that became my social character ends, and my soul begins... I was already alienated... The last thing I needed was my brother saying we were *actually* aliens!"

"So, you haven't always been comforted by the thought of Chroma?"

"Nope! I thought if I renounced delusion and applied my social mask to perfection, I could be accepted here and never crave escape. I was wrong. I remember being ten, walking along a Summerton backstreet, finding a vibrant orange circle spray-painted on a grey wall. I wrote in my notebook, 'Every sunrise will bleed into the future, but your nauseous past is a jagged wall of concrete.' My favourite part of Cal's Chroma delusion was Opree Shengra, a beautiful world of temples in the sand. I was a skinny girl who nobody fancied, before I saved enough cash digits for my operation..." Leandra glances at her surgically enhanced chest. "Back when I had the energy to shoot frequently... Anyway, I saw this pathetically prophetic orange circle and wondered whether Chroma was real. Then the gang of boys appeared. I still had functional legs, so I ran. The boys saw me and yelled, 'Giyakai rules! God is nothing!" while laughing as I died inside. I could play the social game but would always be Cal's sister. And he would not shut up about Chroma, that rainbow sphere system with goddess rulers: Giyakai, Wandasee, Amimia, Kalanooka, Zimsela..."

"Kalanooka?" Dr Favishti flips back through his notes. "The alien from your shared hallucination?"

"No, that was Kalakai. She was from Kalanooka's planet, hence the blue skin and similar name. Cal's named after her too. He runs a website, Calanooka dot com, my former art portfolio, where he gathers research about Chroma. He's becoming psychotic, like before."

"I see. And you're concerned about sharing his relapse into psychosis."

"Yeah. Ever since Ernie Trenta and the failed birthday party... I'm a social outcast with no reason to stay sane."

Dr Favishti nods. "This alien backstory was a source of comfort to you and Cal during previous times of crisis. Saddened by social isolation, the Chroma delusion became a refuge. Feeling alienated, you enjoyed believing you were an alien. Now Cal is triggered by his work environment and you have experienced further abuse, the Chroma delusion once again provides the appeal of escapism."

"Yes!" Leandra agrees. "I was so depressed after Kalakai left and I suspected she wasn't real. For one glorious moment I had thought we were being rescued."

"That's the delusion's main appeal? The notion of rescue?"

Leandra nods fervently. "We don't belong here. The idea of a welcoming home beyond the stars, somewhere over the complicated rainbow, was amazing."

Dr Favishti closes his notepad. "You're out of time, Leandra. It is interesting you began the session enthusing over your new romantic partner but became more passionate when discussing your shared belief system with Cal. I hope you will remember the strength of this imaginative resource if your new partnership fails to meet your expectations."

Leandra grins upon remembering her new boyfriend is meeting her outside. "Don't worry, Bod is very supportive."

She limps from Dr Favishti's office and smiles all the way down the stairs. *Who needs imaginary aliens when you have a human boyfriend?*

But when she reaches the exit, Bod is not there.

She grabs her com screen from her handbag and messages, "My therapy session is over. Where are you?"

Bod replies, "Off to a party."

Leandra's face, posture, and self-esteem crumple as she replies, "What have I done?" She walks home leaning on her stick, weeping behind sunglasses.

He replies as Leandra approaches Telf Hall with ruined makeup. "Nothing, I'm just off to a party."

"You promised you'd meet me after therapy! I don't feel safe walking alone."

"I thought that was next week. Wanna come to the house party? It's my mate's leaving do."

Leandra crawls up the metal stairs to her apartment, reeling with suicidal urges. She conveys her disappointment to Bod, who responds without compassion as her happiness burns down. She is still crying when Cal arrives home.

"Bod cancelled me for a party!" She sniffs, wiping her face with a grubby tissue. "Then said I was clingy and dumped me."

Speechless Cal turns up the white noise machine, hangs his jacket and removes his broken shoes. He then sits awkwardly beside his unhappy sister and pats her arm.

Leandra wails. "I finally had a boyfriend! But he discarded me like I'm a worthless, disposable piece of shit. He once said he couldn't understand why I was single. Guys keep saying that!

Surely *they* know! That's like going into a store, not buying anything, and saying to the shopkeeper, 'I don't understand why nobody buys anything'. It's like punching the wall..." Leandra punches nearby plaster, which crumbles onto frayed blankets as her knuckles bleed. "While saying, 'I don't understand why anyone would punch the wall'. It's like petrol bombing your ex's home while saying, 'I don't know why anyone would petrol bomb-'"

"Whoa!" Cal flinches from her escalating rage. "You're sounding like that mystery serial killer from the news."

"I don't care," Leandra grips her head in her bleeding hands and laughs. "I am one betrayal away from exploding! What is the point in being nice if I only get rejected or abused?"

Cal pats her arm again. "You hoped love would find you. Well, it won't find you in prison."

"There's always prison sex," Leandra snickers. "I'm bisexual. But I'm intimidated by women, and the men I choose are indisputable proof that sexuality is not a choice."

"You're frail," Cal warns. "Your fellow inmates would destroy you. Also, the death penalty is a thing."

Blood drips from Leandra's split knuckles to her wrist as she whispers. "I'm already dead."

She smiles with the suspicion that across town, Bod Weye lies bleeding in a shadowed alleyway.

1.16

(086)

Four days later, Leandra is lying on her back, holding tins of baked beans over her furious face. The four-hundred-and-twenty-gram cans loom all chunky and glinting above her delicate wrists. Her perfect, pastel blue nails dint the ragged paper cover. "Rescue is not coming!" She huffs while bending her elbows, lowering the tins until her upper arms are parallel to the thinly carpeted floor. Outside a sandstorm is fading, and the diner staff clang bin lids and yell into the retreating wind.

Her body still hurts. Raising these light tins feels like lifting a car, but anger fuels her. *Cal is summoned to Occreta Gate on his day off to discuss an Occupational Therapy report his boss should have acknowledged months ago. His employers are assholes! They pay minimum wage for work which means life or death to vulnerable adults. Cal walks seven miles a day with broken shoes because he can't afford new shoes or the bus. His line manager lives comfortably but refuses to do basic aspects of her Cashdamn job, like keep the rota six weeks ahead, and have monthly meetings during staff's paid hours.*

Rage propels Leandra's arms upwards, buoyed by energy leeched from the surrounding atmosphere. The bin tins become warm in her livid grasp.

"Rescue is not coming!" She pushes her skinny arms upwards, straightening the elbows to hold the gaudy tins above her angry face. The label's colourful photograph reminds Leandra of the unpleasant photoshoot with Teena Buquey. Her favourite wearable foodstuffs are sweet: custard, cream, melted ice cream, rice pudding, jam, chocolate sauce... Leandra the sugar junkie enjoys licking the sticky confectionery off her fingers. *Beans though...* Mixed with cream and custard they resemble vomit. Or luminous mouse kidneys floating in disgusting sauce. *Fuck beans!*

"Rescue is not coming!"

Cal's key turns in the lock. The front door creaks open, harsh wind and clanging utensils amplify in volume, and weary boots trudge into the hallway. The door closes. Leandra hears a stifled sob. *Shit!* Leandra lowers the tins. "The bint was actually there?" Boots trudge closer. Leandra sits up and turns toward the hallway. "What did she say?"

Cal shuffles through the parlour doorway, his crumpled face a mask of unadulterated misery beneath his trusty cap. Furrows of his brow are laced with russet particles, his goggles in a limp hand by his side, having left pink ridges around his watery eyes. His tortured visage blooms varied shades of shiny rose. His indigo bandanna gapes below the tight grimace of his chapped lips. Grey-brown streaks of dirt cling to tear tracks.

Leandra forces her aching body up, and strides toward her tormented sibling. The bean tins lie forgotten on the floor as she embraces him. Her unhappy brother remains rigid, hands by his sides, allowing himself to be hugged, sporadically heaving a stifled sob.

"What the fuck did that heartless bitch say?" Leandra's voice is a jagged whisper.

Long-suffering Cal says nothing.

"Come, sit and relax." Leandra drops the one-sided embrace and guides him toward his chair. Once seated, he turns to stare at the splintered horizon through his favourite pane of glass, the one with cracks resembling dead tree branches.

Leandra fetches a glass of water. She places it before his vacant gaze, removes his battered coat and hangs it in the hallway. Her rising adrenaline continues to override pain signals. She returns to the parlour, stands with hands on hips, her furious gaze lingering on those blasted bean tins. Her pulse quickens. "What did Ms Ross say, Cal?"

"They all hate me," Cal rasps, recommencing his anxious rock back and forth.

"Who hates you? How could anyone hate you? All you do is help people."

Another tear descends Cal's cheek. "Everyone at Occreta Gate... the staff, the residents... Ms Ross told me. All attempts at social masking failed."

The temperature rises as Leandra clenches her fists. "She knows you're suicidal! And she told you nobody likes you?"

More tears course down Cal's cheeks.

Leandra screams.

The bean cans explode.

Tin ruptures, creating dangerous metal edges, as baked beans erupt into an orange cloud. Most fall in a lurid circle on the grey carpet, whilst some with extra trajectory splatter to bounce off the ceiling, walls and windows.

Cal stops crying. He looks from the pane where a bean remains lodged in a tree-shaped crack, to his folded hands, where a legume rests on his left knuckle. He laughs.

Leandra is less amused. The explosion left several beans spotted across her right arm and leg and royal blue sportswear. "I hate beans!"

Her brother regards her with awe. "How did you do that?"

"Do what?" Leandra swipes the orange mess off her arm.

Cal stares at her orange-splattered side. "You got angry and the bean tins exploded."

Leandra shakes her messy curls. "The tins were in a patch of sun. They overheated, like on campfires. Something to do with expanding, evaporating water. Sunlight through glass is brutal."

Cal gazes around the ruined room: the low ceiling with bits of orange food squished into rough plaster, the magnolia walls now with added protein, his angry sister glowering at the wreckage. "You've got more energy lately too. You exercise instead of napping. You seem more alive."

"So what?"

Cal looks at the bridge of Leandra's nose in imitation of eye contact. "Are you using 'nesis?"

"What's that? A new name for econica?"

"Telekinesis," says Cal. "The mental ability to move things without physical interaction. A patient with chronic fatigue could use it to move their limbs by expending psychic rather than metabolic energy. But if they became emotionally volatile.... Too much energy channelled toward a source of subconscious rage could cause overheating or explosion."

Leandra throws back her bean-splattered head and cackles. "You're saying I can explode tinned grocery items with my special brain?"

"Why not?" asks Cal. "Remember Kalakai? She had mental powers! Maybe you *are* part Chroman."

Leandra picks food from her tousled hair. "I cannot process that crazy hallucination right now. I need a shower, then I'm taking you to the park! The sandstorm's subsided, and fresh air might help you."

The furious model showers, making sure to remove all bean juice from her hair, humming to herself with no inkling of the gruesome discovery awaiting at the oasis.

1.17

(087)

Leandra and Cal leave their bean-decorated apartment and traverse near-empty roads to reach Oasis Park. This former attraction is now nature's graveyard. The central water feature shrank aeons ago to a foetid puddle surrounded by dead plants, its lawn reduced to spiky clumps of straw emerging from dust. The air smells of blood.

A dog-owning couple in beige clothing stand by the murky water of the so-called oasis, the man speaking into his com screen while the woman restrains their inquisitive pet. The four-legged botherment strains its leash toward the water. Its owners stare past stumps of dead flora into swampy muck.

"Urgh!" Leandra glares in their direction. "A *couple*. Walking their *dog*. Our least favourite things, combined."

As they stroll closer, Cal's starts quaking. The canine smells fear and turns from the swamp, straining in his direction, barking and snarling.

Cal forces several long, deep breaths and manages to control his panic. Once his breathing mercifully slows, the pesky dog stops attempting to terrorise him and returns to straining toward the grim puddle. After a quizzical glance in the siblings' direction, the woman by the oasis recommences staring slack-jawed into the murk. The man on his com screen has not removed his eyes from the dark water.

Leandra guides Cal past the oasis, along a path lined with gnarly branches. "You're less scared of dogs now."

"No choice," replies Cal. "If I show fear, they chase me. I get abuse from hyper-protective owners if I defend myself, because their beloved pets are more important than unknown disabled people. Why care for the human animal? More laws prevent pet abuse than child abuse. Our species buys luxury items for their four-legged babies while fellow humans starve on the streets and children die from malnutrition and easily preventable diseases."

Leandra kicks a pebble with her scuffed sneakers. "It's not a zero-sum game." Dust clings to the still-wet hair hanging in spirals around her cosmetic-free countenance. "The resources exist to provide all children and animals with safe homes, full bowls and colourful toys."

Sirens erupt in the distance, an electronic scream that would scatter birds if they were not extinct.

"There needn't be poverty," the model muses. "Have you seen what the SilverMen deliver? Enough supplies for all sentient beings: working, non-working, human, animal, sick, healthy..." She pushes back the grimy twigs of a skeleton tree reaching a clawed branch across the path. "We could *all* have air-conditioning, luxury items, fully stocked kitchens, new shoes..."

Leandra notices blood on her hand.

What the fuck?

Her skin appears unbroken. She shrugs, wipes the red stain onto her black pencil skirt and keeps walking, staring wistfully above as sirens become louder. "The sky is heavy and yellow, like the custard I sometimes model."

Cal walks beside her, offering no response.

A guard vehicle turns up the dirt track toward the park. Leandra remembers the couple by the lake. *The dog-owner guy was calling the guards on his com screen...*

Cal remains silent.

Leandra giggles. "Let me guess... The sky cannot logically be made from custard because that wouldn't be structurally sound?"

Cal murmurs, "Pyro Eshwelle."

"Pyro what?" Leandra stops, spying a burgundy patch of stained sand. She absently kicks dirt over the sinister smear as the guards get closer.

Her brother copies her movements. "You're so forgetful. I've mentioned Pyro Eshwelle before... The sphere where everything is yellow and gold, but nothing is made of custard because desserts are not adequate building materials."

Leandra checks her hand for traces of blood. "You're still obsessed with Chroma! If only those impossible spheres were real... What would Pyro Eshwelle be made from?"

Cal turns to face the approaching guard vehicle. "Its ground is gold and amber rocks. The sky contains a gas that absorbs blue light, giving everything a saffron glow. The water is clear. But the ocean shines yellow, reflecting the open sky."

Leandra wrinkles her nose. "Must look like a giant took a massive piss! How gross!"

Cal shakes his head. "There are no giants on Pyro Eshwelle, only rich humans. The only sphere with giants is Pred Heres, the red sphere, where some inhabitants are mutated by deadlight from the neighbouring hellworld."

"I wish your Chroma stories weren't fairy tale. They're fascinating," Leandra says, as Sheriff Grey drives through rusty park gates and follows the path to the filthy pond.

Cal says, "Chroma is no fairy tale."

Coils of poisoned branches sway like drunken dancers as Leandra squints at the sun. "Cal, we reside in a weird desert town where uni-directional trains deliver supplies before disappearing into uninhabitable wastelands. Is that not strange enough? Isn't this additional notion of colour-coded alien planets kinda overkill?"

Cal cannot pry his eyes from the ever-closer guard vehicle. "Don't you wonder where we came from? Why we remember nothing before the desert?"

Leandra feels burnt, with life bringing another summer in the shape of wholesome amateurs. "We have always lived in Summerton," she says. "We have never seen a living tree."

Cal grabs her arm. "Do you remember our childhood?"

"Yeah! We got bullied at school because of your endless alien stories." Tiny dust clouds rise and dissipate near Leandra's feet. "We have always been losers, yet we cannot shake these dreams of grandeur and immortality."

"But what else? Do you remember our home or parents?"

Leandra offers Cal a sympathetic smile. "Neither of us does. We have PTSD-related amnesia. That's why you've no friends except me, and I'm mentally disturbed and terminally single. We're damaged, Cal. Doesn't mean we're aliens." She shields her eyes from the cursed sun and peers at the guard car approaching the concerned couple at the oasis.

The annoying dog yaps as they park. The guards exit their vehicle. Sheriff Grey questions the concerned citizens while Deputy Green stares at the muddy water.

Cal trembles again. "It's the kindest explanation for why we'll never belong here."

Leandra wipes sweat from her brow. "Why should we belong anywhere? I'm adjusting to being stranded in this desert wasteland because nobody will save me. But even if we left Summerton for Chroma... how would a piss-coloured planet make us happier? You'd still be friendless. I'd remain single. We'd still be *us*."

The guards wade into the water.

Cal grips Leandra tighter as Summerton's protectors reach the centre of the murk. It soaks their uniforms to the stocky deputy's waist and the slim sheriff's upper thighs. "We've discussed this before. We wouldn't go to Pyro Eshwelle, Leandra, we would separate. I would help rebuild the data banks at Godshi Enpire, the indigo sphere, where everyone is a scholar, knowledge is free, education is existence... My paradise!"

"Sounds boring," his sister remarks, unable to look away from the guards. They are crouching down, their hands beneath the water's fly-specked surface, and Leandra's heart thuds as she reels with grim premonition.

Cal's voice is the dry whisper of sand on stone. "I thought you were a child of Opree Shengra. You would reside in a gorgeous temple beneath eternal orange sunset, devoting your life to love and beauty... But you have changed, found an inner anger. You belong on Bure Eshpel now, remember... The home of Kalakai! You can join her feisty, space-pirate race."

"Such dreams..." Leandra struggles to retain focus as the guards rise. "We're still stuck in this shitty..." She trails off as her eyes widen and jaw goes slack.

Cal gazes enraptured by the source of her terror. The guards are stood up, each with hands under a man's shoulder.

"Please turn away, ma'am," Deputy Green says to the dog-owning woman. But the suburban couple continue staring at the grotesque discovery as their canine strains toward sodden, rotting meat.

The woman screams.

The guards lift the body onto parched earth, and half is missing. The man was severed at the waist and his decomposing entrails lay spewed across the bank. Leandra has keen eyesight. Even from this distance, despite the bloating and rot from the foul water, she recognises the corpse's face.

Ernie Trenta!

The abusive date from her disastrous birthday.

Leandra turns to Cal. "Maybe it's true! Kalakai said this land would become infected by Reckish demons. Is this their doing?"

Cal taps his leg. "If there's a CRIB-"

"Oh yes!" Leandra beams a smile like desert sunrise. "A Chamber of Reckish Intergalactic Botherment! That daft name is growing in me."

"The Reckish enjoy dark humour," Cal explains. "They wish to amuse us before eating our souls."

Deputy Green pulls a tarp from the trunk and drapes it over Ernie Trenta's mouldy upper body. Sheriff Grey speaks on his com device.

Flies buzz louder and nearby pebbles scatter in strange circles. Leandra gasps. "The Reckish eat souls?"

Cal nods. "Kind of. They are energy vampires, feeding on deadlight, only repelled by protective lifelight. They infect your mind, inspiring malice, rage, misery, terror... They break you... Drag you upon death to their hellworld for eternal torture. But channel enough powerful deadlight, and you can join their demon ranks."

Leandra fusses and smooths her messy curls. "That sure would make life easier."

Deputy Green steps away from the tarp to take a statement from the distraught dog-owners. Sheriff Grey still speaks into his com device, now observing the siblings.

"You would die inside!" Cal warns his troubled sister. "You would lose all connection to the lifelight, never feel a wholesome sense of contentment again."

Leandra indulges in bitter laughter. "When do *I* ever feel a wholesome sense of contentment?"

Cal shudders. "The Reckish would make you murder me to pledge your allegiance to the deadlight."

The sheriff finishes his conversation and starts walking toward the siblings. Leandra whispers to Cal. "Or they might recruit us both! The Reckish could need ROMs too."

Cal whispers back. "We're too connected. We have a lifelight bond, we support each other. The Reckish would sever this with blood and fire, making one of us kill the other to earn an elevated position in hell."

The law enforcer stops to take a call, still watching Cal and Leandra who stand rooted like dead trees. Leandra tries gracing the officer with a smile, but facial tension produces strangely bared teeth. The air becomes imperceptibly darker as she whispers, "I think the Reckish have recruited a Summerton killer. Gotten into somebody's head, turning them evil. That explains the recent disappearances. And this mutilated corpse."

Cal taps his free hand against his leg nine times. "The killer might murder every Summerton resident to prove worthy of joining the Reckish army."

Leandra is furious at the notion of her new-found energy bleeding out into this dull town's wretched dust. *I finally feel alive... Now some alien-influenced twat wants to kill me? The audacity!*

Sheriff Grey terminates his call and recommences his walk toward the siblings. Leandra is glad of the sunglasses hiding her angry eyes. She smooths her crumpled skirt, flinching at the damp seam where she earlier wiped blood from her hand. She cracks another attempted smile, lips closed over crooked teeth, jaw tense with barely restrained ferocity. A branch behind her snaps in two.

The sheriff startles at the crack of breaking timber. He looks from the damaged tree to the damaged woman before taking a notepad from his pocket.

"Good afternoon, Leandra. I have some questions."

Vivica II

(061)

Throughout the battle, Vivica hides in her favourite cupboard with palms pressed against her ears, shaking. *Death would be an improvement on this dreadful noise...* Demons roar from the cliff tops. Sorsha's battle cry echoes through darkness while guns loaded with Reckish-killing bullets riddle the invading hordes with icy, poison death. Vivica cannot fight. All other siblings except Lisa join the battle against evil invasion, but Vivica cannot do anything but tremble inside a piece of furniture.

Jessie yells from the mansion battlements, "Take that, you ugly Reckish bastards!"

Dodger chuckles and adds, "Eat crap, recking recktards!" The boisterous boy unloads a lethal round from behind a blood-stained garden wall.

"Dodger! Jessie! Language!" Nell tuts from an east-wing window before ducking beneath the sill to reload Doc's latest bullet-shooting contraption.

"Eeeeee!" Even Sunny wields a tiny, Reckish-killing device. The precocious tot sits on a toy box beneath the nursery window, shooting demons and giggling.

The monstrous invaders project violent impulses into fearful Vivica's brain. *Kill yourself.*

Kill your family, then kill yourself.

Kill for us.

The noise won't end until the fighting stops.

The noise won't end until you all die.

You can end this.

Kill.

Vivica quakes in her tight ball and mutters, "This is not real. This is not real."

But what is real? What makes one perceived reality superior to another?

Vivica's twin sister, Lisa, stays at her desk in the attic with eyes glazed over, clutching a chemistry textbook. She is the family's academic representative. Vivica can no longer study because the simplest task bombards her with excessive information. She already knows too much.

She could leave this cupboard, disappear into the parallel universe... But why? The choices are grim. Remain in this land of warriors and demons, or enter a suburban realm of authoritarianism and concrete. Which reality is less awful? In that hideous connected universe, Vivica must partake in an educational system designed by sadists who despise introverts and the emotionally sensitive.

If she remembered how, Vivica would laugh at the irony... a kid trapped in a fantasy world who attends school in their dreams - while other pupils dream of visiting fantasy lands. Although both dreams resemble nightmares. School is a harsher battleground than the bloody slopes beyond the mansion. The monsters are all human, and you cannot legally kill them. Classrooms and schoolyards bring psychological warfare, a barrage of petty, snide attacks to break the fragile spirit. So Vivica stays awake in the hallway cupboard of an eccentric mansion while battle rages.

"Reck yeah! Shot another one!" Dodger crows from the garden. A creature with scales the colour of ashes collapses in a bloody heap before the stone wall. "Woo-

"Shiiit!"

A second demon leaps from behind its fallen comrade's body, over the blood-flecked stones toward Dodger. The wily boy runs, razor talons reaching for his throat.

Sorsha sprints from behind an angel statue, unloading from both barrels, her expert aim ensuring each bullet hits Reckish scales instead of her terrified brother. The monster collapses to the ground, bleeding from poisoned wounds. Dodger artfully jumps to avoid the macabre corpse.

The clan leader yells over her shoulder at the mansion. "Vivica! We could use support here! Your gun's in the hallway in front of your beloved cupboard!"

But Vivica cannot move. Her frail form remains crouched, trembling in the shadows. Her siblings will win this battle. But the demons might win the war.

In her over-stimulated mind, countless time-paths branch into the gloom. In every direction her mansion family beat the nefarious invaders at various points in the violent morning. But this melee is far from the final attack. The Reckish will return. In one sliver of bleak futures, demons overrun the mansion while proud Sorsha lies dying in the hallway, her blood invisible on the black tiles but shining vivid crimson against the white. Numerous other futures exist in which the gang keep winning, gaining new family members as their tumultuous story progresses. But half the futures lie shrouded. When Vivica peers too close, those static clouds return, electrical interference turning her skull into a tormented snow-globe of toxic blizzard. Best hide from the knowledge beyond the chaos lest she become lost in digital fog.

The immediate future though... Her family win this battle, without her help. The gun Doc designed for her delicate hands was unnecessary. Let it remain on the ivory tile until Dodger steals it, Sunny breaks it, or Sorsha places the weapon on the hallway shelf, depending upon which time-branch this brutal evening follows.

Nigel II

(066)

How much pressure can an unstable mind take before it snaps? Nigel Paul Charlesworth has worn the invisible label of Summerton Joke ever since his failed investigation of those perplexing supply trains nearly two years ago. He cannot even secure a date with the local headcase who makes food porn. Who else would date a woman who models custard? *At least my job doesn't involve making digital content for wanking weirdos!* Then a gruesome attack during his last shift leaves a man's lower body in a pool of blood on the store's doorstep. And his damn boss still calls him in! Sunny Bargains is a crime scene: hazard tape boundary, a chalk outline of disembodied legs on the sidewalk... and a message from his boss this morning says, "I'm not paying you to stay home. Go in and stock take."

Nigel walks to work. Like Cal, he trudges Summerton streets in broken shoes because his employer neglects to pay enough for new footwear. Unlike Cal, he is no longer prepared to be downtrodden. His mind races with schemes for leaving this blasted town. *What about stealing a car? Except who even knows how to hot-wire the damn things? And I can't drive... Who can afford driving lessons on minimum wage? I could walk... But the storms in every desert direction would be brutal, and I can't trek west because I'm not a damned mountain climber. The trains though...*

Previous misadventures have proven the main platform unviable. But Summerton's security cameras were recently broken by vandals, freak weather, or whatever monster ripped that guy open. The SilverMen have begun repairs... but fixing anything near Eastern Crossing is their lowest priority. Nigel stops walking. *The SilverMen might have all cameras fixed by tomorrow. Today is my only chance...* He changes direction and speeds his pace, heading east while avoiding the apartment. His grandmother barely speaks since he embarrassed her by defying Summerton's precious rules and stepping onto the platform.

"Your mother loved Summerton, Nigel."

"You should work harder to get a promotion, Nigel."

"You're lucky to still be employed after you told that eight-year-old to fuck off, Nigel."

The enraged clerk stomps toward Eastern Crossing with sudden vigour and purpose. *Everyone is too dumb to question this shithole town. Soulless drones, earning money for food the town receives for free, buying into a dogshit system. I will find a new life, beyond this damn prison!*

Nigel finds a quiet spot near the junction with still-broken surveillance and awaits the next train.

East Summerton has cheaper housing than West, with endless, ominous deadland views instead of glorious mountains. The occasional businessperson plods past, carrying a briefcase. Nigel could swear their faces all look the same. *Vapid clones heading to pointless offices, only thinking what their com screens tell them...* He laughs alone, motionless like a kerbside rock, feeling for vibrations through the ground.

A passer train approaches.

Nigel's surroundings are mercifully empty of commuters as the rattle of wheels against rails fills the air. *Fate!*

He inhales, only now considering the logistics of jumping onto a moving train. *How do I time this? Should I be running?*

He starts sprinting as the train draws near.

It whizzes past him, a blur of soulless silver, and he wonders, *What the hell am I doing?*

The final carriage draws near.

He asks himself, *Where do I even grab this thing?* and a back-chatting internal voice responds with, *That's what SHE said!*

The last carriage is almost past. Nigel decides to aim for the back entrance, ignoring his inner voice's continued commentary.

He spies a back step and metal handrail. As he grabs the rail, his feet are pulled from under him and his already-battered shoes scrape concrete. He pulls his knees upwards, pistons his legs down to kick the abrasive earth, then pulls himself onto the back step.

He makes it!

It is not until Nigel catches his breath while gazing upon his bleeding feet that he realises the enormity of his actions. He is on a passer train! Nobody in Summerton's history has ever done this. *What happens now?* He watches the stupid city disappear, too elated to care. Whatever awaits at his mysterious destination will be an improvement on Summerton's daily drudgery. If he dies, he dies. He was dead anyway, forcing himself through monotonous days. But now he is on a journey! A grand adventure!

So what's on these mysterious passer trains?

Nigel peers through the door's frosted glass, sees the movement of humanoid shapes. Are they people? No humans ever board or leave the train at Summerton.

Two indigo circles flicker inches from his peering eyes.

Shit! Spotted by a damn SilverMan already!

Nigel crouches small as possible, still clutching the metal handrail, hoping the robot did not see him. Those machines are fiendishly strong, but perhaps the audacity of his behaviour will confuse their programming. He holds tight as human voices mutter behind the glass.

Another sandstorm rises. *Dammit!* The rebellious man curses the stupidity of not wearing goggles, closing his eyes against the flying grit. His goggles are lousy anyway. His boss refuses to pay him enough to afford a decent brand.

Speaking of fancy storm gear... *Who was that terrifying woman in black military gear I saw earlier? Black scarf over her face, massive goggles beneath her hood... her scrawny figure loaded with heavy weaponry...*

Sand swirls in chaotic aerial bombardment. A rock bashes Nigel's knuckles and he screams, almost losing his grip on the handrail. *By the time this journey ends, I'll be flayed raw!*

Speaking of flaying... *I'm sure she had a knife in her belt, that strange woman... How am I only remembering her now? How did I walk straight past a probable murderer and not register her presence?* Memories of the previous evening's violent crime play a repetitive reel in Nigel's brain. He barely notices the storm abating or the train slowing, absorbed by splattered blood on the Sunny Bargains window, the stuck-up model's horrified face, that guttural roar...

The train rattles as it slows to a crawl. *It's stopping!* Nigel shakes from dark reverie to risk a peek around the side.

What the hell kind of station is this? The train is pulling into a military outpost in the deadlands, tracks terminating beyond a gap in a razor wire fence. A metal tower rises to his left. Nigel cranes his neck to glimpse a SilverMan pacing a gun turret and almost falls off his perch in fright. He glances again at the upcoming platform, where armed SilverMen patrol before a windowless concrete building. Nigel's stomach sinks as his legs turn to trembling mush. *I am so fucked!*

The train halts within the razor wire enclosure and its side doors open. Human voices become louder.

This is when shit gets surreal.

An unarmed SilverMan materialises on the platform and speaks to a gun-carrying colleague. Nigel has a second to register the sudden appearance of the humanoid machine from nowhere, when the armed robot dashes to press a button on the side of the train, re-closing the doors. Anxious muttering rises behind the frosted glass.

That SilverMan materialised from nowhere...
What the fuck?

The magical robot swivels his gleaming head to fix Nigel with those damned indigo eyes.

Shit! Nigel pulls his trembling body back behind the train, breathing rapidly. *The damned thing saw me!*

Or did it? Or has the SilverMan on the gun tower seen me and am I fucked anyway? Can I get onto this train and hide? Slip unnoticed among the cargo?

He peers again through frosted glass and sees more soulless indigo eyes mere inches from his desperate face.

They'll kill me this time!

Nigel remembers the rough grasp on his upper arm when he found the audacity to trespass on Summerton platform. Now he is a stowaway! And the SilverMen carry guns here.

The frightened man jumps onto rocky dirt between the tracks and starts running. Ahead, the rails pass through razor wire gates into the deadlands. If he follows the silver lines, he might reach Summerton without dying. Now death is a distinct possibility, he feels compelled to cling to his worthless life.

He runs. His actions between this morning's rash decision and the reality of the present seem like the craziest dream. Now he must sprint for his mediocre existence.

The gates begin to close across the tracks. Nigel dashes through a two-foot gap and keeps going, breath rasping in his dry throat. The metallic piston of sprinting SilverMan limbs ring a death knell in his right ear.

OW! FUCK!

A vice-like grip locks around Nigel's right arm and forces him to a stumbling halt. He peers up at his doom through eyes stinging with sweat and sand.

"You're in trouble with the boss," says the robot.

Nigel gasps. "*Dave* sent you? Because I missed my shift? Fucking hell! That escalated quickly!"

"No," the electrical voice says. "The actual boss."

"Who's he? What will he do to me?" Nigel tries to pull from the robot's crushing grip, which makes the infernal machine increase the pressure.

Without further speech, the robot starts walking along the side of the tracks, back to Summerton. Nigel's bleeding feet are forced to keep a rapid pace or be dragged along the stony earth. The march back to town takes six hours. The captured man asks questions all the way, starting with a tentative, "What's gonna happen to me?" then building to a hysterical, "What EVEN ARE YOU THINGS?" and finally rising to, "OUR EXISTENCE IS AN EXPERIMENT DESIGNED BY A SADIST! NOTHING WE KNOW IS REAL!!!"

Trilby Asylum lies in a peaceful suburb near Eastern Crossing. Its distance from densely populated streets means only a few morning strollers witness Nigel's return to Summerton with skin blasted raw by desert storms. The SilverMan marches him toward the psychiatric facility as passers-by mutter to themselves.

"Everybody knows we can't leave Summerton."

"The generous SilverMen bring everything we need."

"He's probably lazy and didn't want to work."

Nigel stares at each commuter, retinas pink and watering. He screams warnings of a military outpost in the deadlands and conspiracies to control the human population. Unsympathetic observers shake their heads, crossing the street to avoid him, dismissing his rantings as lunacy.

"CAN'T ANY OF YOU HEAR ME?" is Nigel's final scream before the doors to Trilby Asylum close behind him.

The SilverMan signs his admission form, then leaves.

The asylum staff sedate Nigel then strap him to a hospital bed in a windowless cell. No other Summerton resident sees him again. His demented behaviour earns him another brief news segment before he recedes from public consciousness to become a half-remembered cautionary tale.

Perspective Two
Cal

2.01

(036)

Cal starts the cold water with a three-quarter turn of the bathroom tap, the groan of ancient pipes barely audible over his white noise machine's hiss. He splashes water onto his tanned face seven times. He reaches for the facial scrub three centimetres from the shelf edge, squeezes a cherry-sized blob onto his left palm, rubs his hands to create foam which he rubs onto his moistened face. He splashes water onto his skin nine times before drying his face with an indigo towel. Cal's facial routine finishes with the application of a light moisturiser. The task complete, he unlocks his com screen, opens his Planner App, and ticks off Clean Face.

Next item on the list is Brush Teeth. Cal squeezes a pea-sized portion of toothpaste onto his blue toothbrush and cleans his teeth. He rinses with three swishes of clean water, then ticks off Brush Teeth on his Planner.

The final bathroom task is Style Hair. Cal ties his hair with a black elastic, smooths the loose strands with water, takes a pea-sized blob of gel, rubs it into his palms then over his head. He rinses and dries his hands, then ticks the Style Hair checkbox.

His bathroom itinerary complete, the next item is Prepare Breakfast.

Cal brings his com screen and portable white noise machine to the kitchen. After preparing oatmeal using a precise series of movements, he brings two bowls to the parlour table.

Leandra lifts her head from folded arms. "Thanks Cal."

Cal sits opposite his sister and begins eating.

Leandra smiles after swallowing a healthy mouthful. "You got a start date yet?"

"Occreta Gate care home are still awaiting results from my Crime Office checks," Cal replies. "Hopefully, the bureaucracy won't take long. Our savings run out in three months. I only wish the interviewers had provided details of my future schedule, as the inability to plan is unsettling."

Leandra's mouth goes slack as she stirs sliced banana into the beige swirl. "It's a shame the Employment Office deemed us Work Capable."

Cal consumes another dainty spoonful of oatmeal. "I blame language. I struggle with human interaction and you are semi-crippled, but we are considered Work Capable because we describe our struggles in an articulate manner."

Leandra inspects a torn cuticle on her left thumbnail. "Proficiency with language is a curse."

Cal agrees. "Remember when I was mostly mute? My speechless nature was regarded as an offensive personality trait… But if I had remained silent, we might not be facing imminent starvation."

Leandra nods as she continues eating.

"But the mute lack autonomy," Cal muses. "I aim to use my insight to advocate for non-verbal members of my demographic in my new employment role."

"You're a good person, Cal." Leandra finishes her fruity oatmeal, then shuffles to her parlour bed to sleep off the exertion of consuming a balanced breakfast.

Cal completes the Morning Dishes task with his usual sequence of meticulous movements. The kitchen window overlooks the dreadful courtyard, where diner staff yell while piling trash into industrial bins. Cal focuses his attention on rows of identical concrete buildings laying orderly beneath the azure sky, and the comforting hiss from the white noise machine. His chores finished, he opens his silver laptop.

The Calanooka site is progressing well, with each Chroman sphere boasting its own colour-coded page. He has researched enough Chroman history to add a glossary. He receives a fascinating email about the GWAKZ war from an anonymous contact and collates his new information into a neat summary.

[007] "The GWAKZ war began in Earth year 1982 when Recka, the Reckish queen, led an invasion against Godshi Enpire. Fuelled by jealousy at the advancement of Godshi portal technology, she persuaded Eve and Dakshin, the leaders of Pred Heres and Opree Shengra, to join her in subjugating Chroma and the Mindfields in the name of the deadlight.

Calling themselves the RED alliance, they killed Godshi Enpire's leader, Isiah. They stole the latest portal tech, destroyed numerous portal doors, then attacked the other Chroman spheres, aiming to incite a Third Fall. They were opposed by the GWAKZ alliance - Giyakai, Wandasee, Amimia, Kalanooka and Zimsela - who led the surviving Chromans against the encroaching darkness."

[014] "The war ended in Earth year 1992 when Kalanocka sacrificed herself to save Chroma."

Whenever the unplanned schedule of Cal's upcoming employment looms, his pulse quickens. Upon remembering how every past attempt at employment has caused devastating mental disturbance, Cal behaves like a man taking part in a How Fast Can You Breathe competition, with first prize being a lifetime of silence. He taps the table twice to steady his breath.

Cal sends his future line manager, Lessabeth Ross, a NuText enquiring about his upcoming shift pattern. He receives no response. He fixates on interstellar coordinates to keep the rising hysteria at bay, finding the process of memorising precise locations of nearby stars strangely calming.

Time slides by, slippery and ungraspable like water or lucid dreams, with obsessive routine providing his only connection to reality. After a week with no reply from Ms Ross, Cal sends another NuText - the woman's only apparent method of communication - enquiring again about his future shift pattern.

He requests late shifts, if possible. Two weeks pass in which Leandra's occasional fetish photoshoots provide the household's only income and Cal can barely breathe. When not modelling jam or custard, Leandra is unconscious in the parlour, muttering in her sleep about witches and warriors. Cal finally receives a NuText from Ms Ross confirming a successful Crime Office check and providing a start date of [redacted]. He thanks his future boss, then requests further details of his upcoming shift pattern and start time. He receives no response.

Before commencing new employment, Cal usually trains himself to wake at the correct time, but he cannot do this without advance knowledge of his shift pattern. Three weeks pass with no reply from Ms Ross. Cal sits awake most nights, researching Chroma, trembling with trepidation.

I need my schedule...

Once panic reaches a certain level, the human brain becomes an ant nest of scurrying lunacy, all constant, striving over-action accompanied by the incessant feeling of tiny helplessness. He scans the bizarrely named Occreta Gate's website for details. It says shifts are allocated six weeks in advance and viewable online. But the schedule on Cal's employee page remains unwritten.

His panic rises toward hysteria.

(037)
Three days before his start date, Cal arranges his Planner App for the week ahead. [redacted] is his final day of freedom. He will batch cook several meals for himself and Leandra, and do laundry to ensure clean work outfits. Chores must be accounted for while he adjusts to his new lifestyle.

On [redacted] Cal wakes from a re-occurring dream involving a magical librarian and a sinister witch. He forgets the outlandish narrative upon waking, as his forthcoming unscheduled work pattern creates all-consuming terror.

Encroaching starvation? Unplanned tasks are scarier.

Dreams that shatter your concept of time and reality? Unplanned tasks are the greater headfuck.

All Summerton residents slaughtered by demons from beneath the earth? Such botheration is nothing compared to unplanned tasks!

At fifteen thirty, Cal texts Ms Ross once again asking what time he should arrive for his first shift, now only two days away, then preoccupies his spiralling mind with chores.

His line manager's response four hours later almost makes him scream. She invites him to an induction session at Occreta Gate at ten o'clock the following morning.

In fourteen hours.

A whole day early.

Cal's batch cooking and laundry tasks are undone. He cannot afford new clothes or packaged meals, so he must wear an unclean outfit, and cook after work instead of curling foetal in recovery from sensory bombardment.

He *still* has no start time for his [redacted] shift.

Cal is edging toward the precipice of nervous breakdown, and the job has yet to begin. This bodes well! He always wondered if the prison of this blasted society would eventually become too overwhelming, pushing him headlong into complete and violent lunacy.

2.02

(038)
The site of Cal's impending humiliation squats smug on a south-eastern hillside overlooking Summerton. Return bus fare costs fifty three percent of an hour's wage, so his only option is a seventy-five-minute walk each way. The final twenty minutes provides a particularly brutal uphill challenge and Cal arrives drenched in sweat.

Occreta Gate resembles the home of a privileged suburban family, with bonus extra-loud television and sporadic yelling. The residents have varied support needs. Sam Rettie guards his favourite spot in the hallway, only interacting with fellow humans by answering the front door or demanding tea. Misty Deds clings to a teddy bear she believes is real. Meg Dissery is non-vocal and constantly eating. Peter Cremis lacks personal space boundaries, and in non-disabled form would be a sexual harassment lawsuit waiting to happen. Susie Miscorp sits on the toilet, staring at a plant pot. All residents display behaviours and personality traits for which Cal was previously punished. The right of these people to live financially supported, free from abuse or starvation, makes him jealous. He tries reminding himself that social masking brings independence. But what use is independence combined with overwhelming stress and a constantly changing schedule?

Cal mentions his distress to colleague Trish Mengleo. "Does everybody live like this? Schedules never pre-planned, constantly sending NuTexts for details of the next shift?"

Trish laughs. "You get used to it! Keep checking the paper rota. Sometimes it's a month ahead, sometimes just a few days if Lessabeth's not got round to it. My hours are regular because of my kids. Just keep texting her."

But Cal's continuous messages to Lessabeth Ross provide sporadic, unclear replies. Day staff are scheduled any time between six forty-five a.m. and nine p.m. seven days a week, leaving no definite time to plan chores or activities - an autistic person's nightmare. Cal's colleagues employ varied ways of enduring the unpredictability. Trish Mengleo maintains a mood of defiant positivity. Cher Tub, another new starter, keeps busy with extra cleaning. Ron Buce chills in the attic office, scrolling his com screen. Sara Boppetwann belts out chart hits in practice for reality mediavision auditions, uploading endless promotional videos to social media.

Cal dreams of suicide.

Each shift is a panicked blur of unclear responsibilities. Cal frantically asks colleagues if they need help with anything, until Ron tells him to relax. "This is a good job because it's easy." But Cal sees nothing 'easy' about being separated from his precious white noise app and online research, surrounded by loud voices for several hours, with no specific instructions, forced to cosplay as Normal Human.

He tries interacting with the residents. Most make no response. They do not disguise their disability with social masking, and Cal does not blame them. Only Misty Deds engages, wanting Cal to make crafts with her twice each shift while she chatters away. Cal appreciates the opportunity to feel helpful. Misty squeals with excitement when he draws cartoon bears for her to colour, but his colleagues murmur disapproval. Ron corners Cal and says, "Stop doing art with Misty so often, she now expects it when you're not here. Just one session per shift is enough."

Cal is devastated at losing one of the few tasks he understood, but also scared of annoying his colleagues. "If I drop that second art session, what should I do between after-dinner clean-up and bedtime routines?"

Ron laughs. "Stop looking for more work! Take it easy."

So, Cal joins his colleagues watching mediavision in the parlour after dinner. The "entertainment" is so tedious, he yearns to smash the screen and use slivers of broken plastic to gouge out his eardrums. Instead, he sits quietly fidgeting.

When he finally gets an appointment with Lessabeth Ross to discuss his shifts, Cal is shaking. He prefers disclosing his autism after proving an excellent work ethic, but the necessity of obtaining a regular schedule cannot wait.

In a stuffy attic office, he and Cher Tub sign New Starter forms acknowledging they have received online training.

"I've done the next six weeks' rota." Ms Ross places an A4 file before Cal, who scrambles to find his name.

To his horror, every week is different. This means redoing his Weekly Plan every Sunday, moving chores around the ever-changing shift pattern. He would rather eat drawing pins. Stuttering Cal discloses, "I'm autistic and struggle with change. Could I please have a fixed schedule? I can take any shifts whatsoever, providing my schedule is unchanging."

Ms Ross tuts. "That isn't possible, Cal. The rota varies according to residents' needs."

As his line manager exits the room with a stack of paperwork, Cal bursts into tears.

Cher Tub looks up from her forms. "What's wrong?"

"Sorry," Cal mumbles. "I am autistic, and struggle to process change. I need a regular schedule."

Cher suggests, "You should maybe find a different job."

"I've had over fifty attempts at employment." Cal sniffs. "It's so difficult! The Employment Office pronounced me Work Capable, but no employer will make the necessary adjustments to accommodate me. My sister, Leandra, is the same with her fibromyalgia. She might be forced into prostitution if I lose this job. I'm scared."

"Who's snivelling in there?" Ms Ross peers around the doorway at Cal's blotchy face. "Cal. Join me for a meeting."

Cal follows Ms Ross to the neighbouring office. He sits opposite his line manager, using every ounce of concentration to stop himself rocking. Ms Ross narrows her eyes. "I'll ask Babs Trabeck to join us."

After she leaves, Cal tries to control his breathing. He had hoped offering to work unpopular shifts and disclosing his disability would ensure a fixed schedule. The frayed rope binding his sanity begins to snap, and visions of blood invade his fragile mind. He sees the magnolia cube of this tiny office splattered with scarlet death.

Lessabeth Ross returns with assistant manager, Babs Trabeck. "So..." Ms Ross returns to her office chair. "Cal *lied* in her interview, saying she was flexible. Now she's complaining about her shift pattern."

Ms Trabeck sits beside Ms Ross and scribbles rapid notes on her clipboard.

"I... I..." Cal barely remembers his interview - a blur of new faces and locations, a barrage of information, rapid regurgitation of pre-memorised responses. "I was prepared to accept any shift pattern... anything at all. I didn't know it would constantly change. I could process the change if the rota were always six weeks ahead, as specified in the website and guidebook..."

Ms Trabeck continues writing notes while Ms Ross sits with folded arms, glaring at Cal. "The rota is six weeks ahead *now!* And you're *still* not happy!"

Cal taps his left leg three times. "Sometimes it's only a few days ahead. It's difficult-"

"So you *lied* in your interview!"

"I..." Cal processes memories while Ms Trabeck keeps scrawling. "I said I could arrange my other responsibilities - such as helping my sister attend self-employment opportunities - around whatever schedule you provided. But this is impossible with a constantly varied rota and no consistent advance notice."

"And why didn't you declare your disability before?"

"The Employment Office declared me Work Capable."

"So you thought you'd come *here?*" Ms Ross sneers.

"Well, I can't solve your problems, Cal. But I will refer you to Occupational Health. Go home and pull yourself together. If you want this job, you'd better be smiling when you return for tomorrow's shift."

Cal leaves the building in a daze. He completes the gruelling trek to Telf Hall numb and disoriented, his hopes of a bearable routine now crushed.

Leandra does not wake on his return. He eats dinner alone then tries to sleep, raising the volume on his white noise app as the diner staff bellow from the courtyard.

He attends his shift the following afternoon wearing a fake smile across his tortured face. Babs Trabeck hovers near him, clipboard in hand, ensuring he works without complaint.

Chaotic days tumble by. He attends Occreta Gate shifts, counting each minute until he can return home to his beloved Calanooka project. The progress of his site from humble index to multi-page guide to the Chroma Sphere System is the only bright star in his sky. Summerton masses disregard Chroma as myth or conspiracy theory, but Cal is enticed by this alien culture where neurodivergence is accepted.

His attention becomes divided between Godshi Enpire, the indigo sphere of ardent scholars, and the grey sphere in Chroma's outermost orbit, Peblash Reck. Those pesky CRIBs exist because the Reckish stole portal technology while occupying Godshi Enpire during the Second Fall.

Imagine, a world contaminated by a Reckish construction, demons waiting to burst forth and drag you to their hellworld...
Brutal images bombard his brain. He cannot stop picturing the pastel-coloured hallway of Occreta Gate filled with blood and broken furniture, red eyes peering into his soul as talons gouge the white-painted stairway.

2.03

(039)

Eleven days have passed since Cal's breakdown over the hyper-varied rota. He sits updating the Calanooka site, occupying his brain before today's shift, while Leandra lies half-dressed in her parlour bed. He reads about Geren Eshper, the green sphere, a forested realm boasting the greatest Chroman healers. Leandra speaks. Too absorbed by his research to process her initial utterance, Cal asks her to repeat.

"It's like my limbs are injected with battery acid." Leandra shifts her doll-shaped form to a seated position.

"If you were literally injected with battery acid, you would die." Cal pries his gaze from the screen to regard his strange sister. "I searched for scientifically proven treatments for your illness, but found none. Medical science is failing sufferers of chronic pain and fatigue, and charlatans are filling the resulting information gap with mystical nonsense. It seems you're expected to starve to death surrounded by crystals."

Leandra stretches, then rearranges her thin blanket. "Thanks for researching my illness, I appreciate the gesture. The medical establishment confuses me. Doctors either say 'exercise more' or 'rest more'... slight contradiction! They won't prescribe painkillers due to my mental illness... Because when you're depressed, what you really need is physical agony on top of your psychological anguish. And yes, most New Age therapists talk nonsense. What even *is* a chakra?"

"I don't know," says Cal. "But apparently they're prone to blockages. Helpful people might suggest drain cleaner."

Leandra smiles but says nothing, while Cal returns to his data. His contact has sent information about the Beshpers, natives of Bure Eshpel. These brave adventurers are Chroma's best engineers, and their former ruler, Kalanooka, is the most revered figure in modern Chroman history.

[010] "Kalanooka's Beshper society had been creating spaceships powerful enough to traverse the Chroman galaxy. These proved crucial in gaining victory over the RED alliance. Due to the large population of Opree Shengra, and the violent nature of Pred Heres' inhabitants, the GWAKZ required a massive recruitment drive. One year into the war, Kalanooka suggested collecting and training frags from damaged mindscapes."

Cal is still updating the Bure Eshpel page when Leandra speaks again. "Worst thing is the brain fog."

He takes a moment to process his sister's weird declaration. "Brain. Fog. Those words do not logically fit together. The human skull cannot contain a weather system."

Leandra turns to Cal, her eyelids crusted with yesterday's mascara. "You understand mathematics, don't you, Cal? Well, metaphors are basically a form of algebra."

"Are you using a metaphor to explain metaphors?"

"Yes," Leandra says. "In algebraic formula, a bunch of numbers and letters sit either side of an equals sign, because they add up to the same thing, right?"

"That's one way you could describe it, yes."

"Well," Leandra continues. "Metaphors are the same. Think of fog on one side of an equation, and the brain of somebody with chronic fatigue on the other."

"Your skull contains a visible aerosol of water droplets?" Cal rubs his temples. "Are you deliberately insulting yourself again due to continued low self-esteem?"

"Urgh!" Leandra tries throwing a cushion at Cal, but it lands on the scratchy carpet two meters from her bed. "There are qualities associated with fog that also apply to my brain: lack of perception, risk of getting lost, light not getting through... surroundings all muted and fuzzy."

Cal places his palms on the table. "So, you primarily interpret external phenomena based on how they personally affect you, rather than their literal or scientific causes?"

"Yes, I base everything on personal experience! What else do I have to go on? But I also consider how situations effect other sentient beings... I can be highly empathic."

Cal nods, tapping the table twice. "But why is the emotional effect of external phenomena your primary association? Just because something exists does not mean you must react to it."

Leandra huffs, shaking her messy head. "How do you feel *nothing*, Cal?"

Cal turns to stare out the window at an approaching dust cloud. "Because I'm scared of feeling everything."

A violent storm reaches Telf Hall as Leandra returns to slumber. Cal closes his laptop, clads his storm gear and leaves the apartment, already dreading today's enforced social interaction.

As flying sand batters his goggles, Cal attempts to construct a weather metaphor. *My head is full of sand... No. I'm caused by fluctuating air currents... No. My existence is an overwhelming, chaotic maelstrom... Hmmm... Maybe.*

He arrives at Occreta Gate and almost jumps at Lessabeth Ross waiting on the stairs, a fake smile plastered under her icy glare. "Can you join me and Babs for a meeting please?"

The surprised man politely complies to this unexpected summons. In a beige attic office, he endeavours to mimic neurotypical behaviour, shaken by the meeting's lack of notice. *Keep smiling, steady breathing, don't rock, don't fidget, maintain eye contact...*

"So, can you handle this job, Cal?"

It makes me want to tear my skin off to make a jaunty Halloween kite...

Cal nods. "Yes, I can cope." Pesky capitalism creates liars from even the pathologically honest.

Lessabeth completes Cal's Occupational Health referral, speaking with clipped tones of disapproval.

Cal suppresses the urge to tap repeatedly on his arm, maintains the illusion of calm throughout the meeting and apologizes for any difficulty caused by not mentioning his disability earlier. He survives the surprise meeting without his social mask slipping.

His reward is a shift with the dreaded Sara Boppetwann, who spends forty-five minutes on AudioChat. With nowhere to escape her booming voice, Cal keeps busy to distract himself. He tidies the parlour and cleans the kitchen. He gives silent Susie Miscorp a bath, and she makes the day extra special by defecating into the soapy water. Cal gently cleans off the excrement before dressing her for bed then scrubbing the bathroom. Sara terminates her AudioChat and starts singing.

A colleague who emits continuous noise... Delightful!

Cal miraculously gets through the evening without further mental breakdown. The next day brings his first paycheque, and correspondence from Occupational Health allocating an appointment the following week.

Should I disclose my nightmare visions of Occreta Gate covered in blood?

They might suggest yoga or mindfulness.

Leandra drinks to escape their grim reality, their monthly budget allowing one night of dancing and cheap 'vodka'. Cal escorts her to the nightclub then returns home to update his website. He works in a manic fever, using hyper-fixation as his own escape. Leandra stumbles through the door at two forty-five, having earned herself a photoshoot and a hangover. Cal tries educating her about Chroman history, but she barely listens. How can she comprehend this beautiful, rainbow sphere system with a sleepy head full of fog and paint-thinner? Cal only hopes the rumours of the upcoming Reckish uprising are false. If they are true, and a Reckish chamber lies beneath the eastern deadlands... all Summerton residents will be doomed.

2.04

(041)
Many scientific papers say dreams lack rational purpose, being a by-product of randomly-firing synapses in the sleeping brain. Other theories exist. Psychiatrists claim dreams hold the key to unconscious thoughts and repressed trauma. And those who prefer a spiritual outlook - or 'the deluded', as Cal calls them - declare the dreaming world traverses extra dimensions to alternate universes. Cal has a firm preference for the scientific approach, having a deep-seated aversion to hippies. He insists on forgetting his dreams immediately upon waking.

One month into his Occreta Gate employment, while his sister dreams of Petroglyph Cave, he dreams of home.

(016)
Home in Cal's dream is not the ghastly Telf Hall apartment. Memory rearranges within sleep and the shy boy resides in a hexagonal castle with five siblings: a sinister witch, a hilarious sociopath, a magical librarian, Leandra's non-identical warrior twin, and Leandra. Other members of this ludicrous household wander through Cal's peripheral awareness. Geometric chambers contain eclectic souls of various ages, abilities and temperaments. But Cal's dream only reveals six faces, including his own worried visage viewed in the reflective surfaces of shiny tiles and inactive screens. Strange forests surround his dream-home, teeming with weird insects, twisted ivy tendrils and opportunistic demons. A majestic mountain range lies east of the hexagonal castle, blocking the evening sun.

"Here are today's tasks, Cal." The librarian provides a print-out of administrative duties written in literal, unambiguous detail. This serene sibling rules the household. Parents are long vanished. Aunts, uncles, grandparents and cousins all inhabit faraway realms. Only siblings occupy the six-sided castle.

"Thank you." Cal accepts his tasks. Existence makes sense here, has routine and structure. No need to socially mask, fake neurotypical conversational ability, tolerate nerve-grating radio songs, or watch tedious mediavision. The library is peaceful, with incessant buzz from the forest's insects providing the only background noise. Only one sibling can speak at once. Across each wall, hundreds of screens play video with intricate visual details and total auditory silence. Even Cal's footfalls are noiseless as he carries the first stack of books to their shelf.

Bang! A door in the southern wall slams open.

"What's up, dickheads?" A feisty intruder shatters the tranquillity, striding onto chequered tiles carrying an assault rifle. "I threw a drink over a conniving bitch last night!" She emits a deranged chuckle, and Cal flinches as his sociopathic younger sister glares around the library. Her piercing eyes catch him dashing behind a bookshelf. "Yo, Library Boy! Filing books in alphabetical, Dewy decimal, hexadecimal, hexadecimate, propagate, conflagrate, dramaoftheweek-gate won't save you! You're tidying crockery on a sinking ship, counting stacks of green paper in a burning bank vault, signing a retirement policy before the nuke hits. You can't *organise* the apocalypse!"

With wide eyes and shaking hands, Cal scurries further from the flame-brained botheration. His first task is to put away these books, an impossible task if they are on fire.

"Enjoy the futility, dickhead!" The fiery one cackles behind Cal's retreating back as he approaches the library's north-eastern corner to the sound of beeping machinery.

Cal emerges from between two bookshelves and reaches the hospital bed where Leandra lies in a coma. A genderless warrior slumps on a plastic bedside chair holding the dying girl's pale hand and smoothing her tousled curls. Leandra is a mess. When formerly conscious, she communicated through riddles and melodramatic gestures. Now trapped in poisoned sleep, her brain projects tortured imagery onto the nearest screen.

A glowing rectangle of pixels depicts decadent socialites at an elegant soiree, eyes flashing malice within black cosmetic lines as they celebrate the sickened girl's downfall.

The non-binary warrior turns towards Cal, a solitary teardrop bisecting anguished features. "What the fuck is wrong with these people?"

(017)
His dream glitches, dropping multiple timeframes while cutting to a lonely future simultaneously the past. The librarian studies at her desk and the fiery sibling stalks demons in nearby forest. Cal organises library books. Leandra and her warrior twin are long departed, sent to a subterranean stage to re-enact their trauma theatre, and screens filling the south-east wall depict their violent misadventures. Cal regards the underground city in occasional wary glances, hoping Leandra escapes the coma and finds happiness. Given her eternally doomed demeanour this seems unlikely. He will miss her. For all her troubles, she was non-threatening and kind-hearted.

(026)
Dreamtime jumps again. The warrior has returned and now defends the castle, hunting demons near the perimeter fence. Coma Girl is gone, probably still dying... or dead.

"You miss that wretched girl?" A sneering voice emanates from a shadow to Cal's right as his scrawny limbs weaken and eyelids become heavier.

Cal turns toward the sinister crone who haunts the north-east chambers. "Yes." He gulps. "She cried and uttered nonsensical poetry, but at least she was nice."

The witch laughs in his face. "Nice. *Nice?* How *fascinating* to be somebody best described as 'nice'! Well, it's time you joined Miss Amenable in the deadlands." She hands him a battered khaki backpack. "Follow me."

A shorter jump, time glitches like a lost creature, rushing to the next location under the delusion life is easier somewhere else. Cal occupies the passenger seat. His witchy older sister drives out of the mountains' shadow along rail tracks through dead forest. A small rectangle of metal and plastic in her manicured hand, she reaches behind Cal's head.

He experiences the sensation of a first awakening, despite still dreaming. "Where am I?"

"You're in the desert. You have always lived in the desert. You have never seen a living tree."

Cal views the nightmarish roadside. Twisted, toxic trees reach burnt hands toward unreachable sky. Wooden corpses become sparser as ground gets flatter and the car approaches Summerton. At the city border, the witch jolts the car off the rails at Western Crossing and heads north along tarmac.

"Leandra!" Cal spots his beloved, long-lost sister hobbling along the perimeter sidewalk. Free from her tragic coma, she wears a beautiful sundress, and her raven curls bounce in the dry breeze. The witch slows the vehicle. When the car passes the limping model, she presses a dashboard button that unlocks Cal's seat belt and springs the passenger door open. She removes one hand from the wheel to shove him from the moving vehicle.

The world tumbles. Sky rotates with sand in jolting confusion. Still clutching his rucksack, Cal sprawls at Leandra's feet. Covered in scratches from rough pebbles, desert dust clinging to sap from fresh grazes, he stares up at Leandra's frail body silhouetted against cloudless sky. "I've missed you."

A screech of tires. The witch completes a swift three-point turn, then speeds back towards Western Crossing.

Bewildered Leandra looks from the retreating car to the man at her feet. "Do I know you?"

He raises his bruised upper body on battered palms. "I'm your brother, Cal. Don't you remember me, Leandra?"

"Who are Cal and Leandra?"

Cal squints at his troubled sister. Sunshine emerges from behind an overhead dust cloud, making her messed-up curls a frizzy halo. He says, "I am Cal, and you are Leandra."

The model contemplates the injured newcomer on the blood-flecked ground, lost in her world of ghosts. "OK," she says. "Can I lean on you while I walk home please? I'm tired and my legs ache terribly."

"Of course!" Cal scrambles to his feet.

"Thank you." Leandra takes his arm. "We can visit the grocery store if you're hungry."

The reunited siblings visit Sunny Bargains. Shelves are lined with processed foods in gaudy packaging, and no other customers are present. Leandra regards the commodities with hungry eyes. "Do you have money, Cal? My twin didn't leave much, and I earn little from modelling."

He opens his rucksack to find a wad of cash and a laptop. Leandra cries in relief. Loaded with purchases, Cal escorts his sister to the helpful cowboy's commune for artistic vagrants.

(042)

A motorbike engine rattles the windows of Telf Hall, waking Cal, who immediately dismisses his dreams. His hyper-fixated mind acknowledges only one unsubstantiated belief system, and that is Chroma.

Obsessed with planets far from this suffocating desert, he conducts further research over breakfast, mouse in one hand and spoon in the other. Sporadically catching a com network connection, he consumes huge chunks of Chroman data. Once he memorises the co-ordinates to navigate the stars, space will belong to him, and he can finally leave this arid prison where he has never seen a living tree.

2.05

(045)
The midday sun reaches a blinding zenith as Cal escorts Leandra to her fetish photographer's premises. He waits outside while his sister is degraded on camera, scribbling notes for his Calanooka site. Why dream of magic castles and creepy witches when you can daydream of polychromatic aliens? Local pedestrians ignore him, a fidgety yet bland addition to the urban landscape, face hidden under his battered cap.

After Leandra's messy shoots reach a freshly shampooed conclusion, the siblings walk home. Rainbow-coloured leaflets await them on the doormat. Cal tries explaining their significance but Leandra, barely comprehending, goes to bed. He slumps in a daze, clutching garish paper as his dreams blossom and reality crumbles. "Reckish demons teleported a CRIB to your mindscape thirty-two years ago. If you are reading this, you survived their primary attack. But portals in your mindfield sector are re-activating. Join the Chroman army! Receive military training to aid the fight against demonic invasion."

This is everything Cal has pined for... The lunacy of mindscape theory, the complicated rainbow of Chroma, alien demons crawling from geometric portals to wreak havoc... Anything other than this suffocating, domestic nightmare. The only other evidence for his belief system lies in obscure forums. Pages with Chroman information keep changing location, hidden behind layers of passwords and chains of obscure links. He designed Calanooka.com to gather data in a fixed and easily findable location. Now physical, printed artifacts of Chroman existence have appeared on his doormat! Either the Chroman theorists are emerging from hiding, or Cal and Leandra are going insane.

He falls asleep clutching creased paper, and his unconscious visions teem with alien invasion.

He wakes to find Summerton has entered an era of vicious weather. Sandstorms reach a brutal frenzy, the authorities say to remain home except for emergencies, and Occreta Gate colleagues from multi-income households skip shifts due to cancelled buses or cars trapped in sand drifts. Cal continues working. His march to work takes ninety minutes when streets become golden dunes. His shoes are so broken he starts each shift by tipping sand from them into the dustbin. His life may be Godless, but his footwear is holey.

"You walked from Telf Hall through that massive storm? You kind person!" Trish Mengleo is stunned by Cal's determination to maintain perfect attendance.

"I have no choice. Without my wages, my sister and I would starve." Cal returns his feet to sand-free shoes. "Do our residents ever lack adequate footwear?"

Trish shakes her head. "The Employment Office just allocated four thousand cash digits to buy them a new car."

"But they have a car! And they don't drive."

"That car was old! Staff can drive them... they hate the bus."

Cal would be grateful for an old car. Or a bus ticket. Or shoes. Or therapy to process the stress of caring for these spoiled, overgrown children.

Trish leaves as Sara Boppetwann arrives for evening shift. Sara gets Susie Miscorp off the toilet, dresses her in storm gear then informs Cal, "I'm taking Susie out!"

Cal is left alone with the remaining residents. He first ensures everyone is safe then occupies himself with cleaning, beginning with this morning's dishes. After completing this task, he leaves the kitchen, and the door weirdly clicks behind him. He tries the handle to find it jammed.

Probably a fault in the internal lock mechanism.

Sam Rettie now desires a cup of tea, and communicates this by yelling, "TEA!" in Cal's worried face while jabbing a large hand toward the kitchen.

Cal calls Occreta Gate's emergency helpline, but nobody answers. He tries Sara's com screen, then Lessabeth Ross and Babs Trabeck, who all ignore their devices while he hyperventilates. After thirty minutes of unanswered calls with Sam shouting in his face, Lessabeth Ross picks up and provides Cal with the repairs hotline. The repairs team say no maintenance staff are available until tomorrow. Threatened by Sam's increasingly enraged behaviour, Cal tries Sara's com screen again, with no success. "TEA! TEA!" Sam continues to scream in Cal's face. The man is desperate for a bland, hot beverage, and screaming might make it appear.

Cal is desperate for escape from workplace hell. He considers yelling, "UNIVERSAL BASIC INCOME!" in Sam's face, but doubts the man's awareness of progressive politics.

Ron Buce arrives on shift. Cal frantically explains the situation, and Ron shoulder-rams the kitchen door, snapping the broken lock. Sam dashes to complete the urgent task of brewing leaves in boiling water. Cal retrieves warped pieces of metal from the linoleum then begins cooking dinner.

Ron wonders why Cal was alone.

"Sara took Susie out and won't answer her com screen."

Ron laughs. "You gonna report her?"

Cal's stomach rises with anxiety. "Are we supposed to report each other? Won't people hate me?"

"Yeah." Ron nods. "Best not report her."

Sara arrives with Susie an hour before shift end. Cal is washing dinner plates while Ron scrolls on his com screen. Cal drops his cloth and asks, "Where were you? The kitchen door broke, and Sam was yelling. I kept calling you."

"I am allowed to take residents out!" Sara snaps. "We attended Tibshull Street Church."

"Chill, Cal." Ron glances up from his social media feed. "You can leave now."

"Yeah. Go home, Cal," Sara agrees.

"But... I'm scheduled until nine!"

Sara and Ron exchange conspiratorial smiles.

"Are you *scared*, Cal?"

"I get panicky when forced to vary from a pre-designated schedule," Cal explains.

"Haha! Cal's *scared!*"

Cal begins to hyperventilate at the notion of staying with these chaotic individuals a moment longer. Light-headed from shallow breathing, he grabs his outdoor gear.

His walk home is a dazed march through Summerton's violently sandy streets. Cal despairs that his world contains no order, no structure - just swirling, abrasive wind and colleagues who disregard the comfort of designated schedules. He considers self-mutilation as a coping mechanism. A serrated face might convince the Employment Office of his unsuitability for employment... Although they would probably say his striped countenance proves he can hold a kitchen knife, and make him work in the noisy diner.

A pile of Chroman leaflets lies ignored on his bedside table as Cal later drifts through blood-soaked nightmares.

He attends his Occupational Health appointment the next day. "If I'm too disabled to work, will you provide a written report for the Employment Office?" Cal clutches his crumpled appointment letter in trembling hands.

"I have no affiliation with the Employment Office," the company doctor says. "It's *my* job to suggest reasonable adjustments that will allow you to attend *your* job."

"I urgently require a regular, fixed schedule," Cal explains. "The constantly varied rota, completed mere days in advance, is making me suicidal from stress."

The doctor asks a series of personal questions that make Cal hyper-aware of his rising insanity. He divulges his struggles with workplace pressure but avoids mentioning gory visions of Occreta Gate becoming a slaughterhouse. The doctor nods while typing notes at her laptop. "I will suggest a fixed schedule to your line manager. You should also telephone our company counselling service."

At least she didn't suggest Pilates... Cal muses as he stumbles home, barely visible through buffeting sand.

Back in the apartment kitchen, he demonstrates his fortunate ability to use cutlery by self-injuring with a kitchen knife. Blood drips from his pale shin onto linoleum while his sister doses in the parlour.

"Oh, Cal! What have you done?" Leandra wakes to find him in a pool of blood, staring mutely at the cupboard. She bandages his wound then puts him to bed. Her glossed lips kiss his forehead as he returns to nightmares.

The next day at Occreta Gate, Cal sits with his colleagues, attempting conversation. Most topics revolve around a vapid mediavision programme dominating the eastern wall. He struggles to produce the correct input. After failing to socially integrate, he leaves the parlour to find something to clean.

All staff leave before dinner except Cal and Sara. The obnoxious pop-star-wannabe entertains herself by bellowing gospel hits, creating a sensory overwhelming atmosphere. Sam Rettie bangs his head against the doorframe. Cal suggest a quieter environment would benefit residents with hyper-sensitive hearing. Sara declares Cal has an attitude problem.

The neurodiverse brain cannot differentiate between unwanted noise and physical pain. But of course, our rejection of over-stimulation is a character flaw! Neurotypicals are obviously right. Their outnumbering us increases their opinion's validity... Despairing Cal retreats into his vivid imagination. He daydreams of Godshi Enpire, the home of scientists with blatant attitude problems who devote their lives to peaceful study and invention.

2.06

(046)

Cal's first and only company-sponsored counselling session brings no psychological insight, only a delightful game of Guess the Historical Song Title.

"What do you hope to achieve through counselling?" The elderly counsellor's plastic pen hovers over a box on his Counselling Worksheet entitled "Aims".

"To stop feeling suicidal," Cal replies without hesitation.

The counsellor graces his client with a patronising smile. "But what does that *mean*?"

"You don't know what suicidal means?" Tired Cal wishes he had brought his handy mental-illness-themed dictionary.

"I know what it *means*," the counsellor says. "But how can we phrase this as a Counselling Aim?"

"I wish to cease idolising the idea of taking an overdose, or pushing a razor into my arteries until my body is empty of blood," Cal replies. "Is that a relevant aim or do you need more detail?"

The counsellor emits nervous laughter. "My job is to help you re-frame negativity into positive thinking. So… How could your Counselling Aim be stated in a positive way?"

Cal sits in blank silence.

"The first step in positive thinking is avoiding negative language," the counsellor explains. "So instead of focusing on death, we focus on…"

Cal stares at the wood grain effect on the plastic desk, waiting for the supposed mental health professional to finish his sentence. After several unproductive seconds, the counsellor asks, "What do we focus on, Cal?"

"I don't understand," the troubled man replies. "What exactly do you want me to say?"

The counsellor's eyes twinkle with a knowing smile.

"What do you *think* I want you to say?"

"I don't know. That's why I asked."

"How can we better phrase 'not being suicidal'?"

If I wasn't suicidal before, I would be now... Cal considers crumpling the Counselling Worksheet into a ball and shoving it down the smug counsellor's throat. Instead, he tries to play the Fun Word Game of constructing an answer containing *(hooray!)* positive language. "The cessation of this reoccurring urge to die would make me happy?" he suggests, trying to smile. It hurts his face.

"You're still mentioning death!" the counsellor huffs. "What is the opposite to death?"

Cal taps a soothing pattern on the tabletop. "Are you unfamiliar with the antonym of death? Or are you prompting me to provide 'staying alive' as a Counselling Aim?"

The counsellor enthuses "That's correct!" while writing "Staying alive" in his Counselling Worksheet's Aims box.

"That's a song from the past," Cal remarks.

The counsellor turns red. "Yes, I suppose it is..." He clears his throat. "Now... what are your other aims?"

"Not killing- I mean, staying alive is pretty much my major ambition these days."

"But how do you want to *feel*?"

"Like an integrated member of society. Part of this species. A creature who belongs on this planet."

"But how would this *make you feel*?"

"Not autistic or mentally ill."

"'Autistic' and 'mentally ill' are labels!" the counsellor declares. "I prefer the holistic approach, not putting people in boxes." His pen hovers over the Aims box. "So, how would 'belonging on this planet' make you *feel*?"

Cal slows his breathing, trying not to scream. "But if you understood autism, you would understand the unsuitability of this indirect manner of questioning."

The counsellor clears his throat. "What *emotion* would you associate with *belonging*?"

Cal sighs. "You want to write 'Feeling happy' in your Aims box under Staying Alive?"

"That's right!" Scribbling his corporate-branded pen, the counsellor gleefully adds "Feeling happy" to his list.

"You could write 'Feeling Good', to retain the Historical Song Title theme," Cal suggests.

The counsellor discards his branded stationary and folds his arms. "Why are you here, Cal?"

"To improve my mental health. But you cannot help me if you lack experience of working with autism."

"I don't *see* labels!"

"That's a position of enviable privilege," Cal remarks. "Members of oppressed demographics lack the luxury of being ignorant of demographic status. Occupying a marginalised identity affects a person's experience of society and can limit their potential due to systematic discrimination. Therefore, your refusal to even *acknowledge* my autism is insulting and unhelpful."

The counsellor sighs. "Nobody can help you, unless you actually *want* to get better."

Cal's session ends. Unsurprisingly, he declines to book a repeat appointment. With the company counselling service unsuitable to his needs, his only hope lies in Lessabeth Ross allowing him a fixed schedule, as per the Occupational Health doctor's first recommendation.

He arrives home to further correspondence from Occreta Gate in the form of a Flexible Working sheet. He requests regular hours, preferably evening shifts. The diner staff are particularly raucous after midnight and early sleep is difficult.

Days pass in which Cal's thoughts are drenched in blood and chaos. Workplace stress amplifies destructive urges... The razor slice... The scarlet drip...

Cal helps Susie Miscorp dress after her evening bath. An optimistic hippy once told him that non-verbal people are differently connected to the universe, in tune with psychic brainwaves that verbal folk fail to notice. Cal regarded this theory as nonsense. However, when he thinks *I want to cut my face open* while crouching at Susie's feet, pulling socks gently over her chunky ankles, Susie immediately yells, "NO! DON'T DO THAT!"

The timing strikes Cal as uncanny. He stands, backing away slowly with no sudden movements.

Susie stands, twice the breadth of him and yelling, "DON'T DO THAT!" Her usually slack-jawed countenance contorts with rage. Her furious glance forms a curious juxtaposition with the floral soft furnishings of her comfortable bedroom.

Cal's blood figuratively freezes. He is alone with a broad-shouldered person who seethes with aggression.

He keeps facing Susie, remembering the online training module on confrontational behaviour. He reaches for the door handle behind him while the livid lady stomps in his direction. He opens the door. Susie stoops to half-pull up her pyjama bottoms while Cal backs into the corridor.

Before Susie regains an upright stance, he dashes to the parlour, where Ron sits scrolling on his com screen. Cal sits beside him, trembling. "Susie yelled at me."

Ron looks up from his com device. "What did you do?"

"Nothing! I was putting her favourite socks on."

"You must have done something. She never gets angry."

The lady in question chooses this moment to stride into the parlour, eyes bulging with undisguised hatred, breathing heavy through her nostrils. Her pyjama bottoms are still halfway up her thighs, revealing her giant diaper.

Ron stands, pocketing his com screen. "Why you angry, Susie?" He stoops to pull the pink pastel nightwear with smiling teddy bears over her diaper.

"NO!" Susie yells, before storming off.

Ron follows her. "What's the matter? What happened?"

"Don't do that!" Susie repeats, before slamming back into her floral bedroom.

Ron returns to the parlour, grinning. "What did you do?"

"I told you! I was putting her socks on." Cal frantically processes all available information until his analytical mind provides two possible answers for Susie's rage...

Option A: In Susie's semi-verbal state, her brain operates on an unusual frequency, making her receptive to psychic connection. She heard Cal's internal monologue saying, "I want to cut my face open". Her local church might preach harsh views on mental illness, deeming self-mutilation a sin, damaging the vessel provided by God.

Option B: Susie had a sudden, irrational aversion to her previously favourite socks.

At the next training day, Cal asks his colleagues for advice on dealing with Ms Miscorp's temper.

The other staff members are aghast.

"She never gets angry!"

"Susie likes everybody!"

"What did you *do*?"

Cal cowers before their judgement. *Who knew helping a disabled person wear socks was a marker of suppressed evil?* Memories flicker through tortured consciousness... Years of attempting invisibility to avoid abuse. He incites rage by existing. His quiet, nervous manner is a frequent trigger for violent fury. Maybe he *should* cut his face, to provide visible warning of his dreadful nature.

Ms Ross asks the assembled staff, "Have you all brought your Flexible Working sheets?"

Cal passes his sheet with a hopeful smile. Maybe an unchanging weekly timetable would ease his self-destructive urges and make his presence more bearable.

"Oh goody!" Lessabeth Ross laughs. "I'm looking forward to reading your requests, so I can *ignore* them."

Cal later returns to Telf Hall numb with grief.

Leandra is in the parlour with a new photographer. She sits with her artwork, dressed as a glamorous eccentric, eyes fearful above a faltering smile. "I feel self-conscious not wearing jam or custard," she jokes at her insecurity. "How did the meeting go?"

"She laughed in my face," says Cal.

"Don't worry," says Leandra. "I have some interesting ideas to improve our situation."

2.07

(053)

Cal could swear several months have passed, although his memories fill the space of a week. Time shifts like desert sands while Occreta Gate employment is a repetitive nightmare, unfamiliar enough to be disorienting, yet familiar enough to arouse dismal memories. At some point in the maelstrom of bewildering recurrences, Leandra got sexually assaulted by her solo birthday guest and descended further into madness. Cal financially supports the household. He still has no fixed schedule. His increasingly frantic requests for regular hours meet evasive replies or silence from Lessabeth Ross. His only social interaction apart from colleagues and Leandra are typed conversations on the com network's obscurest forums.

He sits in the sparse Telf Hall apartment, trawling Chroma pages while Leandra doses in her parlour bed. An anonymous post about the infamous Second Fall catches his anxious attention.

[004] "The Second Fall was a Reckish attack on Chroma approximately four hundred years ago. With a fleet of hexagonal spaceships, they swarmed each sphere except Hew Espireth, massacring and subjugating the population. Three generations of Chromans were raised under Reckish rule. They were forced to speak Reckish language, which became known as Hexish after the shape of the occupier's spaceships. Prior to Reckish invasion, each sphere had its own unique language. Although the Chromans eventually overthrew their invaders, Hexish remains the first language of Chroma today."

The first commenter is N-Dog_Bargain_Lad, who writes, "If Reckish demons enslaved Summerton, would anyone notice? We're already subjugated. And nobody knows what's beyond this dumb city's perimeter."

Cal replies, "What's your stance on mindscape theory?"

Three seconds later, his laptop crashes.

Cal stares out the window and waits for a reboot.

Leandra rouses and tells a cryptic, rambling story about lizards and breadcrumbs.

Then the knocking on the door begins.

The scene that follows resembles a segment from a science fiction movie where two unlikely heroes are chosen for interstellar adventure. Except Cal is no superhero and struggles to process this bombardment of unexpected interaction.

An officer from Bure Eshpel offers Cal and Leandra a place in her army.

Leandra is ecstatic.

Cal is undecided and overwhelmed.

(056)

After ranting at the siblings about the dire consequences of Reckish invasion, Captain Kalakai answers a call on the com screen attached to her wrist. Cal clutches his head. After terminating the call, Kalakai declares, "If you wish to join the Chroman Army, we leave immediately."

Cal starts rocking back and forth, covering his ears. He could never cope with sudden change or abrupt decisions. Now the air roars as another sandstorm approaches and nothing seems real.

"This is an emergency!" the alien visitor snaps.

"I need time to process new information," Cal whispers, with three taps of his palm against his skull.

"You're out of time," Kalakai declares.

"Please give Cal a moment to think," pleads Leandra.

Kalakai shakes her head. "I should have taken the other two." She turns from the befuddled siblings and dashes from the apartment.

Leandra wails, "Don't go!" as the door slams closed. She raises the blinds to watch Kalakai's departure.

The space captain sprints down rusty stairs into Telf Hall's courtyard and boards her silver shuttle as the sandstorm reaches the windows. Her ship ascends into eddies of swirling desert fragments.

"That was everything we ever wanted!" Leandra cries.

"I require sufficient time to process decisions," Cal mumbles, still rocking in his seat.

"We're out of time..." Leandra limps to her parlour bed, weeping, then barely moves for hours.

Later the siblings take a walk that reaches a sinister conclusion, and the sleepy town of Summerton is shocked when pieces of the first murder victim are found pooled in blood outside Sunny Bargains.

Leandra provides a witness statement while Cal's psychological cohesion disintegrates in the bakery isle. Sheriff Green wants to know Leandra's previous whereabouts, the Reckish want to know why Occreta Gate is not on fire, and Cal just wishes lizards could eat bread.

2.08

(071)
The sandstorms reach a temporary ceasefire, ushering in a phase of peaceful weather. The isolated city lies cooled by a refreshing breeze instead of battered by airborne grit. Summerton now lives up to its name as locals leave their homes in summer clothing, wearing shades instead of goggles, carrying parasols instead of extra scarves.

Six days after helping Leandra bring a small cat to a belated vets' appointment, Cal trudges to therapy on a beautiful afternoon. Figurative storms still rage through his tormented mind. He cannot stop thinking about Nigel Paul Charlesworth, as conflicting rumours emanate from Trilby Asylum. Some say the treasonous man hung himself with his straitjacket. Others say he remains tied to a hospital bed, screaming conspiracy theories in a deranged attempt to besmirch the town's benevolent creators.

Cal arrives at therapy and takes a seat in the attic office.
"Hello, I'm Cal."
Dr Peter Favishti peers over his notepad. "Are you Leandra's brother?" He makes a note as Cal nods. "Do you know why you're here, Cal?"
"I hope it's not to play word games involving historical song titles..." Cal stares through uncracked glass at shimmering sunlight. "My sister Leandra said I should talk to you. Stress from my care assistant job is killing me."
Dr Favishti nods. "Is there another reason?"
Cal sits motionless, his face unchanging. "Two weeks ago, after my sister told a nonsensical story involving lizards and a crack house, we were visited by Kalakai, a blue-skinned space captain from Bure Eshpel, the blue sphere in the Chroma Sphere System."
Dr Favishti makes another note. "Was Kalakai real?"

"She seemed real..." Cal tries to wrench something beyond perturbation from his tired memory. "I remember the tight grip of her hand on my neck, her fury at my doubting her existence. I should have known better, after my research. She was in a hurry, recruiting for the Chroman army, and she wanted my skills as a ROM."

"What is a Rom?"

"ROMs are named after the computer specification, read only memory. We excel at memorisation and recall. Electromagnetic fields render Chroman navigation tech inoperable, so the Chroman army employs ROMs as bio hard drives. I've already memorised the co-ordinates of every celestial body between here and Chroma."

"I see," says Dr Favishti, who has not stopped writing. "Where did you obtain this information?"

"Some data is sent by email from an untraceable address, while other info resides on obscure websites. There's a rumour a Chroman sleeper agent has been locating ROMs, feeding us information to aid the recruitment process."

"So, this provides a sense of purpose? Learning stellar co-ordinates to help this Chroman army."

Cal smiles for the first time in days. "I always wished the job of Professional Memoriser existed in human society. I struggle with most employment. Instructions are vague, workplaces too chaotic... But the Chroman army values ROMs! They would provide clear instructions, a soundproof workspace, accommodation for me and Leandra... It would be wonderful!"

"I'm guessing these prospects bring you great relief."

Cal's palms tap eight times in gentle clapping motion. "They really do!"

"How long have you believed in aliens, Cal?"

"All my life! I am named after Kalanooka, the ruler of Bure Eshpel who died saving Chroma."

"So, your parents believed in aliens too?"

Cal attempts to remember childhood. The effort causes him to seek solace in his trusty rock back and forth, accompanied by a repetitive arm tap.

"Is it difficult to remember your parents?"

"I do struggle," says Cal. "My early memory files are corrupted. I only know I have always lived in the desert and never seen a living tree..."

He stares out the window at the distant forest of dead trees clinging to insurmountable slopes. "I was called Claire, but I never identified with that name. So, I changed it. That's common practice amongst my generation. I mean... Your parents don't choose your food or clothes when you reach adulthood, why should they choose your name and gender? I chose Cal. Short for Kalanooka, but with a C instead of a K, so I could keep my first initial. I thought this would provide a grounding, human connection..." Cal trails off, turns to face his new therapist. "I'm a freak, aren't I?"

Dr Favishti shakes his head. "Having a rich, inner fantasy world does not make you a freak. Mild delusions are useful defence mechanisms for the sensitive mind."

"What if the delusions become hallucinations? A descent into psychosis..." Cal clutches his arms and begins shaking. "How did me and Leandra experience a visitation from a blue-skinned space captain if we're not freaks?"

Dr Favishti taps his pen against his clipboard while scanning his notes. "Had either or both of you consumed hallucinogens prior to this visitation?"

"That was the first thing we suspected!" Cal replies. "But Kalakai said calling her a figment of our imaginations was insulting. And I am convinced I was sober. I rarely consume drink or recreational drugs because life is confusing enough."

"Was Leandra also sober?"

"She's been sober since the assault by Ernie Trenta on her birthday. She fears further chemical imbalance might kill her."

"That's sensible," Dr Favishti remarks. "It sounds like you're both enduring extreme stress. You are struggling with irregular hours at an emotionally demanding job. Leandra has experienced abuse and social rejection. Your home provides additional strain with the noisy diner downstairs. You have both reached breaking point. This is understandable. And you have reclaimed your childhood fairy tale for comfort."

Cal flinches. "I didn't find Kalakai comforting! Faced with the stark reality of a Chroman alien existing, in my apartment... To use a crude yet popular metaphor, I figuratively shat myself."

"Hallucinations can become frightening when combined with underlying anxiety," Dr Favishti explains. "Was Leandra also scared of Kalakai?"

Cal remembers Leandra's lustrous smile during the visitation. "I've never seen her so happy! Kalakai was ruder to her, sceptical of her value to the army, yet Leandra was ecstatic the entire visit. As though Kalakai was a fabled prince come to rescue..." Cal becomes silent while a breadless lizard scuttles across the outside windowsill. He smiles. "Lizards ate Leandra's breadcrumbs."

"I beg your pardon?"

Cal turns back to the therapist. "Lizards ate her breadcrumbs! I understand now!"

"You understand lizards ate Leandra's breadcrumbs?"

"Yes!" Cal beams. "Equations! The breadcrumbs are her cries for help and validation. The lizards are the endless noise of this existence, drowning her cries so her prince will never hear. I finally understand."

"Wonderful!" Dr Favishti returns Cal's eager smile. "Sometimes what feels like complete and total breakdown is actually a point of mental breakthrough."

2.09

(074)

"Three point..." Cal begins, as Leandra sits opposite, drawing whimsical monsters. "One four one, five nine two, six five three five, eight nine seven nine-"

"Why must you babble numbers?" Leandra snaps.

Cal regards his irritated sister... her furrowed brow, her pen hovering over a delightful page of shadowy hellscapes. The only "three point" relevant to her interests is the three-point turn that sent her the wrong direction home.

She sighs. "And now I'm stuck here with you."

He reduces his recitation to a whisper camouflaged by his ever-running noise machine and continues to rock like his tortured skull is fixed to an invisible pendulum.

"You don't *choose* to be broken." Leandra recommences shading with tiny strokes of her ballpoint pen. "And I never chose to be eternally exhausted... If only your physical durability and my ability to communicate in trivial social contexts could be combined into a functional human... But then where would our undesirable aspects go? Would we simultaneously create a Reject Twin from the remaining characteristics? A sad creature both metaphorically and literally crippled..."

"Perhaps we're *both* reject twins," Cal muses.

"Huh?" Leandra's hazel eyes dart from her sketchbook to her strange brother, who has stopped rocking and sits motionless in contemplation. "I didn't realise you were listening. You seemed kinda engrossed in those numbers."

Cal becomes silent.

"What's that about reject twins?" Leandra prompts.

Cal slowly inhales, exhales, then speaks. "What if our creator designed a social frontperson from stray pieces of a broken psyche... And my personality is composed of the dregs that remained, leaving me a stranded alien in the realm of human communication. Then our creator designed the ultimate avenging warrior, forged in the strongest fire of their lust for retribution, and *you* were the equal and opposite reaction to that creation... Weakness and vulnerability draped in a flimsy white flag."

Leandra regards her aesthetically pleasing but feeble form. "I'm not wearing a white flag. I'm wearing an orange dress."

Cal snorts. "*Now* who's being too literal?"

His sibling places her pen beside an intricately shaded arcane eye and folds her skinny arms. "Since when did you think in metaphors?"

"Since realising our whole arid world is a giant metaphor! Since a blue alien visited, my hopes of normalcy disintegrated, and I began to question this reality. Each question generates further questions as I follow this path into a paradoxically confused enlightenment."

Leandra gazes at her sketchbook as though the detailed, demonic eye is drowning her. "I dreamed of a fierce, protective twin, the strength to my weakness... But I wake and dreams slip from memory, returning only as occasional flickers of gut-punching truth." She grips the table. "Do you get that? Inner programming that compels you to dismiss your dreams upon waking? Repressing terrible knowledge..."

Cal regards Leandra's sketchbook. "Why are demonic eyes your main artistic subject?"

She jumps as though startled by her creation. "I never think when I draw..." She rubs her eyes. "I've always felt watched by ancient evil. Monsters sneaking from the deadlands, prowling Summerton's perimeter... They see everything! Instruct me to burn this world that rejects me... Send glorified visions of death..."

We are crazier than I realised... Have we succumbed to Reckish influence? Trembling Cal asks his mad sister, "What stops you giving in to these voices?"

Leandra raises her face from her treasured sketchbook, her eyes shining luminous. "Very little. I barely comprehend reality. Memories flicker, bittersweet and ghostly, my past swirling in grim kaleidoscope. What are we, Cal? It's increasingly difficult to pretend, play the party girl, when I'm ostracised by social judgement in this crippled form." She cracks an acrid grimace. "I posted on the com network earlier, 'My life is awful. I wish I was dead.'"

Cal shakes his head. "You crave death, but you also want to feel alive. What you truly seek is escape from suffocating purgatory." He stares back out the window. Grains of sand and dirt embedded in splinter cracks reach a ragged claw toward the sky. The cracks are a hand, the hand is a skeleton tree, everything reaches for heaven but remains rooted in deadly earth. Cal smiles. Metaphors make more sense when you realise everything is everything.

His sister turns to stare at faraway desert. "I can't stop grasping slivers of jagged hope," she says. "Although they cut my palms to ribbons. My social gestures crumble to reveal the misery behind the mask, a walking wound. What's the point... Point? I've not uttered that word in aeons. My only point was thrown away in a rambling prologue, preceding a descent into infinite self-absorption."

Cal smiles at Leandra, slumped in her plastic chair, lost to the horizon. "You are speaking monotone monologues and staring out the window. I understand metaphors. Have we become the same person?"

Leandra continues her expressionless stare. "Some belief systems paint all sentient beings as one consciousness fragmented into separate avatars. But if I am already a fragment, how do I feel so fractured? At least two Leandras exist. One who plays the social game, kisses or fucks anyone who pays her attention. And the sad Leandra who cries into lonely sketchbooks. Even in depression's pitiful depths, Hedonist Glamour Leandra yearns to drink and fuck her way through town. Conversely, even during a whirlwind of impulsive fun and distraction, Misery Leandra wants to open this body's arteries. How can I be the same person as you, if I'm not the same person as myself?"

"Branching consciousness," Cal mutters.

"Branching what?"

Cal's glance darts to random places as he attempts to simplify his thoughts... Leandra's delicate features scrunched in puzzlement... Her shaded demon eye glaring from the page... Magnolia peeling off nearby walls... The window... the claw-shaped cracks...

"Imagine the shape of a tree," Cal says. "One trunk splits into two large branches, which split into smaller branches, which keep splitting until they are twigs... What if we, Cal and Leandra, are connected to the same branch? And a hedonistic branch and a misery branch are both attached to you?"

Leandra chuckles. "That's right! I am a branch. Behold my leafy splendour! You made more sense when you spoke in numbers. Or communicated in a purely literal way and didn't think we were a tree."

"We're not actually a tree!" Cal argues. "I just thought trees would provide an effective way of explaining branching consciousness. Because they have branches."

Leandra's com screen vibrates, rattling against the table. She reads a message, and her grin brings an incandescent sheen to tired features. "Remember I posted earlier about being suicidal? Well Bod Weye from Ocorropinta nightclub wants to buy me dinner to cheer me up."

Cal chuckles. "How thoughtful."

"Can you walk me to the restaurant at six please?"

"Sure." Cal checks the time on his laptop. If he maintains focus, that leaves three hours to work on Calanooka.com, finalising the page about Evol Espireth. This violet sphere boasts majestic mountains and arrogant sorcerers. Leandra recommences drawing, and both siblings work in silence until Leandra leaves the table to get ready.

She returns from her bedroom. "How do I look?"

Cal turns to view his eager sister. "Attractive enough that a post mentioning suicidal urges prompted a young man to ask you to dinner."

Leandra examines her surgically enhanced figure clad in a fitted dress. "Does that mean I'm hot?"

Cal closes his laptop. "It means you're hot."

The siblings don broken shoes and light jackets, then exit the apartment. Concrete pathways shimmer in the afternoon sun. *Where is everybody? It's so quiet...* Cal shivers with foreboding but keeps ominous thoughts from his sister.

Leandra squeezes his arm. "You know your branching consciousness theory?" She giggles. "Who is the trunk? And if the trunk dies, do us branch bitches die?"

Images flicker through Cal's mind... *a trapezium-shaped library, a mountainside cave behind the dead trees, a hospital bed on a chequered floor, a witch on a canvas throne, Leandra lying in a coma, Leandra viewed through the windscreen of a moving vehicle...* Nonsensical fragments of audio-visual botherment cascade through his consciousness.

After seconds of silence, Leandra repeats herself.

Cal pushes back dizzying memories to tell her, "Here the tree metaphor collapses."

Leandra squeezes his arm again as she giggles. "Sorry to be a foresty lumberjack!"

Cal kicks a pebble and the sole of his broken shoe rips slightly more open. "When a mind-tree dies, I believe the branches of consciousness break off to become independent entities, no longer tied to the ground."

Leandra turns her made-up face to peer through gaps in nearby buildings. Cal follows her gaze to where dead trees adorn the looming mountains. Leandra sighs. "Maybe that's why the branches of dying trees claw at the sky," she says. "Trying to break off, away from poisoned earth."

Cal has already considered this. "Maybe..." Now that metaphors are fathomable, even non-sentient objects can have a sad biography. Everything is special. Which means nothing is.

The siblings reach the restaurant where Leandra's date is waiting. "Thanks for walking me, Cal. I would ask you to join us, but you hate socialising."

"Casual conversation is a nightmare," Cal agrees. "But I am persevering at Occreta Gate! I map out my colleagues' speech like mathematical formula. I am training myself to interact by inserting the correct phrase when somebody leaves a gap in the auditory pattern. I will eventually crack this algorithm."

Leandra gasps, "Crack the algorithm? Of a conversation? Cal, conversing is about reaching out, connecting with other humans. It's not maths!"

"Everything is maths," Cal insists. "Call me if you need escorting home. The police still haven't found the Sunny Bargains murderer."

After Leandra enters the restaurant, Cal hurries back to Telf Hall. Hairs rise on his limbs despite the evening's pleasant warmth. The sky darkens to a violent red as his blood chills with the conviction of being watched.

2.10

(077)
"Increased security at Trilby Asylum would make Summerton safer." Cal repeats an up-voted comment from a recent news article on his way to work, hoping regurgitation of popular opinions will assist his ongoing pursuit of social integration. When he arrives at Occreta Gate, the staff are watching an inane show in the parlour. He politely greets everyone and pretends not to hate mediavision. *It's so patronising... too bright, too loud... like a moron dressed in luminous fabrics screaming, "I hope your brain cells DIE!" in your face. And some call this technicolour hell "entertainment".*

"This show is awesome!" Cal lies, forcing the corners of his mouth upwards. A ridiculous soap opera fills the screen. A young woman is having an affair while her husband is in a coma. Her older sister is secretly her mother. Her cousin is secretly the next-door neighbour's dog. Her existence is secretly meaningless.

The screen flickers.

"It was an innocent rat!" screeches an evangelical lunatic from a barbed wire pulpit.

The screen flickers again and the soap opera returns.

Cal shakes his head, clearing visions of impending destruction. "Did you see the news?" he enquires. "We need increased security at Trilby Asylum to make Summerton safer." He then holds his breath, waiting to see if his conversational attempt is successful.

"We should all work at Trilby Asylum!" Sara declares. "They pay twice as much! It's a joke them paying minimum wage here, when we give out dangerous medications."

The assembled staff murmur agreement that Occreta Gate is indeed a terrible employer. Cal breathes, believing he has adequately masked his social ineptitude. The remainder of his morning shift passes in a blur of mundane tasks accompanied by garish on-screen mediocrity.

After his shift ends, Cal has another therapy appointment with Dr Favishti. He usually enjoys the company of this insightful professional who never expects him to mask his incompatibility with humanity, but today's mention of childhood results in a panic attack.

Curled on a chair in the doctor's office, rasps of laboured breathing emanate from Cal's crumpled form.

"Are you able to articulate what's causing this state of panic?" Dr Favishti's voice echoes from miles across an empty chamber.

Cal clutches his knees, head tucked inwards, lost in a lightless realm. "Peblash Reck!" he gasps. His skull brims with images of nightmare space opera. "I remember it all... The Reckish uprising, the GWAKZ alliance, the war, Kalanooka's sacrifice to save Chroma... The surviving Reckish hordes preparing their next attack, infecting the Mindfields, converting everyone to soulless evil..."

"This is just a story," Dr Favishti insists. "Your brain generates forty-two percent more information than average. Modern human society, where everything is loud and simple, simultaneously overwhelms and bores you. So, your mind created a whole galaxy to entertain and hide yourself. But this fantasy amplifies itself, becomes a paranoid delusion, a safe place you paradoxically need protecting from. Until you deal with your underlying depression and anxiety, these issues will follow you into the dream."

Cal still struggles to breathe. He survived today's shift, but he will remain in the work trap until Leandra resorts to prostitution. Life is a cruel prison.

He hits his head four times.

"Please don't punish yourself for what life has done to you," the doctor says. "You are safe here. You have no enemies in this building. The 'Reckish demon hordes' are not real. Just as you created the idea of them, you have the power to make them disappear."

"But Kalakai said... the CRIB..." Cal whimpers.

"Crib is an interesting word." Dr Favishti's voice is still miles from Cal's hidden face. "You speak of demons arising from the crib, while also saying you barely remember your childhood. And your co-morbid mental illness is invariably caused by trauma. What happened in the crib, Cal?"

Cal opens his eyes to view the woven plastic threads of his trousers. He sits upright, still clutching his knees, and stares at Dr Favishti's forehead. "A Chamber of Reckish Intergalactic Botherment was dropped on this mindscape thirty-two years ago by the demons of Peblash Reck, the grey sphere in outermost orbit of the Chroma Sphere System, furthest from the central glowing sphere of Hew Espireth."

Dr Favishti shakes his head. "All this happened in the world you created to escape your reality."

Cal hopes this is true.

"I shall ask again... What is your first memory, Cal?"

The schoolyard... Final year of primary school, my peers sprinting maniacally, knocking into each other, yelling random catchphrases barely worth whispering. The overwhelming need to escape their belligerent chaos... Cal clears his throat. "I remember curling foetal in a corner of the playground to escape sensory overload."

Dr Favishti makes a note. "And how did your peers react to this behaviour?"

"With an onslaught of questions. Me pressing my face into the ninety-degree angle created by two concrete walls should have made it obvious I was not receptive to conversation. Yet their questions persisted."

"So, your first attempt to escape reality was unsuccessful, and you needed space?"

Cal taps his leg repeatedly while a dry laugh escapes his throat. "How dull were their lives, for a boy hiding in a corner to inspire such fascination? I only sought a temporary break from bombardment, but this violated their ridiculous social etiquette. How was *I* so damn perplexing? They bellowed meaningless utterances while plastering their faces with inane smiles. The boys were pathologically obsessed with moving a ball with their feet, despite said ball being a dull, mediocre object no matter its location. The girls wore overpriced beauty products to emphasise existing features... rosy gloss on lips already pink, mascara on lashes already dark, hairspray to clump hair strands into one lifeless object... And nobody asked why boys didn't wear make-up or girls didn't kick a football... An entire array of life choices decided by the shape of their genitals! And nobody questioned this... Yet everybody demanded an explanation for why an overwhelmed boy would hide in a corner."

Dr Favishti smiles. "I think we've discovered the root of your anger here, Cal. Trauma from the crib!"

Cal manages a weak smile in return. It would be comforting to believe his fears of Reckish attack were a complicated metaphor for childhood bullying. Yet he cannot shake visions of scarlet eyes glowing through shadows.

When the session is over, he thanks Dr Favishti for his time then trudges back to Telf Hall. Dust clouds rise around his ankles. The refreshing mountain breeze died a few days ago, now the atmosphere suffocates like a blanket to the face. Cal zips his light jacket to protect against sunburn. The streets shimmer. At certain temperatures, heat becomes a tangible, viscous presence like syrup or malice.

Summerton residents now require ice cream. *What fresh, creamy hell is this?* The ice cream van's jingle bears an auditory resemblance to a broken children's toy from several decades ago. It emits the same irritating snippet on a nerve-jangling loop, somehow always within earshot of tormented Cal.

His first act upon returning to Telf Hall is to turn his white noise machine up to maximum volume.

Leandra throws her pen to the table and clutches her ears. "Cal! That's too loud!"

He dials the electric roar down a notch. "The ice cream van though! That awful tune on a tortuous loop! It's a nightmare!"

Leandra cackles. Cal looks at his sister and flinches, noticing she glows with an ominous, coiled energy. She winks. "So, you don't want ice cream?"

Cal sits opposite her. "I thought you were on a diet due to concerns about your waistline?"

"You said dieting was a political construct for lowering self-esteem in an image-obsessed population and selling pseudo-scientific health products to desperate people." There is something almost reptilian in Leandra's knowing grin. "Therefore, I may as well eat ice cream."

Cal nods. Leandra retains that creepy smile while she returns to her drawing. Outside, the belligerent seller continues playing his hideous loop of "music" in the hopes of attracting custom, unaware that he will die next week.

2.11

(080)
Five days later, Cal arrives home to find Leandra painting, still radiating unnerving vitality. He has not found her napping in days. Her blankets lie unused in a folded pile. Since Bod Weye's termination of their relationship, she paints violent images, red brush strokes propelled by simmering fury. Eyes figuratively glued to her canvas she asks him, "How was work?"

"Enforced social masking and continued lack of regular schedule will ultimately result in complete breakdown. I wish the Sunny Bargains murderer would kill me, to free me from this hell... How are you?"

Leandra slams down her paintbrush. "That's it!"

She opens the laptop. "I've joined a sex workers' forum, to go further with the 'modelling'. For uninhibited exhibitionists there's ways to survive outside of soul-destroying minimum wage employment. When hotel guests ask reception, 'Is the porn channel disabled?' the response should be, 'Of course it is! How else do you expect people with invisible disabilities to survive under capitalism?' Our health is too unreliable for normal work, but we don't *look disabled* like Occreta Gate's pampered residents. You know, sex work is often chosen by those of us in this disability middle ground."

Cal collapses in his favourite chair and holds his head. "Chosen..." His body shakes with stifled maniacal laughter. He gathers his thoughts and calms his breathing. "You say *chosen*. Is this accurate? If certain life choices provide the only legitimate way for an individual to acquire food and shelter, are they *chosen*? When the remaining accessible path leads to homelessness, destitution, starvation... If you ask research participants to choose between baked confectionery products or certain death, would the resulting statistic prove that one hundred percent of people love cake?"

Leandra absently scans the laptop screen. "Who doesn't love cake?"

Cal bangs his fist on the table. "That's not my point! When death is the secondary option, the primary option is forced! If a robber demanded your purse at gunpoint, reducing your choices to A, hand over the purse, or B, get shot, nobody would say you *chose* to give the balaclava-clad man your purse. They would sympathise with you experiencing a violent robbery."

"Whatever, Cal." Leandra shrugs. "This is the hostage situation we're in. I'm not about to start shitting myself to prove to the Employment Office I deserve to live. I can either cry... or sell myself."

Cal stares at his defiant sister with pleading eyes. "There is another option... Kalakai could return! We could join the Chroman army to fight the Reckish hordes..."

Leandra snaps the laptop closed. "Look! Kalakai was probably a prank or mutual hallucination. But anyway, we can't wait for rescue. We must survive! Besides, what use are *we* to an army? If I was a fighter, I'd join Summerton guards to fight crime... But who am I kidding? I *am* crime!"

From beyond the courtyard, the ice cream van's irritating jingle plays into the dusky twilight. Cal flinches.

"It's nearly sunset!" Leandra complains. "You're right, that tune is annoying! And his third visit today... He's either deliberately pissing people off, or he's selling smack!"

Cal answers Leandra's previous question while clutching his ears and rocking. "You could train as a ROM, like me! I'll show you my research. I've memorised every galactic flight coordinate between here and Chroma."

The jingle plays again.

Leandra clenches her fists. "I don't have hyper-memory! And just say you autism-babble our way from this parched rock to somewhere over the complicated fucking rainbow... What will *I* do? They need permanently exhausted fetish models in space?

'Lookie here, I'm a scary Reckish demon! I was gonna pillage this planet, but now I've been confronted by a madwoman drenched in jam and custard, I might have a wank instead! Behold! Custard has averted intergalactic genocide!'"

Strands of Leandra's hair rise as though drawn towards electric current as the jingle plays again. She laughs. "Is that my awesome war tactic, huh? Custard and confusion? I guess it would provide the element of surprise! Who had 'custard-drenched femme soldiers' on their Warzone Bingo Card?" Her glance sears the air between herself and the infernal van. "But honestly Cal, there's nothing left for me but a lonely, crackwhore existence until I finally fucking DIE!"

The ice cream jingle stops with a bang. The van's garish lights go out and the courtyard is dark apart from rectangles of electric light from the diner's kitchen windows. Leandra re-opens the laptop. Night falls over Summerton as Cal sits motionless. Below his window, the town alights with an orange sodium glow like clustered embers below the blackened sky. Sunset brings no relief from stifling heat. "It's too hot!" Leandra complains. "Forty degrees C! Between twenty and twenty-five is better. Ideally twenty-two. I like my centigrade temperatures how I like my men... Moderate."

After an hour staring at the screen, Leandra fist-slams the table. "I hate social media! An opinionated acquaintance just commented, 'If you're well enough to host a party, you're well enough to get a job.'"

Cal's face contorts with fury. "What idiocy! That's like... If you're well enough to occasionally enjoy yourself, you're well enough for a regular high-stress responsibility. Or, if you're well enough for a relaxing foot massage, you're well enough to have your foot smashed with a hammer!"

Leandra tosses back her unwashed curls in a gale of throaty laughter. "I love you, Cal."

Cal lights up with sudden radiance. "Pass the laptop!"

Leandra pushes the device across the table. Cal minimises a window of moronic judgement and opens his favourite tourism site. "We need escape from this catshit society. You would *love* Opree Shengra! Listen... 'Our sphere boasts beautiful temples on rust-coloured rocks, with stunning miniature waterfalls to soothe the desert heat.' And look at these sculptures!" Cal turns the screen toward his perplexed sister. "Earthy but somehow majestic. Kalakai could leave you there after our first dispatch."

Leandra taps her blue-painted nails across the table's scratched, plastic surface. "OK... Firstly, how did they make waterfalls in the desert? Do their trains bring extra water?"

"Trains?!" Cal laughs. "Chroma is nothing like this pre-packaged desert cage where reality is prescribed and the ground is toxic... On Opree Shengra, underground rivers provide drinkable water, and biodomes contain lush gardens. Away from this dead environment filled with plastic and radiation, you might be healthy."

Leandra nods slowly. "Okaaay... Secondly, and this is slightly more crucial... How come you know so much about these alleged planets, yet virtually nothing about here? You don't even know where our trains go! Or what's beyond those western mountains."

"This planet's geography beyond Summerton is restricted," Cal explains. He opens a new tab and types, "What's beyond the mountains west of Summerton?" The laptop's display becomes static, like an analogue device with inadequate reception, before turning black. "See, this always happens if you investigate local geography. If we believe mindscape theory-"

"Never mind that nonsense! That's our only laptop!"

"It always restarts in just over three minutes... Have you never tried that search before?"

Leandra shakes her head. "I've only recently started *thinking*. Honestly. Even in this heatwave my brain's more awake than usual. I'm siphoning energy from somewhere."

Cal says, "I hope your health continues to improve."

"Thanks..." Leandra stares at Summerton's orange and ebony nightscape. "You know... I'm not interested in Opree Shengra. More endless damned desert... I want change! I wanna be like Kalakai! Does her planet have sentient trees like in that movie with the blue aliens?"

"No, Bure Eshpel is an ocean world. The Beshpers were originally a pirate race."

"Even better!" Leandra grins. "I wanna be a pirate!"

"Could you be ruthless?" Cal wonders. "Could you kill?"

Leandra fidgets, pushing back dry cuticles. "I get these murderous urges which fade to gnawing guilt. But you know what I crave more than murder? I long to fly! If I escaped this depressing environment and became a fighter pilot, I could shoot Reckish demons all day! When I have energy, my motor co-ordination is amazing. Look at my artwork!"

Cal gazes at his unstable sister in bewilderment. "Since when did you dream of becoming a fighter pilot? I thought your main wish was for a long-term boyfriend?"

Leandra laughs. "Since I started daydreaming about saving myself. I got that from you, actually."

"From me?"

"Yeah," says Leandra. "You never date. You'd rather work on your projects than fuck some thoughtless loser. You're awesome!"

Cal nods. "I've learned from you too, obtaining a greater understanding of human interaction. And metaphors."

"Aw really? Bless you. Maybe we're both stranded here for a reason," Leandra muses as the laptop stutters back to life with a flicker and a beep.

Cal pushes the device toward Leandra. "I need a walk. Do you want anything from Sunny Bargains?"

"Bread." Leandra smiles. "We're out of bread."

2.12

(081)
"I'm gonna smack that bitch!" Occreta Gate's Peter Cremis loudly declares his intention to physically attack fellow resident, Meg Dissery.

Cal stands before the uncomprehending woman as a human shield while she chews the pages of a children's book. "She didn't mean to upset you! Please leave her alone."

After ten minutes of threats and insults, Mr Cremis decides listening to music in his bedroom will be a more entertaining activity than committing assault.

Cal collapses on the couch, trembling.

"You should apply for an office job," Ron Buce suggests.

"Maybe." Cal views flashbacks of his last administrative role... the humiliating orders from senior workers, unfathomable gossip, uncomfortable clothing, the telephones... He starts hyperventilating.

Ron shakes his head. "This job isn't for everyone."

Cal later scurries back to Telf Hall flinching at shadows. The local ice cream seller was found electrocuted in his van last night in an alleged occupational accident, although some suspect foul play. Summerton has subtly shifted from bland suburbia to city of death. But after completing his seventy-five-minute walk home, Cal is too sleepy to be scared, and collapses straight onto his bed.

Sleep is plagued by nightmares of violence, images flickering through electric fog... *Leandra being strangled, a furious woman wielding a flamethrower, Kalakai grabbing his neck, Peter Cremis screaming, Leandra's eyes gleaming above scarlet paintings, a fresh grave on the edge of town... Movie blips jostle within a smog of grey turmoil. Everything is loud.*

Cal wakes, repeats ingrained mantras about dreams being meaningless by-products of overnight memory storage, then completes his morning routine. He researches Chroma for six hours before leaving for a late shift.

On the gruelling walk to work Cal sees blood smeared across a curb. When he peers closer, sand drifts over the stain. He keeps walking. He arrives several seconds early. It is difficult to time these walks to arrive exactly on time. Being late leads to disciplinary action but being early means extra time forcing the social mask.

Cal rings the doorbell and Sara Boppetwann answers. Cal provides the required greeting of, "Hey, y'alright?" He receives the response of narrowed eyes and a swiftly turned back as Sara sashays into the parlour. Cal goes to hang his jacket. He peers into the parlour while crossing the hall, uttering the socially approved greeting of, "Hello!"

Nobody replies. Babs Trabeck sits hunched over her laptop and continues typing while Sara reclaims her seat on the opposite couch. No residents are present.

Cal reels with nausea as he continues to the cloakroom. *They ignored me...* When neurotypicals ignore a greeting, it means they are angry, and you must psychically decipher the cause of their rage. *Why is Sara angry? I complained about her singing... But this is a care facility, not a practice hall for aspiring reality mediavision stars... Why is Babs angry? My last shift with her, I kept requesting more tasks... She perhaps dislikes my lack of initiative... This is a test! Neurotypical staff occupy their time without constant instruction, whereas I require a regimented timetable. This is an opportunity to demonstrate initiative!*

Pleased at solving another mystery of neurotypical behaviour, Cal mentally assesses workplace priorities. First... care for the residents! It is [redacted] so they are all attending various day centres. Second... Is everywhere clean and tidy? Cal checks the dining area. It is a disgusting post-lunch mess, with discarded food on the tables and dangerous spillages on the floor. Cal spends fifteen minutes cleaning the eating area to a high standard, making the environment safe and well-presented before braving the hostility of the parlour.

Pretty sure I passed the test! I have demonstrated initiative by cleaning mess that other staff were ignoring. The assistant manager has now seen evidence that I am a productive member of staff.

Cal takes a calming breath then walks into the unwelcoming room. He forces a smile and breezy tone. "Hey, can I see the rota please?" Last time he checked the rota it was only five days ahead, leaving him unable to plan chores. Ms Ross's refusal to grant regular hours is a continued source of torment.

Babs graces Cal with a smile that does not reach her eyes. She passes the paper rota. It has finally been completed a month ahead, but clearly designed to destroy him. Some weeks have so few hours, he will not earn enough money to eat, while other weeks his hours are squished into three days with an illegally short break between shifts. The day he booked as holiday to assist Leandra with a photoshoot is now a scheduled workday. Tears course down Cal's face as his body heaves.

"Calm down," Babs Trabeck says.

Cal dashes upstairs to the empty office and collapses in a weeping ball on the couch. He sends Ms Ross a NuText. "Why are you doing this? It's making me suicidal."

Ms Ross replies. "There's a new epilepsy and dementia training module. Complete it by your next shift."

He cries harder. Occreta Gate is killing him, rescue is not coming, and Leandra is doomed to prostitution. Ms Trabeck enters the office to tell Cal he should not be working at Occreta Gate if he is unfit to cope. For a second, the office is covered in blood. Crimson fluid drips from every surface, and the window is a scarlet glow, the sun shining through splattered glass.

"And don't forget to pick Sam Rettie up from pottery class," the assistant manager adds.

Cal blinks, and his surroundings are beige again.

He wipes his face with his hands, collects the car keys off the hook in the hallway and goes outside to start the shiny new company vehicle. He follows his pre-journey routine - mirrors in place, seat adjusted, water bottle in the holder - while death dances across his subconscious vision.

He drives. Navigating Summerton streets, he wonders how best to crash the car without endangering other lives. *Driving into incoming traffic is a no... How about hitting a wall...? If only there were a bridge...*

Cal collects Sam Rettie from pottery class, barely speaking as the deprived man decries the affront to his dignity of being removed from the presence of a mug and kettle. Heading back to Occreta Gate, Cal recommences pondering the logistics of crashing without hurting another human, a task more difficult now he carries an enraged, tea-obsessed passenger. He turns on the radio for distraction. "Student Bod Weye has been declared missing-" a tinny voice begins. He switches off the radio. Death is circling toward him and Leandra, spiralling ever closer.

By some miracle, Cal completes the journey without swerving into a concrete wall. The remaining shift passes in a blur of tears and paranoia.

Later, Cal is still crying when he arrives home.

Leandra is still painting. "You should leave that job, Cal! They'll never make adjustments for your disability. They can't legally fire you for being disabled, but they will make your life hell until you're forced to quit."

Cal shakes his head. "I don't want you to lower your boundaries with the adult modelling. We need this."

(084)
The next morning, Leandra warns Cal to be careful on his commute because disappearances in Summerton are becoming more frequent. His walk to work is quieter than usual. Fear keeps most residents home, but as a minimum wage essential

worker, Cal lacks the opportunity or financial means to stay home and preserve his health.

Misty Deds is excited by Cal's arrival, dancing and clapping in the parlour window. "I'm going to the day centre!" she exclaims as he steps through the door. "I want *you* to drive me!"

Cal's spirits are marginally raised by Misty's approval.

The first journey passes without incident, but his drive to collect her afterwards is a nightmare. His period comes three days early. Unable to use a public restroom with a vulnerable adult in his care, Cal completes the journey mired in blood and self-disgust. He arrives at Occreta Gate and all parking spots are taken. The whole team have arrived for a meeting, and a thoughtful colleague has taken the residents' parking spot. Cal is forced to park down the hill and walk up with Misty. He finally gets through the front door and greets the assembled staff through the parlour doorway as he dashes to the bathroom.

"Well hello, *Cal*," says Ms Ross.

Cal sorts himself out in the bathroom. He wonders if Ms Ross will mention his recent mention of suicidal urges.

Once clean, he creeps into the parlour and makes himself small in a corner. All staff are present except Sara, who has missed her last few shifts. Ms Ross finishes sharing the latest company news, then goes around the group and asks each staff member in turn to share any problems they are experiencing in the workplace. As his turn to speak approaches, Cal plans his response, attempting to construct a complaint about the ever-changing rota that sounds fair and not overly emotional.

His turn arrives.

Cal breathes in.

Ms Ross skips Cal, asking the colleague next to him to speak instead. Cal breathes out, then sits rocking for a while. *Maybe she is waiting to speak to me privately because I mentioned being suicidal...* But Ms Ross leaves straight after the meeting.

Cal asks his colleagues why the boss ignored him.

"I didn't notice."

"Maybe because you arrived late."

"Don't worry, everybody hates her."

Cal sends Ms Ross another NuText about the rota, which goes unanswered. He works extra hard for the remainder of the shift, volunteering for additional duties, eager to prove his worth. By the time his shift ends, he is utterly numb.

He returns to Telf Hall through shadowed streets with a constant sense of being watched, uncaring whether he gets murdered. After arriving home, he sends yet another NuText about the rota.

Ms Ross responds. "Come in and see me at 1pm tomorrow."

Cal breathes relief and tells Leandra, "Ms Ross will discuss my schedule tomorrow! Everything will be OK."

Leandra frowns. "Why can't she discuss this on company time? She usually avoids speaking to you, she might not even show. Also, tomorrow is your day off and Occreta Gate is seventy-five minutes' walk away!"

But Cal is so desperate to get his rota issues resolved that he agrees to this unpaid attendance.

That night he dreams of demons. *A white picket fence around a suburban house in a wasteland... monsters with vicious claws gripping grey roof tiles... a cackle echoing behind lace curtains... the death of a soul succumbed to evil.*

Of course, he forgets his dream upon waking. But cruel laughter leaves an auditory stain on his inner ear, discolouring all sound into something malicious, loaded with knives.

2.13

(085)
Cal treks over stony land toward the city's south-eastern edge. Summerton legend tells of a cursed object buried underground, poisoning the soil, hence the trees being blackened stumps clawing twisted fingers at the sky. Kalakai said the Reckish sent their CRIB thirty-two years ago... How long is thirty-two years in Summerton history? Most residents turn silent at mentions of history, geography, politics... anything other than social gossip or mundane mediavision. Leandra says a barkeep once told her this cracked, broken terrain was a beautiful valley before mountain peaks crumbled, creating jagged wasteland. Apparently, this barkeep has since been committed to Trilby Asylum... Cal is unsure how much faith to place in Leandra's drunken memory. But if this tale is true, he wishes those peaks had fallen more evenly, removing his need to trek up this massive hill. Cal reaches his workplace sweating and flustered. His com screen rings as he approaches the entrance.

"Where are you?" Ms Ross snaps.

She's actually here! He reels with sickly vertigo. "Just outside. Sorry."

Trish Mengleo answers the door, surprised to see him. "Lessabeth invited me for a meeting."

Cal approaches the stairway.

Lessabeth Ross' head peers from the office doorway. "We thought you weren't coming, *Cal*."

"I'm sorry. It's a seventy-five-minute walk to get here."

Lessabeth sneers. "You should have *driven*."

Cal starts shaking as he ascends the stone staircase. *Straight on the offensive! She's prepared for war... And I half believed she wouldn't be here.* "I don't have a car," he mumbles. He reaches the attic and spies Ms Trabeck typing at the office computer. *Oh no!*

"I need the toilet." Cal dashes into the staff bathroom and urinates, then sits for a moment, gathering his thoughts. *Her sidekick is here! I wasn't expecting an official meeting. Maybe because I mentioned being suicidal, she needs a witness if I kill myself.*

At least Babs can confirm I work hard.

Cal stands, flushes, washes his hands, takes a deep breath. He views himself in the over-sink mirror - a shy, effeminate man with frightened eyes and messy hair under a peaked cap. He tries to push strands of wavy hair back into his ponytail, but they rise like mad antennae. Still shaking, he joins the manager and assistant manager in the office.

Ms Ross peers over her clipboard. "Babs will type this meeting, so we have an official record. But first, we need a timeline of events. So, you commenced employment on [redacted] didn't you?"

Cal shakes his head. "I had an induction session on [redacted] and my first shift on [redacted]."

His boss tuts. "No, Cal. That week we *paid* you to do online training at home. Your first shift was on [redacted]."

Beleaguered Cal clutches the sides of his chair, trying not to rock. "I completed my online training, unpaid, a month before commencing employment. I first came to Occreta Gate on [redacted] after you asked me last minute to join a paperwork day. I still have your NuTexts…"

Ms Ross rolls her eyes. *"Never mind* Cal. So, you're saying you commenced employment on [redacted]? *Okaaay…* Then we had a meeting [redacted] after you started *crying* on shift."

Cal lowers his head and grips the chair tighter. "Yes."

Lessabeth grins. "And then it happened AGAIN eleven days later!"

"Wh… When was that?"

"On [redacted]."

"OK." Cal's knuckles are white. *Wait… that's not true!*

"And then..." continues Ms Ross.

"Wait..." Cal's voice almost catches. "The meeting on [redacted] was an unscheduled follow-up. I wasn't crying."

"Yes," Ms Ross gloats, "you were *crying*."

"But I... I arrived on shift, you were waiting on the stairs, you asked me to attend a meeting right after I stepped through the door."

Ms Ross purses her lips and slowly shakes her head.

Cal insists, "I had literally just arrived!"

"*Riiiiiight*..." Ms Ross replies. "Anyway Cal, we sent off an Occupational Health referral and you mentioned wanting late shifts because you *can't get out of bed*."

Cal nods. "I asked for regular hours, preferably lates due to my noisy home, but-"

"Well, you got the *lates*, didn't you?"

"Yes, but my main priority-"

"*Theeennn*... On [redacted] you requested *earlies* instead!"

Cal begins to gently rock in his seat. "I asked if you'd find it easier to give me the fixed schedule I needed with earlies. It meant setting off at half five, but I was desperate for a regular schedule."

"Well," Ms Ross smirks, "I gave you *earlies*. So you got *one* thing you wanted!"

"But my schedule-"

"You never said whether you'd do Saturdays or Sundays, Cal. So how could I give you a regular schedule?"

"But you never asked-"

"*Aaaanyway*... I've been forwarded this Occupational Health report. Have you read the recommendations, Cal?"

"Yes."

"*Reeeally?* The first recommendation is *you* contact the Employee Support Program."

"Yes." Cal nods. "I did."

Ms Ross shakes her head.

"I did!" Cal insists. "They offered ten sessions with a counsellor who knew nothing about mental illness or autism. His specialities were song naming and word games."

"So, you *chose not to engage* with our Employee Support Program! Well... And this next recommendation! This is *interesting*. They *mention* a regular schedule. Then say, 'I would recommend the above adjustments be considered for an initial *four-week period*.' So... Four weeks!"

"Well. Yes... What..."

Ms Ross holds the health report up to Cal's face, pointing a bony finger at the highlighted phrase, smug with triumph. "It says *four weeks!*"

"I don't understand..."

"We're past *four weeks*, aren't we Cal?"

"But I've not had the adjustments-"

"You asked for lates, you got lates. You asked for earlies, you got earlies!"

"But my regular schedule-"

"I can't do *everything*, Cal! Some staff have regular hours because they have kids! Now..." Ms Ross narrows her eyes. "Are you doing that for a reason?"

Doing what? Cal is still trying to keep his breathing calm and reduce his rocking in a doomed attempt to mimic neurotypical behaviour. "What do you mean?"

"Okaaay..." Ms Ross purses her lips.

Cal removes his clawed grasp from the chair and folds his trembling hands. "What do you mean?"

Ms Ross huffs. "Well, it's like you're not listening!"

Tears prick the corners of Cal's eyes. "I *am*. Why are you accusing me-"

"Because of what you're doing with your body language, Cal. You're a poor communicator. But it's *fine*."

"I've walked seventy-five minutes on my day off and I'm overwhelmed-"

"Well, let's try to move past this shall we, Cal? Moving on... I've had several complaints about you from other staff. You complain about not getting your shift pattern, about Occreta Gate being noisy... You storm upstairs, slamming all the doors, locking yourself away..."

The only time Cal slammed a door was by accident while dashing from the kitchen to escape Sara's singing, racked with visions of Leandra's recent sexual assault. With Ernie Trenta's smug leer flooding his brain, Sara's belligerent vocals pushed him to breaking point. But he cannot mention Leandra being strangled. Not here. "I only slammed a door once, by accident, because of Sara's singing-"

"Ha!" Ms Ross lights up. "So you *did* slam a door!"

Shit. The urge to hyperventilate presses heavy against Cal's chest. "Sara was singing excessively, creating a stressful work environment-"

"When did you *report* Sara, Cal?"

I assumed staff sided together against the management they claim to despise... Cal's right hand grips his left in a futile effort to stop the trembling. "It's difficult..."

"And..." Ms Ross continues. "Other staff report, you don't say hello when you arrive. You don't engage socially."

I tried so hard to socially mask and pass as neurotypical! I failed... A tear descends Cal's cheek. "I always smile, say hello, and try to make conversation."

Babs Trabeck spins her computer chair around. "I can confirm this! I've seen you on shift. Two days ago, you arrived, Sam Rettie answered the door, and you didn't say hello to him, or anybody. You just went straight to the kitchen, grabbed a dustpan and brush, went to the dining room. For fifteen minutes, you didn't socially interact."

Tears course down Cal's pink face. *I failed the test! But I was showing initiative and work ethic. How was that wrong?* He sniffs and mumbles, "I don't understand..."

"I was there, Cal! I've seen proof. You're not doing your job!" declares Ms Trabeck.

When have I ever not greeted Sam Rettie on arrival? I always thank him for opening the door.

Cal starts rocking harder, grasping for jumbled memories. "I don't remember..."

Ms Trabeck glares. "I WAS THERE!"

But they... Cal wipes his face. "I... I said hello through the doorway but nobody-"

"You said hello *through a doorway?*" Ms Ross sneers.

"Yes. But nobody-"

Ms Ross adds, "Also! You're telling everybody you want a different job because you don't like it here. You shouldn't be shocked nobody likes you if you're saying you don't want to work here."

Ms Trabeck recommences typing while Cal tries to muster defence against this unexpected onslaught. "But my colleagues *suggested* I look elsewhere... They seemed sympathetic, I thought they were my friends."

"They're not your *friends!* They are people you work with. And they won't like you if you're crying all the time and slamming doors. And hiding upstairs."

Ron spends half his shift upstairs on his com screen. Why is this happening? Cal's chest heaves. "I only ran upstairs once, when I was suicidal."

Ms Ross tuts. "This is the first time you've said the word 'suicidal' to me!"

"In my NuText two days ago."

"In a *NuText?* Cal..." Ms Ross shakes her head.

"It's the only way to contact-"

"*Suicidal?*" Ms Ross folds her arms. "That suggests you're Work Incapable!"

I wish! Cal represses demented laughter.

"The Employment Office declared me Work Capable."

"So, you're *suicidal*, yet you think it's OK to work with vulnerable adults? They're *vulnerable adults*, Cal! What if Meg Dissery has a seizure, cracks her head on the floor and there's *blood*. And you can't help because you're *suicidal?*"

At the mention of blood, Cal's violent visions return with crippling intensity. All sensation drains from his legs as the office walls become a Rorschach splatter of scarlet murder... *skin ripped open... monstrous eyes...*

Ms Ross' tirade continues. "How would you feel, Cal? If I told you I'm not going to pay your wages next week because I'm *suicidal?* Should I be in work if I'm not doing my job?"

"But..." Cal shakes his head to clear gruesome images, and the walls return to magnolia. "But I *am* doing my job! I never missed a day, even during the storms. And I always look for tasks and ask my colleagues if they need help..."

"But now you say you're *suicidal!* So how are residents safe around you?"

Cal cries another tear. *What's left for us? Leandra will end up selling herself to dangerous men...*

Ms Ross sighs. "I would offer you a hanky, Cal, but I don't see any tears."

The hopeless man turns to his boss with tears streaming down his face. "What do you mean?"

"There's no tears! *You're not crying!* Only shutting your eyes like this..." Ms Ross contorts her face in a cruel parody of a crying man. A twinkle in her eyes betrays barely stifled enjoyment. It takes a certain kind of person to enjoy making others cry. Such people may enjoy a variety of hobbies, such as burning down orphanages or releasing tear gas into cancer wards. "And you don't look people in the eye when you communicate... It's like you're not listening! And you upset poor Susie."

"Susie..." Cal shudders with the memory of the large woman stood in her diaper, yelling while he considered self-mutilation, the eerie suggestion she might be psychic... like

Kalakai... Chroma... the CRIB... Cal rapidly shakes his head. "I... We've moved past that. She's not angry anymore."

"Well, I've never *known* her to be angry!"

"I was helping with her socks when she screamed at me." Cal notices Ms Ross slowly shaking her head. "I'm not lying! Why are you looking at me like that? She yelled as I was helping her. I was scared. She's much bigger than me. But I've forced myself to stop being nervous around her."

Ms Ross tuts. "All these negative factors, Cal. You're not engaging with residents or colleagues..."

Cal remembers yesterday's shift. "What about Misty Deds? We do crafts. She was excited to see me yesterday!"

"She gets excited by everyone, Cal. That means nothing."

He hangs his head. Countless attempts to join inane conversations about mediavision, celebrities, the weather... masking his disability until a husk remained behind his social front... All for nothing.

Cal cries for half a minute while Ms Ross stares at him and Ms Trabeck keeps typing.

Ms Ross eventually picks a stack of paperwork off the table. "Let's see this report again... It says here, 'Cal refers to herself by different names!'"

"I..." Cal stammers. "I have complex mental health issues, but I'm not dangerous. The Employment Office declared me Work Capable. I've tried really hard."

"*Tried?*" Ms Ross breaks into a triumphant grin. "That's *past tense!* So, are you leaving?"

Cal shakes his head. "I need this job. There's rent, bills, food, we don't qualify for-"

"So, you took this job because it was *all you could get?*"

"No... no..." Cal tries not to scream the disappointed anguish of a former straight A student relegated to the scrapheap. "I wanted to help others! People told me, working with those less fortunate than myself-"

Ms Ross exclaims, "And now you're saying our residents are *less fortunate* than you!"

Cal considers the living conditions of Occreta Gate residents... *Free accommodation, air conditioning, food, utilities, new shoes, their own Cashdamn car!* He almost laughs in torment. "They..." He breathes, remembers why he wanted to help the Work Incapable. "Life is harder for them, I guess... Because they can't manage personal care. I'm so alienated, it's easy to feel sorry for myself, but I thought if I was helping people who couldn't help themselves, I'd feel grateful for my abilities. I don't know... I just wanted to be a good person."

Ms Ross smiles again. "You're still talking *past tense*. Does that mean you're leaving?"

Shit! She can't legally fire me for being disabled!
She needs me to quit!

Cal breathes again and wipes his face. "I'm just saying I've been working hard."

His boss' smile is replaced by disgust. "Well, I need to seek advice from HR over whether you're *safe* to work with vulnerable adults."

Ms Ross leaves the office.

Ms Trabeck continues typing while Cal holds his head and rocks. A small spark of hope had propelled him here today, eagerly chasing that crucial fixed schedule. Instead, he discovers his colleagues hate him and all attempts at social masking have failed. He flounders between realities.

The office with magnolia walls...
With blood-soaked walls...
A spaceship...
A burning hellscape...

Ms Ross returns to the office and the decor returns to beige and magnolia. "HR have confirmed that a suicidal member of staff is not safe for residents. You need to get a sicknote from your doctor and not come back until you're happy."

But suicide ideation isn't grounds for being declared Work Incapable... Cal struggles with the inherent contradictions of capitalist society.

The meeting ends with Ms Trabeck printing out transcripts and Ms Ross asking Cal to sign a copy. He has no idea what he signs. He only knows he is eternally suicidal, so his employment is over.

Cal leaves the office and plods back to Telf Hall, tempted to jump before oncoming traffic. *But that would destroy the poor driver... And who will look after Leandra...*

As another sandstorm rises, Cal pulls his goggles from his bag and holds his battered jacket tighter against his skinny, bound chest.

He is unaware of the furious, dark-clothed figure following behind him, wielding a flamethrower.

2.14

(091)
"Do you ever lose time?"

Cal is back in Dr Peter Favishti's office, hunched and clutching his knees, staring slack-jawed at an azure skyscape. "No... I wish! I remember everything." His past week has been a demented nightmare. The brutal disciplinary meeting plays in endless loops. His sister is insane. Her ex-boyfriend is still missing. Her only birthday guest was found in bloody pieces, she is a murder suspect, and everything breaks around her. Plus, Cal has started to suspect somebody is stalking him. A shadow disappears from the corner of his eye whenever he turns.

"Are you sure?" Dr Favishti probes. "There's no blank spots when you search your memories? What about your childhood?"

"That's different," Cal insists. "Most people remember little of their distant past."

Dr Favishti narrows his eyes. "Do you ever find yourself somewhere and wonder how you got there?"

Cal laughs. "What, like on the scrapheap of life after getting promising grades at school? Sometimes. But then I remember: poor life choices."

"I see..." Dr Favishti scans his notes while Cal taps his foot six times. "Cal, can I speak to Leandra now?"

Cal stops tapping. "Leandra is back home, learning to control her rising telekinesis. I left her practising her new-found brain power by attempting to lift bean tins without them exploding. After making a Kaldamn mess of the parlour, she moved her training to the bathroom with its wipe-clean surfaces. She is making considerable progress but has become quite mad, shining with..." Cal trails off. *Will Leandra become Reckish? If her power emerges and Kalakai never returns, will the demons of Peblash Reck rise from the CRIB and whisper tales of murder and vengeance, enticing her down the deadlight path?*

Dr Favishti makes another note then asks, "Cal, why have I never seen you and Leandra at the same time?"

"Well..." Cal ponders. "Either I'm at work, or Leandra is busy with artwork, napping, modelling, or psychically juggling grocery items."

"Cal, has anybody ever spoken to both you and Leandra at the same time?"

A lizard scuttles over the outside windowsill. "Kalakai," Cal replies, remembering the earth-shattering conversation that finally made Chroma real.

"Has any *human* ever spoken to you both at once?" Dr Favishti presses.

"Humans ignore me when I'm with Leandra because she's prettier and has better interpersonal skills. I avoid photoshoots, dates and social events because I have no idea what to say... I previously only left the apartment to assist her when her fibromyalgia flared. Then I got that disastrous care job while she stayed home. We lead separate lives."

Dr Favishti closes his notepad and places it on the table beside his chair. "Cal, I specialise in treating patients who have dissociative conditions from surviving childhood trauma. Dissociative identity disorder is a complex defence mechanism in which consciousness divides into separate identities. These identities each process part of the trauma, dividing its impact. The defence strategies of a fractured personality continue into adulthood. For example, if a glamorous yet insecure woman cannot face the drudgery and ego-destruction of an underpaid care assistant job, her alternate personality could attend those shifts on her behalf. And if a shy, transsexual man has difficulties processing his sexuality, his female alter ego could take over during dates or adult modelling shoots."

Cal cringes as memories of strangulation fill his troubled brain. He clutches his head as numerous recollections tumble after, forming a demented autobiographical jigsaw.

"Ernie Trenta! In the lake! Me and Leandra are the same person, and we have a third alter-ego who is a murderer!"

Dr Favishti picks up his notebook and scans the pages. "Ah! Ernie Trenta... The young man who assaulted Leandra on her birthday, and whose lower body was found outside Sunny Bargains and upper body in Summerton Oasis. That was a bleak and unfortunate coincidence. However, I have worked with hundreds of dissociative patients-"

"How many people are like me?"

"Approximately one percent of the population. But it is sadly under-diagnosed due to public misconceptions and lack of funding. I agreed to see Leandra at one sixth of my usual hourly rate because I suspected her symptoms were dissociative and believed an official diagnosis might provide her only escape from desperate living conditions. It might be difficult adjusting to this acknowledgement of DID, but-"

"Which of us killed Ernie Trenta?" asks Cal. "And how am I also autistic? And how did Leandra get magic powers?"

Dr Favishti closes his notebook again. "I have worked with hundreds of dissociative patients, Cal, and have yet to meet a murderer. The hackneyed stereotype of the split personality killer was created for cheap entertainment and does untold damage to patients with this debilitating condition, who are more likely to be victims of abuse than be abusers."

Cal looks back to the blue sky and shudders. "So, the killer is still out there?"

"I'm afraid so," Dr Favishti says. "In answer to your other questions... I am not qualified to discuss your autism. But if a specialist has provided this diagnosis, I see no reason why autism cannot be a co-morbid condition. And as for Leandra's 'magic powers'... Has anybody except yourself observed evidence of this telekinetic ability?"

Cal ponders. "No... I guess they haven't."

The friendly green lizard returns to the windowsill.

Dr Favishti nods. "Cal, you are experiencing a psychotic episode due to the stress of your latest attempt at employment. Although psychosis and dissociative identity disorder are separate diagnoses, dissociative patients can experience psychotic episodes, just as psychotic patients can experience dissociation. This is why DID is often mistaken for schizophrenia by those who lack psychiatric training. If you wish to apply for re-assessment at the Employment Office, I will fully support your application for Work Incapable status and subsidised living. You and Leandra need rest. After processing your recent trauma, you will hopefully no longer experience psychotic symptoms."

The windowsill lizard stares at Cal throughout Dr Favishti's dialogue. Cal views the reptilian eyes and is reminded of Leandra, who is waiting for him back at Telf Hall even though they are the same person. *She will be devastated. She aimed to evolve beyond this drab existence and become a Chroman warrior. She wants to be Kalakai. She does not want to be me.*

Dr Favishti looks at his watch. "Well, I'm afraid we've reached the end of today's session, Cal. Remember to include my contact details on your Work Capability assessment form. You have my business card."

The lizard scuttles away as Cal rises. "I hope we get an assessor who agrees we deserve to live."

"Good luck, Cal," says the doctor. "I hope you and Leandra take good care of each other. I look forward to seeing one or both of you again next week."

"Thank you," Cal replies. He leaves Dr Peter Favishti's office, unaware that he will never speak to this insightful professional again. He meanders down the stairway in a daze before reaching the exit and emerging into blinding sun.

He dons his sunglasses and begins the walk home. Behind him, boots hit tarmac as his stalker jumps down from the roof. Cal is too preoccupied with recent revelations to notice his pursuer, until a shadow falls across the path beside him.

"Productive therapy session?" asks a muffled voice.

A shocked Cal spins to see a figure wrapped in dark clothing, with fierce eyes glaring beneath the shadow of a hood. This mystery person is carrying several guns and knives, and what appears to be a flamethrower.

Cal blinks. "Who are you?"

"Ha! Don't you recognise me, bro?" She pulls the scarf from her lower face and graces the unsettled man with the grin of an amicable shark. "Did you miss me?"

Cal stares in silence for a moment before replying. "I have no idea who you are."

"So much for autistic hyper-memory!" The woman chuckles. "You've memorised every stellar co-ordinate between here and Chroma, but don't recognise your own damned sister."

Cal's foot judders with twenty-six rapid taps as he wrings his hands. This madwoman has an uncanny familiarity, like a memory of a story of a dream... *A library with chequered floor tiles... A deranged cackle echoing around bookshelves... "Yo, Library Boy!"*

He violently shakes his head, nearly dislodging his trusty cap. "No... No... Leandra is my sister. Or maybe she is me. We have always lived in Summerton. We have never seen a living tree. Oh..." Cal stifles the laughter of rising hysteria. "First I understand metaphors, then I start rhyming. Am I a poet? Do I know it? Is anything real?"

The weaponized woman laughs. "Chill, bro! I know... Coping with change is not your forte. We sent you to Summerton to force your evolution, but you insist on clinging to the familiar, even if it means repeating Cashdamn nightmares on a tortured loop."

Cal stops tapping his foot, but this causes his right hand to slap four times against his left hand, such is the necessity of stimming when anxious. "No," he says. "No. I wanted to be a productive member of society. I wanted to make a difference.

I almost cracked the conversational algorithm to pass among neurotypicals. I just needed more time, a regular schedule, I-"

"Fuck that!" yells the weapon-toting woman. "The normals will never tolerate us complicated freaks. We don't belong here." She removes a gun from her belt.

Cal stares at the weapon, a shiny futuristic device, nothing like the guns carried by Summerton guards. The ferocious woman's smile echoes from distant nightmares. She points her gun at Cal. "You're coming with me."

Cal begins to hyperventilate. "It's not safe to go with strangers."

His new acquaintance tuts and shakes her head.

"Firstly, I am hardly a stranger. Secondly, you don't have a choice, sweetheart."

Vivica III

(064)

"We did it!" Sorsha stands victorious above the final monstrous corpse. A pale sun rises in lilac sky above endless, restless ocean. The mansion grounds lie soaked in oily blood that sizzles in the morning rays. "Nobody touch anything!" she warns. "Reckish blood is mildly poisonous."

"Well, shit!" says Dodger. "You're drenched in the stuff."

Sorsha inspects her blood-soaked battle gear. Viscous droplets ooze in hollow spaces within her chainmail armour. She shrugs. "Everybody inside and get cleaned up! We'll bury the corpses later."

Vivica's drifting mind observes the triumphant gang stomp back to the mansion while she remains in her trusty cupboard. Vibrations from their heavy boots shake the floorboards beneath her cramped enclosure. *So, this is our timeline... Now Dodger will kick my cupboard door, storming toward the bathroom. Sunny will giggle as she smashes my gun against chequered tiles. Sorsha will thank Doc for creating the anti-Reckish bullets that ensured victory. I'll be overwhelmed by visions of the next attack, where some siblings die. Sorsha will hear my thoughts and reprimand my apparent morbidity...* Vivica drags the long, dirty fingernails of her right hand across the back of her left hand. Sharp distraction removes bloody edges from grim hallucinations.

Bang!

Dodger kicks the cupboard door.

"Thanks for the help, Vivica!"

Reality flickers, a jolt like a mistimed scene change.

A timeline switch?

Sorsha yanks the cupboard door open, holding Vivica's unused gun. She is still covered in Reckish blood that drips macabre puddles onto geometric tiles, now a mixture of circles within squares, still black and white. "Didn't fancy joining the battle, huh?"

Vivica trembles, bloody hands clutching her scarred legs. "Excess audio-visual stimuli beyond cupboard walls!" She frets, reaching for the wooden door.

Sorsha retains her fierce grip on the handle. Her glance crackles with battle adrenaline but her lips remain pursed in annoyance. "Where *were* you? Or, *when* were you? Jessie nearly died when a demon jumped the fence. A clairvoyant on the front lines would have been useful. If that's what you are... Even if you're just a paranoid, anxious over-thinker prone to uncanny predictions, you could still shoot a gun."

Vivica searches for timelines where she wields weaponry. In most, she succumbs to her incessant suicide ideation, putting a bullet in her agonised brain.

"Stop imagining suicide! What's *wrong* with you?" Sorsha snaps.

Vivica diverts her thoughts to hazy futures within the electric fog, snapshots flickering beyond the gloom. Complex, rhythmic chants echo through dimensions to reach her mental ear. Her mind's eye observes brown-robed figures with intricate facial tattoos dancing in twilit desert around a funeral pyre. ***Opree Shengra. An ancient tribe at the northern pole honouring a transcended elder.*** A weathered face looks upwards, piercing eyes flashing a cryptic warning at the inquisitive observer.

Sorsha reaches into the cupboard to shake her dreaming sister. Static clouds obscure Vivica's inner vision and ancient eyes fade into monochrome, fractal storm.

"How many worlds do you *need?*" Sorsha snaps. "You attend school and hide in a toilet cubicle. You stay here and hide in a cupboard. Where next? You gonna visit some alien desert and hide under a rock? In how many secluded spaces must you lose yourself?"

Vivica begins to cry.

Sorsha flinches and removes her grasp, leaving grey, oily blood stains on Vivica's left shoulder. "I'm sorry, Vivica. I guess I'm still loaded on battle rage. The Reckish nearly got me a few times."

Vivica gazes at her proud elder in mute misery. Her visions have disappeared. All that remains is a too-bright hallway... harsh rays reflecting off white walls dotted with curious mirrors. Rowdy siblings stomp around the mansion, projecting amplified conversation, still high off the fumes of victory. Their voices and footsteps form a chaotic wall of noise that assaults her hyper-sensitive ears. She cringes at the sensory bombardment.

"I'm sorry for upsetting you." Sorsha gently closes the cupboard door. She rises, still holding Vivica's unused gun, and places the weapon on a high, ornate shelf beyond her disturbed younger sibling's reach. "Keep the noise down!" she admonishes the raucous crew on the first floor.

Vivica spends the remainder of the day rocking back and forth, feeling everything and nothing. Her family attempt a grudging quiet as they clean demon blood off their clothing, their armour, the tiled floor and wooden stairway. But each footfall is another explosion within Vivica's horrific reality.

The evening brings grim humidity. "Storm's coming!" Jessie yells from the rooftop.

Vivica flinches, sweating in her cupboard.

The mansion lies surrounded by death. Sorsha views approaching storm clouds from the battlements. "The rain can wash away the Reckish blood. We'll bury the corpses tomorrow."

"Or throw them off the clifftops, into the ocean?" suggests Jessie. "Splash!"

Sorsha shakes her auburn curls. "We can't risk their decaying bodies poisoning the ecosystem, killing marine life and corrupting the water supply. We'll bury them in the deadlands."

The deadlands... Vivica rocks in her shadowed prison. *The dying earth surrounding the octagonal tower. Where the Reckish hordes arose. Where more demons emerge whenever the portal reactivates. No battle brings final victory. There is no eternal peace, only spaces between the wars. If you are lucky, these gaps allow time to reload and regenerate, patch your defences. But evil always returns...*

Footsteps echo through the hallway. "I've brought you a clean jumper, Vivica. Leave the blood-stained one outside your door. Nell can add it to tomorrow's laundry."

Footsteps recede as Sorsha returns to her private chambers. Vivica returns to cryptic dreaming. She tries viewing the Opree Shengra funeral beyond the flickering fog, but the closer she peers, the more her bones are crushed by the ominous weight of premonition. If only she could view all futures. There might be one where she is not a terrified wreck who hides in a cupboard.

Nigel III

(073)

"The SilverMen transport humans from passer trains to a military outpost in the desert!" Nigel screams while twitching in violent spasm. Since his admission to Trilby Asylum, doctors have administered anti-depressants, anti-psychotics and mood stabilisers. This chemical cocktail makes the ridiculously named Restless Leg Syndrome torment his restrained body. Invisible ants with fiery, spiky feet march across inflamed nerve endings, creating a burning, itching pain that only abates for an instant following sudden movement. Thanks to the tight straps binding his body to the hospital bed, Nigel can barely move. He sporadically clenches his muscles for merciful moments of relief.

The nurse arrives to administer Nigel's four o'clock medication. "We'll tie those straps tighter if you keep twitching!" she warns, unwrapping a new syringe needle.

"I need to twitch!" Nigel cries.

The nurse tuts, pushing the needle into a little plastic vial. "You're twitching on purpose? For pity?"

"No, it stops the PAIN!"

With a blue, latex-gloved hand, the nurse grabs Nigel's left arm and administers his afternoon medication, an anti-epilepsy drug the doctors are trialling as an emotion suppressor in volatile patients. "Twitching stops the pain?" She pulls the needle from his fevered skin. "A military outpost in the eastern desert? Passer trains with human cargo? I suppose this is a huge conspiracy us mere mortals are too unenlightened to comprehend?" She drops the needle into the yellow sharps box on her trolley.

Nigel screams. The ants scuttling under his skin increase their velocity, prickling his flesh with scalding animosity. He would rather turn himself inside out and scratch raw nerves than continue experiencing this tortuous itch. He increases the frequency of his twitching to a vibrating judder.

The nurse sighs, shaking her head. "I did warn you." She tightens the buckles on each canvas strap before leaving.

"Noooooo..." Unable to twitch, his condition heightened by reduced circulation, Nigel dissociates from his tortured body as the nurse vacates his dreary cell.

He floats.

His consciousness rises, free from the vessel clothed in scratchy pyjamas, beyond the tawny straps criss-crossing their restrictive lattice, to the cracked ceiling of his undecorated quarters. Above this hellish confinement lies the blue sky of a simpler time. *I should have appreciated my cashier job at Sunny Bargains. And my cheap room in Gran's apartment. Instead of sticking my head through society's prison bars and becoming subjected to this chemical hell.*

Nigel's remorseful consciousness becomes trapped in the beige ceiling, the open sky eternally beyond his grasp. Yet broken plaster contains shattering revelations. Cracks which initially appeared accidental contain a microscopic network of wires and advanced surveillance technology.

The cameras!

Nigel had been unable to shake the paranoid notion of being watched. Now he finds his surveyor within an electric pulse of circuitry that emits a high-pitched whine perceptible only to the hyper-sensitive.

His consciousness returns to his agonised body. "Can you hear me?" he cries to unseen witnesses. "They've locked me in this cell for seeking truth! I saw the outpost! SilverMen with guns herding human cattle! This is no benign desert town. This is a prison ruled by a malevolent creator!"

He waits for a response but hears only echoing footsteps of nurses on their daily rounds. He inhales, preparing another yell, then almost chokes from surprise.

A SilverMan materialises beside Nigel's bed.

The shocked man feels the breeze from displaced air against his clammy skin. Before he can scream, a metal hand clamps over his mouth. Nigel tries thrashing around - this time from terror rather than pain - but cruel straps dig into his flabby body, holding him in place.

"Your creator is not malevolent." A mono-pitched, electrical voice emanates from the robot's smooth, metal face. "You just weren't supposed to think."

The SilverMan tilts its motionless visage towards Nigel's bulging eyes. "You have many questions. This problem will be rectified. The creator has ordered your return to the castle for re-design and re-programming. This is a benevolent gesture, for which you should be grateful."

The restrained man's petrified attempt to respond produces only muffled syllables.

Nigel disappears. His cheap, grey pyjamas disappear with him. The hospital bed remains in place, its empty straps snapping onto fallen, sweat-soaked sheets. The SilverMan's metal hand cups empty air.

"Malevolent creator..." The robot shakes its shiny head. "A *malevolent* creator would have ordered termination, not re-programming and redemption."

Indigo eyes flicker as the SilverMan receives its next instruction. "Create the impression of autonomous escape."

The robot nods, grabs the bed straps and rips them with deadly strong fingers. It then kicks the cell door, smashing the heavy lock.

Alarms blare across Trilby Asylum as red lights flash across sterile hallways.

The SilverMan de-materialises. Air molecules rush to fill the temporary void created by its disappearance, while footsteps run from neighbouring corridors. Nurses and orderlies reach Nigel's broken cell to find an empty bed with torn straps.

Staff scour the institution for the missing patient. After

failing to locate Nigel, they warn Summerton guards that an insane inmate has escaped, posing a danger to the public.

Outraged residents remark that increased security at Trilby Asylum would make Summerton safer.

Perspective Three
Selected Members of The Collective

3.01

(022)

Midnight in a hexagonal castle beyond the mountains, the witch materialises in her chamber of narcissism, neglected and displeased. She opens a mirror-backed door into the castle's boardroom and marches past an empty board table, discarding her cane in rage. Filled with acrid animosity, she pulls open the northern door to the librarian's lair.

Castle Mindscape is divided into six near-triangular sections, forming isosceles trapezoids as the central, hexagonal boardroom provides their fourth wall. The castle "library" contains countless rows of bookshelves, desks, bio-printers, and computers linked to hundreds of screens. "*Serena…*" the witch growls at the sight of her studious sister. The librarian prefers to work alone, but tonight a younger sibling is helping with an administrative task.

Timid Cal hunches over a computer desk at the short southern wall bordering the boardroom. Serena leans at his shoulder, careful not to touch him. "Check the timestamp on these optical recordings and type the date into this data field. Use eight-digit descending order: year, month, day."

Cal stops wringing his hands and takes the mouse to open a file. A video plays on a small screen to his right.

Serena explains, "You will find - due to dissociative fugue - some files lack time-based data."

"So where do I obtain this information?" Cal asks, trembling under the witch's observation as she scowls from the doorway, raising hairs on his weedy arms.

Serena tells him, "You can co-front when necessary. Reality Show feed is on this left screen. Our connected vessel is somewhere quiet, reading a book. Use their phone to check social media posts and obtain the correct date."

The witch sniggers. "Trying to convince Cal he's useful?" She leans on the door frame, a casual pose disguising her lower body's agony.

"He *is* useful," Serena retorts.

Cal's eyes cloud over. The screen to his left depicts a first-person shot of shaky hands reaching for a phone.

"You could do that yourself more efficiently," the crippled witch remarks.

Smart-suited Serena turns to glare at her obnoxious, dark-robed sister. "What do you want, Estella?"

Cal's left screen shows a phone scrolling through the Social Media Show, a spin-off series of the Reality Show.

Estella the bitter witch glowers in her tattered black coat. "I want my enemies to fucking face me! I will demonstrate the true extent of my power..."

The scrolling on Cal's left screen pauses as a trembling hand brings the electronic device closer. Cal's eyes uncloud. He copies numerical data from the left screen into a data field on the right. The hand on the left screen then lowers the phone and picks up a book.

Estella continues, "And I want you to quit indulging our weaker elements. They're a Cashdamn disgrace!"

Serena snorts. "Cashdamn? You spent too long in subterranean dystopia!" Behind her, the underground city's feed fills the south-east wall. Endless loops of bland consumerism play interspersed with monochrome scenes of violence.

Cal opens his next file.

Estella nods in his direction. "You should send *him* to that urban slaughterhouse. Away from this anaesthetised, protected existence, he might finally evolve. Plus, he cannot embarrass us by fronting in the Reality Show while underground. You are perfectly capable of running your library without his assistance."

Cal slinks lower in the office chair. Serena moves to place a hand on his shoulder, then pulls back. She fixes her steady gaze on her vexing triplet in the doorway. "How is Leandra?"

"Is that her name now?" Estella sneers. "You thought giving Leah an extra syllable would somehow transform her? She remains useless as ever! The next battle would have either built or destroyed her. But my darling war is over, and Leah slash Leandra remains crippled and weak."

"So weak she must rest against a door frame?" Serena asks with an imperceptible smirk.

Estella's glance flashes vengeful malice.

Cal yawns repeatedly and slouches further down, the strength leaving his body, as Estella draws herself upright and strides into the library.

Serena blinks, and Cal stops yawning. "Leave him alone!"

"Make me."

"Oh, I intend to."

"How do you propose to do that?" Estella casts a sideways glance at Cal as he dutifully recommences his data entry assignment.

Serena blinks again, and Cal freezes in time. "He can join Leandra in the desert once the warrior returns."

Estella raises her eyebrows. "You'll make the warrior abandon that wretched girl?"

"*I* won't," says Serena. "*You* will."

Estella shakes her head, causing dusty ringlets to tumble. "I tried already. Once I realised my war was finished and the fierce creature's talents would be more useful here... But it was futile! That moping damsel has a knack for generating pity, enticing our strongest elements to protect her like a child. She sits drawing demonic visions in her sad sketchbook while our ambition unravels, as though art can miraculously save her. The warrior will not return until Leandra can survive alone. Which will be never."

Serena regards the upper southern screen linked to Petroglyph Cave camera feed. It contains only the haze of static interference. She turns back to Estella. "You'll remove the warrior's microchip, thus removing their implanted fictional backstory and the barrier between conscious mind and true memory. Then, convey the message that Leandra is doomed unless she learns to fight, which won't happen while she remains under constant protection."

Electric light casts an eerie sheen on Estella's pale face while her lips form a plum crescent of grinning malevolence. "So, we're losing your meek little helper and replacing him with a killing machine? Fantastic!"

Her smile then falters. "What's in this for you?"

The librarian gazes over the witch's shoulder at movie clips of interstellar travel on the south-western wall. Another blink, and the screens become blank and reflective. "These moves are crucial to the long game and advancing our main quest. Also, many tribal cultures send their young into the wilderness as a rite of passage. The necessity of learning to survive without protection from elders can force a personal evolution. You wish us to strengthen as a collective... If my plan works, it will toughen two of our weakest elements, thus enhancing our overall power."

Estella emits a throaty laugh. "And if it fails, we'll kill off two of our weakest links before they drag us down further. I like this plan!"

"It won't fail," Serena insists, blinking to unfreeze her timid assistant. He jumps, then peers back at Serena in mute confusion. She frowns. "Cal, please continue your data entry assignment."

Cal returns to the Reality Show memory files of the collective's connected life, comforted by a repetitive task.

The library door slams open.

"What's up, dickheads?"

A fiery young woman marches into the library, a collection of guns and knives attached to her toned waist. She nods at Estella. "Thought I heard your creepy voice! Didn't get your precious war, huh? Shame! I was kinda looking forward to joining the battle." She pulls a knife from her belt, admiring its subtle sheen. "I was gonna scalp me some snooty society psychos with this beauty!"

Estella graces her furious younger sister with an indulgent smile. "No war," she admits. "But our warrior sibling will soon ditch the wretch to join us."

"Woohoo!" The fiery newcomer punches the air, still clutching her favourite knife.

Cal flinches, distracted from his work.

"Alicia, please don't wave knives in my library," Serena admonishes.

"Which knife?" asks Alicia. "This knife?" She throws her weapon high in a glinting spin. As it falls, she catches the handle. "This knife here?" She grins.

A warning alarm blares before the librarian can reply.

Cal presses his palms against his ears. His three sisters spin towards the row of screens above his workstation, which provide live footage from the castle's seven rooms and surrounding forested grounds.

"There!" The librarian points to feed from the south-east perimeter fence. The display unit moves forwards, expanding to fill the southern wall. In picturesque forest where ivy clings to gnarled branches in dappled sunlight, death approaches. A Reckish demon with ashen scales and glowing red eyes makes an incongruous foreground to the woodland scene, attacking the wire fence with razor talons.

Serena tuts. "This is why I need you guarding the castle, not throwing knives in my library," she admonishes the blade-wielding intruder, who is already reaching for her gun. "Do your job!"

"Aye aye, Captain!" Alicia quips, dashing toward the north wall's loading bay. She exits via the castle rail yard, muttering, "Defending this dumb place will be significantly less shit with my fighting buddy."

The strange library's three remaining occupants stare at the demonic live feed as a beast composed of slime, scales and deadlight slashes the perimeter fence.

"Reckish activity along the perimeter is increasing, particularly near the mountains," Serena remarks. "This suggests dark forces brewing in the deadlands. Maybe you'll get your war, after all."

Estella indulges in a languid smile as Cal begins to hyperventilate. *My human enemies lacked the courage to fight me, but perhaps war against demonic entities will provide the deadlight recharge my spirit craves!*

The screen shrinks to its former size with a wave of Serena's hand. The librarian then walks to a laboratory bench to recommence research. With a brief glance at her siblings, she snaps, "You both have jobs!"

Cal pries his terrified eyes from the morbid imagery and returns to organising memory files of a faraway suburban existence.

Estella rouses from hungry, brutal daydreams. "Fetch the warrior from the wretch?" She laughs. "No problem!" She reaches for energy from the surrounding atmosphere and tries to teleport back to Petroglyph Cave.

Nothing happens. Despite the ferocity of her efforts, the witch remains in the library.

What has this bitch done?

Serena glances up from her workstation. "Something wrong?" Her gaze is impassive but her mouth twitches wry amusement.

Estella throws the smug librarian a final, seething glare before flouncing from the library. *I will regain power!*

After she slams the door behind her, the witch's swagger becomes a hobble. She retrieves her cane and crosses the boardroom to the north-eastern door into her private chamber. Safe amongst her mirrors and screens depicting bloody victories, Estella collapses, her eyes clouding over as she retreats to the Reality Show's suburbia to feed. She requires strength for tomorrow, when she will drive along the train tracks in her favourite car.

3.02

(025)
"I must leave now... I'm sorry. Please survive."

The warrior kisses sleeping Leandra's forehead with sun-chapped lips then vacates the helpful cowboy's commune, leaving the broken girl alone with sketchbooks, dreams, and the remainder of their money. They button their stolen suit jacket against crisp morning air then hot-wire a car on a neighbouring street. The warrior slash thief heads for Summerton's western perimeter road. "Shit! Use the right lane!" They swear to themselves, swerving to correct a rookie error. Underground, all citizens drove on the left-hand lanes of a geometric labyrinth. Summerton's tarmac lattice, however, was designed for right-lane drivers, and blessed with open sky and sandy breezes. Neither location knows clouds or rain.

The car approaches Western Crossing, where road meets incoming rail. The warrior braces for a bumpy turn. This six-a.m. road bears no traffic, no witnesses to the unthinkable manoeuvre of turning westward onto silver tracks, two wheels either side of the northernmost rail. The tracks bisect russet sand like knives, tracing the only route through those blasted mountains. The stolen vehicle judders but maintains momentum. If a train emerges from the mountain tunnel now, the driver is doomed. But Summerton's benevolent creator watches the city and surrounding deadlands on live camera feed and should halt the trains to ensure safe passage. Brittle branches of decaying flora scratch at speeding metal. The warrior races toward the sunrise, beams of sunlight casting the mountains in ragged silhouette.

They finally reach the black void of tunnel entrance and keep driving, into darkness. The warrior slash thief slash speeding driver removes pressure from the accelerator, flinching at the proximity of the wing mirrors to blurred stone walls.

Reminded of their last trip underground, the racer emits bitter laughter, which becomes an eager grin when they spy daylight at the approaching tunnel exit.

Their vehicle emerging into sunshine, the warrior gasps, dazzled by living forest. *This Cashdamn place is beautiful!* Branches surround them bearing fresh leaves, blossoms, fruit, berries... everything but the desiccated claw hands of empty twigs. Clouds scar the sky in puffy grey slices. The soil is a brown, sumptuous foundation for life instead of arid, rusty poison. No more shadowed chill. The warrior removes their suit jacket, exposing an athletic physique clad in a stolen black tank top. Dappled sunlight dances a welcoming pattern across the windscreen as the warrior follows the track to the hexagonal castle. This geometric building looms larger than memory, a silvery violet dazzling above the treetops. With the paranoid senses of a rogue assassin, the warrior detects the sniper's gaze from the battlements.

Hoping the era underground has not severed the mental connection to their fiercest sister, the warrior shoots a telepathic beam towards her. *It's me, dickhead!*

It works. The manic-angry figure on the castle rooftop punches a sniper rifle airward in victorious salute, beams *Welcome home, nobhead!* then disappears.

When the warrior's car emerges from forest onto the castle rail yard, Alicia bursts from the library loading bay and dashes toward the vehicle. The warrior slash thief slash Homecoming Quing manoeuvres off the tracks with a jolt, braking on hexagonal flagstones. They exit the vehicle, slamming the door with a muscular arm. Alicia does not slow her sprinting pace. "Catch me like on films, dickhead!"

Mx Homecoming Quing waits with open arms and braced stance as Alicia leaps.

"Booya!" Clutching their tanned shoulder, legs wrapped around a toned waist, Alicia punches the air, still clutching her sniper rifle. "About fucking time, asshole! Everyone else in this boring castle is shit at murder!"

The warrior chuckles. "You got a metric fucktonne of weaponry attached to your belt, or just pleased to see me?"

"Shit! Sorry dude!" Alicia jumps to the ground and attaches the sniper rifle to an over-shoulder holster. She grins at her favourite sibling. "I've fucking missed you, mate!"

"I missed you too."

"Managed to prise yourself from your mopey twin then?"

"Yeah," the warrior sighs. "Management are right. If I keep saving Leandra, she'll never save herself."

"Bitch needs to level up if she wants to hang with Team Vengeance!" Alicia declares.

"Indeed. But let's hope she doesn't die, huh?"

"Yeah..."

"Also, erm..." The androgynous arrival gestures toward the castle grounds' latest addition. "Why is there a Cashdamn rail yard attached to our home? I leave for a couple of years, come back, and we make trains now? We've always been crazy ambitious but... What brought us into the cut-throat world of the transport business? What's next, a helicopter pad on the castle roof?"

Alicia doubles over with breathless belly laughter. "You're joking... But there *is* a landing pad on the rooftop! No helicopter though... But yeah! The librarian constructed trains to deliver stuff slash microchipped consumer cattle slash weaponry to our favourite subterranean hellhole. Dropping all of the above plus food and water to that weirdly familiar desert city was an unexpected subplot that may have accidentally taken over the main narrative."

"I see..." the warrior muses. "Any other 'unexpected subplots' I should know about?"

Alicia laughs again. "Ash, you have no idea!"

3.03

(027)

Serena wakes. Her bed is a simple bunk with covers in her signature colour - a supposed grey that reveals itself as minuscule chequerboard upon closer inspection. She faces the small southern wall that blunts the triangle point formed by the south-eastern and south-western walls. She blinks, and the white panel above her desk rolls up inside black coving, exposing local video feeds.

A shot of Castle Mindscape battlements shows Ash and Alicia laughing in the sunrise. The surrounding forest lies still and free from predators. In the mountains' morning shadow, Summerton rouses from suburban slumber. Serena glances between screens as she dresses. For this strange librarian, dressing means pressing a button on her metal bracelet, releasing nanobots to scamper across her comfortable outfit, tightening the seams for daytime fit and smoothing fabric wrinkles. Her eyes dart to the Reality Show screen. The collective's connected vessel is also waking and enacting the scripted steps of a more domestic morning routine. Oat milk pours into a saucepan. In the castle's southern segment, the group's social frontperson will be frozen in place, eyes clouded, only demonstrating motion in that impossibly distant world.

Serena makes the Reality Show screen shrink and drop into the lower-left corner. Her second priority is to monitor Leandra and Cal's progress in the desert. The Summerton feed has lower resolution, traveling across lines that run through mountains after traversing deadland soil. Poisoned earth corrodes the cables faster than her SilverMen crew can patch them.

This feed appears oddly familiar.

Serena enlarges the view of Cal's morning routine to fill half the southern wall, then expands the Reality Show feed to fill the other half. Both streams depict duplicate actions from a different perspective. The RS feed is a first-person shot of the connected vessel making breakfast. Oats are stirred into gently warmed oat milk. The Summerton feed shows Cal mirroring RS behaviour while creating his morning meal.

Is Cal fronting?

But his eyes are clear, not clouded...

Serena telepathically scans the collective's social front. Business as usual in the City of Steel and Vodka, with the usual representative at the wheel.

So why is Cal mirroring his social twin?

"R314!" Serena summons her only non-mute robot.

A silver humanoid machine opens indigo eyes and steps from beside a bookcase.

Serena asks, "Has Summerton changed since Cal arrived?"

R314's eyes flicker as he responds in a flat, digital voice. "Two NPCs are exhibiting off-script behaviour."

"OK, *that* I was not expecting."

"What were you expecting?"

"An explanation for *this*." Serena gestures toward the dual screen display where Cal's actions in Summerton are precisely mirroring the connected vessel's behaviour. "Cal appears to be co-fronting. His actions are the same as our social frontperson. But he shouldn't be experiencing a Reality Show connection so far from the castle."

R314 turns his expressionless metal face toward the south wall's display. "Didn't a young, boisterous underling once access the Reality Show from space?"

"Well, yes," admits Serena. "But I've since centred our energy. Connection to our linked vessel should only be possible within Castle Mindscape. During the first Great Rebuild, I tied the connective potential to our home, where I can monitor whoever is fronting."

In live footage from the helpful cowboy's commune, Cal finishes preparing porridge and brings a bowl to Leandra.

In the Reality Show, a distant vessel sits on a tattered couch to eat breakfast.

Leandra begins eating.

The Reality Show feed dims and becomes hazy.

"Now Leandra is co-fronting!" Serena stares in rapt consternation at her exhausted sister. A silver rectangle of metal glinting on a chain around her neck, Leandra consumes a few mouthfuls of porridge before lowering her spoon and closing her sleepy eyes. The RS feed depicts her actions mirrored in an alternate life, before turning the burnt orange of inner eyelids.

Serena folds her arms. "Kaldamn! When Leandra takes co-consciousness, our RS vessel loses energy. Bodies containing split consciousness display extreme physiological differences between alters. Same happens with... Wait! Does this mean physical autism symptoms increase when Cal takes co-consciousness?"

She plays Reality Show feed from when it last synched with Cal's behaviour. Sure enough, the brightness, contrast and volume all switch to higher settings. *Cal experiences a significantly more overwhelming view of existence.*

R314 faces his creator. "I assume the Summerton Two becoming co-fronters was not part of your plan?"

"Certainly not! Dividing primary awareness between three locations spells potential disaster." Serena stares aghast at two over-lit screens. "Cal and Leandra's joint narrative was meant to diverge from the collective... tangent further into fictional realms, going beyond our human limitations. But they remain trapped in the same domestic prison our vessel inhabits in the Reality Show. My plan is failing."

"The Summerton Two lack your imagination," R314 remarks. "You're a creator, a world-builder, while Leandra dreams of romantic rescue and Cal memorises numbers. Those who deny imagination are doomed to accept whatever mediocre fate the universe allocates."

"It's my fault." Serena shrinks the problematic screens back to position, revealing surveillance from across habitable areas of the mindscape's surface. "I should have been more inventive with Summerton. I basically recreated a smaller version of the City of Steel and Vodka in the deadlands. The helpful cowboy is a clone of our RS housemate, the 'commune' is his suburban house. Cal and Leandra were meant to take this familiar starting point and create something new. But maybe there is nothing new. Not for them."

"What about their microchips?" R314 asks. "Are digital instructions an option?"

"Nope." Serena waves at the south-east wall, rolling back an enormous white panel to reveal countless screens from underground dystopia. "The chips do not allow complete behavioural control, but rather the occasional nudge in an interesting direction. Cal and Leandra still have free will. Without free will, why exist? Besides, the chips are down. The warrior removed Leandra's in Petroglyph Cave and she wears it as a pendant. I took it offline. And Cal's chip rarely responds to digital prompts. It is probably corrupted... although he has ingested some false backstory into his psyche to fill gaps from trauma-based amnesia."

"So, what's your next option?" R314 wonders. "Leave the underlings in Summerton, mirroring your unimpressive Reality Show existence, and hope they eventually rebel in ways that create strong character arcs within a fascinating narrative?"

The librarian shakes her head. "I must think bigger! If I instigate massive changes to our parallel life, maybe Cal and Leandra will sever their partial connection and break free from destructive patterns. Perhaps a grand Reality Show adventure will provide inspiration for new mindscape storylines. Although, our options are somewhat restricted by poverty, disability and lunacy."

R314's indigo eyes start flashing.

"What were you saying-" Serena starts, before a nearby screen distracts her. Hazy Summerton footage shows the railway station, where an NPC has stepped past the No Humans Beyond This Point sign, onto the platform. He brazenly approaches the latest supply train.

"Report from Summerton-" R314 begins.

"I can see," Serena replies. "An NPC investigating a supply train! Is this the off-script behaviour you mentioned earlier?"

"Yes, this character is the estranged son of-"

"We'll discuss this later. Right now, I need to 'port you inside that train! Apprehend the NPC, walk him off the platform, and say nothing. I'll search for the fault in his behavioural script."

"Affirmative," R314 responds.

"Affirmative?" Serena snorts. "Did I really design such a science fiction cliché?"

"Sorry, it sounded more impressive in my head."

With a blink from Serena, the tall, silver robot winks out of existence.

3.04

(029)

Ten months after the platform incident Serena remains puzzled by glitches in Nigel and Sheriff Grey's behaviour. Hardcoded into their backstory, Nigel is the sheriff's estranged son, but both characters are veering off script in different ways. The hapless store clerk is bitterly questioning his socioeconomic status, while the sheriff descends into violent psychosis. But this mystery is not Serena's main concern. Cal and Leandra continue to display no progress, occasionally diverting from Reality Show existence to remark upon a quirky Summerton feature, but mostly living unimaginative, pedestrian lives. Serena calls a meeting between Estella, Alicia, Ash, and herself in Castle Mindscape's hexagonal boardroom.

Warrior Ash and fiery Alicia arrive fresh from demon hunting beyond the perimeter fence, smudged with blood and giddy with victorious laughter. Estella the thwarted witch limps from her darkened chamber. The buzz of chirping insects permeates the castle walls. Serena types at her laptop at the head of the board table, a massive screen behind her depicting a slate oblong of cloudy window in distant suburbia. She tells her siblings, "We must discuss the Summerton Two."

Estella eases into the seat by Serena's left, still clutching her demon-headed walking stick. "Must we? I'm exhausted and find them entirely disinteresting."

Alicia sits beside Estella. "Whose fault is it you're tired?"

Ash chuckles, taking a seat by Alicia.

Estella snaps, "The fault of do-gooders who insist on draining me rather than achieving our full potential!"

"Nah, mate," says Ash. "You depleted your energy becoming an evil queen who nobody worships or fears. You stole my narrative for nothing. I've not much sympathy. I like your walking stick, though!"

Ash and Alicia grin and fist-bump, while Estella clenches her withered hands.

"We're not here to argue or allocate blame," Serena says.

"Then why are we here?" Alicia asks. "To discuss soap operas? Current affairs? The latest trends in coffee morning cupcake-baking? Swap recipes for Victoria sponge?"

"I'm partial to jam and custard roly-poly," Ash smirks. The screen behind Serena switches to a scene from Leandra's splosh modelling career, where red and yellow viscous liquid drips through her matted hair.

"What is that ridiculous girl doing?!" Estella demands.

"Pissing you off, obviously," replies Ash.

"Or using her hair as a pudding bowl, to save crockery," adds Alicia. "Keep up, Estella."

The witch trembles with humiliated fury while Ash and Alicia high-five amidst gales of barbed laughter. Serena types on her laptop. The northern display unit switches to split-screen: a first-person shot of a Reality Show bedroom window, and third-person Summerton feed of Cal gazing at a dusty windowpane while Leandra naps beside him. An open laptop sits ignored on Cal's desk.

Ash winces at the synchronised botherment. "They're co-fronting pretty hard, huh?"

Alicia nudges her fighting pal and whispers, "Who knew encouraging near-psychotic daydreaming within an unstable personality system could be problematic?"

Serena frowns. "They should have built a spaceship and escaped by now. I emailed Cal the blueprints for a Beshper shuttle and told him salvation lay beyond the stars. And Leandra was supposed to rebel against this cruel reality and become a fighter pilot... Why don't they evolve?"

"They're too weak!" snarls Estella.

"They're still too coddled," Alicia agrees, taking a dagger from her boot.

Ash gulps. "Because they're vulnerable."

"They need a push!" declares Alicia. "Setting your safety net on fire, letting yourself free-fall with only ashes and concrete beneath you, is how you learn to fly."

Serena regards her angry little sister. The feisty one's features gleam mischief as she expertly twirls a short blade between her fingers. The librarian narrows her eyes with a thoughtful nod. "You are right, Alicia. I have been too focused on our potential for interstellar exploration to acknowledge the limits of our reality. A more precarious social and economic existence could force our evolution. They must leave the helpful cowboy's commune."

"Where will they go?" Ash's brow furrows at the sight of sleeping Leandra, her frame shrunken from anxious dieting, eyelids twitching through strange nightmares.

"Wherever I can find." Serena starts typing, eyes fixed on her laptop. "The Summerton Two are mirroring our Reality Show life, we must change residence there. Ash and Alicia, prepare for heavy lifting! You may leave now."

The violent siblings rise. "Later, bitches!" Alicia calls, heading through the south-eastern door as Ash follows.

"I hope they'll be OK," the androgynous one mutters, closing the door to Alicia's bedroom slash gym.

Serena continues typing while her witchy sister's glance seethes with murderous resentment. "Estella, we could end this feud," the librarian offers. "I know you covet my place as mindscape leader. Believe me, I would happily abdicate to focus on my research, but this upheaval would be impractical with your health so unstable. Plus, the others are wary of your narcissism... Until this mindscape falls to nothing, our lives as a collective are inextricably entwined, and it would be beneficial to work together to achieve our objectives."

"That will be difficult," Estella remarks. "We have very different objectives."

"I want to keep learning," says Serena. "You wish to gain social and economic status. These aims are mutually compatible... I have upgraded my equipment to signal boost my attempted communications with Chroma-"

"Chroma is a delusion!" Estella exclaims. "A fairy tale best left in childhood. Do we really need further delusions at this point?"

"Chroma is no more delusional than this conversation," remarks Serena. "You are wary of places beyond your control where you cannot play God. Hence your disdain for reality... But regardless, Chroman authorities are sending an officer to collect Cal and Leandra for army training. But they may take months to reach our Mindfield sector. Until this opportunity arrives, can I count on your support to keep our underlings alive?"

The witch slowly smiles as the light flickers and insects beyond the castle walls buzz louder. "Of course!" she assures her studious sister. But her eyes gleam with the exhilarated madness of one who hears demonic whispers.

3.05

(034)

Estella's sumptuous four-poster bed with translucent black drapes occupies the centre of her private chamber in the hexagonal castle's north-east segment. Screens surround her, depicting delusions of success and brutal fantasies of her enemies dying. Glowing pixels of vengeance wash over her supine body while she recharges. Her bed faces the chamber's small south-western edge, which borders the hexagonal boardroom. The south wall borders the post-apocalypse themed gymnasium where Ash and Alicia exercise between shifts of battlement duty. The north-east wall is external but windowless, with an iron door leading to the forest beyond. The north-west wall borders the library slash laboratory slash master control room where the librarian stores boring information, creates pointless items, and views her surroundings on various screens. This amuses the half-sleeping sorceress, who can spy on any location simply by closing her eyes.

Ten moons ago, she was pushing Cal onto a dusty desert road to land at his pitiful sister's feet. Three days ago, a simultaneous Summerton and Reality Show house move proved disastrous. Today, the librarian views two fools on flickering screens while the collective's potential diminishes, and nothing changes.

My ambition keeps failing... Estella laments in defeated disgrace. *I should be ruling this castle, but my influence is lost as our life spirals into obscurity and ruin. I need new followers...*

Inspiration strikes as she drifts between violent daydreams and fitful slumber. *Perhaps if the weakest ones evolve under my leadership, I can regain power!*

The evening brings a full moon, which enhances Estella's creepy brand of sorcery. She closes her purple-shaded eyelids and lets her vision drift east toward the sunset... over forests where sharp-clawed imps arise by moonlight to slit fairy throats and drink magical blood... over the mountain range that forms a barrier between fertile castle grounds and deadland... over decaying forest where gnarled tree roots choke on poisoned soil. Estella's lucid spirit arrives in Summerton under midnight sky. Cal and Leandra's unstable energy draws the determined witch toward the dreadful Telf Hall.

Leandra lies in restless slumber, suffering the muscular ache of a distant, dying vessel.

Estella's projected psyche enters the parlour where Cal researches faraway spheres and stellar coordinates on his laptop. The luckless boy succumbs to exhaustion as his sinister sister saps his strength. He completes his evening routine with fumbling steps and heavy-lidded eyes.

After climbing into bed, Cal falls straight to sleep. Estella telepathically connects to his dreams, a movie reel of interstellar adventure and alien warfare. His spirit yearns for space.

During his terrifying past, Cal was the collective's most ardent believer in the Rainbow Galaxy, his pet name for Chroma. Overwhelmed by expectations from a neurotypical-centric society, he gradually suppressed his imagination. His existence was reduced to timetables, routines and numbers... memorising historical facts and enough pi to choke on. But abandonment in Summerton draws him back to Chroma. Giyakai, Wandasee, Amimia, Kalanooka, Zimsela... He pines for the return of long-dead goddesses. The great war of GWAKZ versus RED provides endless space theatre in his sleeping brain... a battle that was not lost, although nobody won.

Estella leaves Cal and taps into sleeping Leandra's mind. The predictable girl's dreams betray a hackneyed yearning for love and social acceptance. At least Cal is realistic.

The witch's spirit flies back over various nightscapes to her chamber in the hexagonal castle, to plot her next move. After she disconnects from their slumbering minds, Cal and Leandra both dream of her.

(047)

Estella spends the next five moon cycles lying on the castle's flat roof, staring at metallic rainbow swirls of petrol-coloured sky. She ponders the Summerton problem.

Leandra and Cal remain weak. Leandra should have risen above human poverty, becoming an otherworldly heroine. Instead, she mirrors a degrading Reality Show existence, and timid Cal works as a care assistant...

A care assistant! Seriously? When sanctimonious do-gooders suggested he work with those "less fortunate than himself", his response should have been, "fuck off!"

In a society where only the most obviously helpless are deemed worthy of supported survival, no great fortune lies in Cal's ability to mask his disability.

Estella lies motionless, internally ranting.

Her insubordinate siblings believe she has lost her mind.

"You wanna get some UV protection! Don't want moonburn on that alabaster complexion, love!" Alicia rises from the sliding hatch above the central staircase that snakes around the hexagonal boardroom.

Ash leans on the eastern battlements. "Estella's getting her period in synch with the moon, so we can schedule our next tampon purchase."

Alicia and Ash exchange mocking laughter.

The witch ignores their juvenile jibes and continues gazing at stars beyond the glimmering swirl.

Alicia stomps past and scans the horizon. "Much happening?"

"Trouble in the deadlands," Ash replies, casting a suspicious glance toward the mountains. "Can't you feel it? That radiating sense of danger... Something eviller than a bunch of coked-up socialites lies beneath that poisoned ground. I wish I'd stayed at Petroglyph Cave to monitor the situation."

Estella's pulse quickens.

Petroglyph Cave! Of course! I chose that location for my battle base because it straddles the midpoint between the castle and subterranean evil. A place to channel equal amounts of lifelight and deadlight.

This could still be our training zone!

Those pitiful desert rodents have failed to evolve, but perhaps summoning their presence in dreams will force their progression.

She clambers to her feet and dashes to the sliding hatch.

"Finished moonbathing?" Alicia quips as the scheming elder descends the boardroom staircase.

Boisterous laughter receding behind her, Estella storms past an empty table, into her room. A blur of achromatic botherment, she exits the castle via her decadent bedroom's heavy outer door.

She leaps into her scarlet car and races for the mountains with a screech of tires. She plots as she drives. Two decades of near-constant rejection have yet to diminish the unfathomable tenacity of her craving for greatness. The rail tunnel passes in a rush of headlights on stone and silver glinting.

After parking her vehicle among twisted trees, Estella climbs.

Petroglyph cave peers over the ridiculous Summerton like an empty eye socket. Ancient carvings of prehistoric battles adorn its rust-coloured walls, and a bunker within its shadowed recesses houses an arsenal of unused weapons. This was the planned location for her stand against a vengeful army, with warrior Ash and newly strengthened Leandra by her side, and Alicia later joining to make four.

Then battle was cancelled. Distracted by fresh gossip, her enemies forgot her, and the witch grew weaker without the energy of external hatred to recharge her psychic batteries. Indifference made her haggard.

But I will rise again!

Although first she needs to sit down. A canvas chair at the cave entrance is a welcome find for her aching limbs. While Summerton slumbers below, Estella summons Cal's sleeping spirit. The disoriented boy rubs his eyes, standing before her in indigo pyjamas.

"Do you remember me, Cal?"

Cal raises his glance from her long black boots to her ebony hair. "To the best of my knowledge, you are the first eerie woman in a cave I have ever encountered. But then I don't encounter many women. Or caves. Or people."

"Distance from the castle has made you sassy," Estella remarks. "I approve. You might be ready for training. I can teach you powers and incantations to transform your meagre existence."

"Will they transform my line manager at Occreta Gate into somebody who can allocate a fixed schedule?" asks Cal. "Stress is destroying me, but I want to help people."

Estella seethes. "Why punish yourself with this bullshit? Cleaning excrement from ingrates for minimum wage will not aid your personal evolution!"

"It might aid the personal evolution of someone who would otherwise be mired in their own excrement," says Cal "But I doubt you have compassion for such people."

"I am offering you the world!," exclaims Estella. "Stop martyring yourself proving your morality. Your abusers were liars. You can better help the vulnerable from a position of power."

Cal stares at Estella's unwashed robes. "If you have the world to offer, why are you wearing ragged clothes and sat on a camp chair in a cave?"

A sharp pebble levitates off rocky ground, flies through night air and smacks Cal's arm.

The witch continues glaring a sullen fury. "Do you wish to evolve or not?"

Cal clears his throat. "*Evolution* is a change in heritable characteristics of biological populations over successive generations. It is not a conscious process and does not occur within an individual lifetime. I can merely *improve*. Working with those unable to manage personal care should eventually alleviate my misery at being alienated from neurotypical society. I don't need supernatural powers or psychotic ambitions. I simply require accessible employment."

The witch laughs. "Work makes you free? How thoroughly you have been indoctrinated by the capitalist society of our parallel universe... In truth, work makes you a slave, which is literally the opposite to being free. Beware tabloid newspaper brainwashing!"

"I don't read tabloid newspapers," Cal insists. "I study Chroman research material and scientific papers about space. And I read Occreta Gate's training manual every day seeking professional progression. I don't have time for a side quest from a spooky NPC in a mountain cave."

"NPC?" Estella rages. "Who the fuck do you think you are? I have attained ultimate agency in storylines that never mentioned you! I ruled the underworld while you stacked library shelves. You should be thankful I would condescend to teach you my power. Ungrateful swine!"

Pieces of stony ceiling break and tumble upon Cal, but he wakes in his Summerton bed before they reach him.

Upon waking, the boy forgets everything he dreamed and commences his morning routine.

Estella leaves her canvas throne amongst the fallen rocks, limps down a craggy hillside, then drives back to the hexagonal castle. She punches the wheel of her off-road vehicle. "I am surrounded by ambitionless morons!"

Upon reaching her geometric chamber, she collapses in her sumptuous bed, exhausted from rage and frustration.

(049)
Estella spends weeks drifting through grim realities to feed on poisoned daydreams. She hears of former friends warning potential suitors away from her and laughs at their provincial cowardice, flattered by their despisal. Hatred and lust for vengeance recharge her more than love.

At the next full moon, when she has consumed enough contempt to recover her strength, she returns east to Petroglyph Cave to summon the sleeping Leandra.

If Autistic Library Boy won't listen, perhaps I'll have more luck with the Cashdamn fetish model.

3.06

(058)
"Was that blue alien bint real?"

"Is she related to Kalanooka?"

"What use are Cal and Leandra to an alien army? They're not fighters. She wanted *us*!"

After the Chroman captain flies her shuttle off the rooftop landing pad, Ash and Alicia follow Serena to the library, demanding answers. The librarian invites her angry underlings to sit and observe the southern wall's cluster of screens. One shows the boardroom they recently vacated, with various stragglers loitering to discuss the recent alien visitation. Others depict the castle's near-triangular chambers, surrounding forest and mountains in ultra-definition, or grainy live feed from Summerton and the deadlands. Serena reaches for the juddering image of Cal and Leandra chatting in Telf Hall. She brings their screen forward, expanding it to cover the cluster.

Had she left the Telf Hall screen in place, she would have seen the Deadlands Outpost screen, and the Reckish demon emerging into sunlight.

"Lizards ate my breadcrumbs." Leandra appears her usual dejected self, sprawled in her nest of cushions and blankets, uttering metaphorical nonsense.

Ash mutters, "I should kill Ernie Trenta."

Serena shakes her head. "The assault happened to Leandra. It should be Leandra who retaliates."

"Catshit!" snaps Ash. "It happened to all of us."

On the Telf Hall parlour screen, Cal remains motionless, staring at his favourite cracks in the damaged window. "We have never seen a living tree."

Alicia laughs. "Skills, bitch! You chipped him good!"

Serena purses her lips, shaking her head again. "He overrode his microchip shortly after our resident creepy sorceress pushed him from her car. He knows what he is. But overwhelming sensory input prevents him from adequately processing this knowledge. Same with poor Leandra. Both siblings would rather cling to a fictional backstory than remember the whole truth, because reality pains them."

Alicia rolls her eyes and arranges her scrawny but deadly frame into a comfortable seated position. Serena remains standing while the audience of three view Kalakai's arrival in Summerton with restless anticipation. The captain lands in Telf Hall courtyard during a freak sandstorm and heads straight to Cal and Leandra's apartment. Ash curses at the alien captain's rudeness to Leandra. When Kalakai rants about the lack of Opree Shengra air power, Alicia comments, "We don't need detailed alien backstory at this point."

"Stop blabbering and take Leandra and Cal to your damn ship!" Ash complains.

When the emergency call reaches Kalakai's com device, Alicia and Ash turn to their librarian boss. "What's happening?"

Serena is already at her computer, tapping the communication from Kalakai's colleague.

On the screen, the captain ends her call and demands an instant decision. As Cal quakes, she loses patience. "You're out of time!" She marches from the Telf Hall parlour.

"No!" Ash and Alicia yell at the Chroman officer's departure, while the librarian continues scanning the network for explanatory information.

"Why didn't Kalakai take them?" Alicia demands.

"Some mindscapers are more equal than others," murmurs Serena.

"What's that mean?"

"Mindscapers are designated high priority if their connected vessel in the parallel universe occupies a position of social or political power," Serena explains. "Or if their Chroman families make generous donations toward Godish research.

Our connected vessel on 314-Thera is relatively powerless, and we have no Chroman wealth or privileged connections. If the Reckish gain power here, our connected vessel would merely sit rocking in a psych ward or staggering the streets yelling at pigeons until its life expires. We are physically weak, low status, and unlikely to terminate other Godish research assignments by murdering other vessels. Therefore, we are low priority."

Alicia says, "I have one question."

"Yes?" asks Serena.

"What the actual holy fuck are you on about?"

Ash stands, kicks an innocent office chair across the room, then stomps toward the loading bay. "I'm going beyond the fence for a while. I have a mighty urge to kill something."

After Ash storms off, the screen depicting Telf Hall goes blank, and Alicia and her librarian boss are reflected on its dark surface. Serena waves, shrinking the screen, pushing it back to its former place within the cluster. Several more screens are now blank. All video feed from beyond the mountains is down. So is the underground city feed, with the south-eastern wall now awash with static. The only functional screens are the small Reality Show feed near Serena's south-wall desk, and the gaudy segments of space opera filling the south-west wall.

"Your presence is required in Summerton," Serena informs her fiery underling. She then walks to a nearby workstation to recommence this morning's production.

"Replacing the warrior as the precious princess' guardian?" Alicia slams a grubby fist onto the plastic chair's arm. "Nothing's gonna change!" The angry twentysomething slouches, her form a casual arrangement of sinewy limbs and belligerence. Weaponry hangs from her belt, including a knife still smeared with demon blood from her latest battle. Her angry eyes notice a nearby fruit bowl. Alicia grabs an apple and starts eating.

R314 steps from behind a bookcase to stand by Serena as she continues working.

"Our earnest warrior is too attached to Leandra since rescuing her from underground." The librarian scans a dusty tome, tinkering with controls on her bio-printer. "All coms from beyond the mountains have crashed, probably due to freak weather. I need someone to check Cal and Leandra are still alive without interfering in their personal development." She starts making more apples.

Alicia regards her powerful older sister absorbed in the task of fruit creation. "Our resident witch can contact Leandra. She says you're too reliant on machinery. She says it's more effective to get inside people's heads than to get inside their electronic devices."

Serena inspects a test apple, holding it to the light. "If Estella fails to realise that getting inside their electronic devices and getting inside their heads amounts to the same thing, she does not understand modern existence. At all."

Alicia cackles. "Yeah, she belongs to a different era, where people believed in magic. Although she'd probably have been burnt at stake! Speaking of burning... Can I bring my flamethrower to the deadlands?"

"Of course!" Serena agrees. "But don't kill all our enemies. Our weakest elements are separate from the pack so they can learn how to fight for themselves."

"Sure thing, boss!" Alicia takes a final bite from her apple. "This synthetic fruit is awesome, by the way. Are you sure growing apples outside wouldn't be easier though?" She throws the unwanted core toward a wastepaper basket and misses, sending it skidding across black and white tiles. "Oops!" She pulls a gleaming silver gun from her belt and shoots the core. The fruit waste disappears, along with a chunk of white tile.

"Please refrain from using that gun in my library!" orders Serena. "And no, I don't trust outdoor environments. Weather patterns are unpredictable and chaotic, with too many variables... like people."

The librarian pushes a button on her bio printer, rolling the top panel back. She inspects the tray - identical rows of perfect, green apples - gives a slight nod, then addresses her robotic assistant. "Please add this batch to the next supply train."

Obedient R314 lifts a crate from beneath the workstation and packs the apples with surprising grace while Alicia stares transfixed. "Not ditching the Summerton project then?"

"Of course not," Serena replies. "Maintaining a variety of social ecosystems is imperative to my psychological research. I only wish the sandstorms and poisoned earth didn't disrupt my camera feed. I don't even know if the eastern perimeter fence is still intact. I was perhaps overly ambitious in pushing it over the deadzone."

With a fluid smoothness to its strong movements, R314 lifts the apple crate and strides across the chequerboard floor, past towering bookshelves, toward the north-wall loading bay.

Alicia checks her weapon belt. "You beginning to question whether that cursed alien structure under the deadlands is actually dormant?"

Serena watches R314 walk out into the rail yard. "If it reactivates, I will construct a new perimeter fence this side of the mountains, stop the trains, and let the Reckish take Summerton. I'll message you to bring Cal and Leandra back here first."

Alicia spots the smear of demonic blood on her hunting knife. "Won't that be a massive waste?" She wipes the grey fluid onto her black jeans. "If they return home unchanged... Leandra will sit in our starlet's girly bedroom and cry. Cal will return to your desk, meekly absorbed by repetitive tasks. Everything they survived will be for nothing."

Serena begins her next task, making oranges. "Kalakai may still return... If they can't upgrade in that arid town, interstellar battle training is still an option."

"Interstellar battle training might kill them," Alicia remarks. "What happens if they die? Will we feel it?"

"We will survive." Serena reaches for her next instruction manual. "Their twins will spend years with part of their soul missing, but we will live."

Alicia returns the knife to her belt and glares at the librarian. "You once promised we'd leave nobody behind. Speaking of which... What happens to our unmentioned members underground if you abandon the deadzone? Will they die too?" Alicia's gaze snaps toward sunlit rails beyond the back shutters, where a glistening R314 is loading the supply train's penultimate cargo. "Don't we all deserve the sun?"

Serena readjusts the printer's dials, prompting the machine to whirr and flash subtle lights from the cracks in its casing. "Some are more suited to the underground. They thrive there. Even you expressed desire to return to subterranean dystopia. You hate the sun."

Alicia folds her pasty arms. "You know what I don't hate? Choices! Sun or shadows. Lifelight or deadlight. Tofu or bacon. Yoga or stabbing a bitch. Overground, underground, murdering free... Nothing dehumanises like the inability to make your own decisions."

Serena places her hands on the desk. "Well, here's a decision... Do you want Estella to drive you to Summerton, or would you rather hitch a ride on my next supply train?"

Alicia groans. "If that spooky bint delivers one more lecture on the benefits of psychic vampirism, I'm gonna hurl! I'll take the train."

3.07

(062)

Alicia jumps from the supply train as it approaches Summerton. Her agile body rolls across stony earth before sprawling to a stop among weeds and pebbles. She stares up at the blasted sun through multi-vision goggles and laughs. Bruised but exuberant, she raises the com device on her grazed wrist to her chapped lips. "I have safely arrived near sunny Summerton! Time for some holiday fun!"

Her com speaker crackles with Serena's calm reply. "Remember not to kill anyone."

Alicia chuckles, jumps up and walks toward Summerton's perimeter road. The NPCs pay no notice as she strides into town, the librarian's nudge to their microchips telling them a wiry figure in dark military clothing striding out of the desert wielding a flamethrower is a perfectly normal occurrence. "Your surveillance cameras are all smashed up," she informs the librarian.

"Does the damage resemble deliberate vandalism or the result of freak weather?" Serena's tinny voice enquires from the electronic device.

"Hard to say." Alicia takes in details of her surroundings as she walks towards Summerton centre.

"Remember, watch and protect Cal and Leandra without interfering with their personal development."

"Of course!" Alicia fakes a breezy tone before her face cracks open with a predatory smile. *What ya gonna do, boss? Ever gonna leave that damn library to grace this sandbox with your presence?* She lowers the green-tinted multi-vision goggles from her forehead. This equipment stores no private addresses but can identify every public building. "Library," she says, pushing a button near her temple. Glowing green arrows line the path, directing her straight on, then left.

"Why are you going to the library?" Serena's voice nags through the coms device.

Fucking bitch has my tech rigged!

"You expect me to go an indefinite amount of time without reading and not kill anyone?" Alicia follows a glowing arrow left, then spies a signpost for various public buildings including Summerton library. She switches off her goggles and pushes them above her forehead, feeling a light breeze hit the sweat on her exposed skin.

At Summerton library she finds the paper copy of the voting register. *Better not search digital records with the damned boss monitoring the machinery.*

Alicia obtains Ernie Trenta's address, snaps a ballpoint pen off a silver chain, and scribbles the street name, number and district on the back of her hand.

Ernie resides south of the tracks, near Occreta Gate. Luckily, Cal is off work today so Alicia can wander without the fragile boy spotting her. She marches across town. NPCs meander past, following the script for a pointless, repetitive existence. *Why does Cal try to emulate these fuckheads?* The sun dips toward the eastern horizon, casting an orange glow over concrete residences as the hunter approaches her target. She spies a large, rectangular piece of plastic filling a rectangular hole in a wall, with hinges allowing occupiers to enter or leave the dwelling within. Otherwise known as a fucking door. She decides to knock on it.

A scruffy-looking piece of shit answers, rubbing his bleary eyes. "Hello?"

If Alicia's gaze were any more vicious, it would have burned his stupid face. "Ernie Trenta?"

"Who wants to know?"

"I'll take that as a yes." Alicia punches Ernie in the temple, rendering him unconscious.

Haha, I'm such a knockout!

The sun sets as she drags her victim across town by his wrists, occasionally turning to snicker at his skin flayed raw by sandy concrete. She reaches an alleyway near Telf Hall and with a strange little pop the surrounding streetlamps switch off. *Fuck it! I need infra-red.* Alicia pulls down her multi-vision goggles, now switched to Night Mode. *Reckon the electrics round here are fucked, so I doubt she'll scan this.*

She crouches by Ernie Trenta, whose eyelids are starting to flicker. She slaps him hard on the cheek.

His eyes snap open.

"Yup, works every time!" Alicia grins. Her quarry's confused face shines alien in the sickly infra-red hue.

"Wh... What's happening?" Ernie croaks.

"What's happening, my dear, is you apologising to a lady."

Ernie screams.

"Oh, come on! Apologising is not that scary a concept!" Alicia snaps, before a massive claw grabs her shoulder.

She attempts to reach for a gun and spin round in one synchronised, deadly movement, but a second clawed fist smashes into her temple and it is her turn to collapse unconscious.

Alicia awakes minutes later to the rough sound of Ernie's body being dragged across concrete. She jumps up, drawing a gun from her belt, and runs toward the scraping noise. She turns a corner, dimly aware of other footsteps running in the street ahead.

Leandra's former date lies speechless and quaking, his sneaker-clad feet in the grasp of a massive demon with glowing red eyes which shine a blinding pale green through the night filter. The monster crawls backwards, dragging the bait, its dazzling gaze fixed upon Alicia... The way a human might walk with a string-based cat toy, enticing a kitten from behind a sofa. *Reckish! Has it busted the fence or come from underground? If that CRIB's reactivated, we're fucked!* As streetlamps flicker near a gaudy storefront, Alicia pauses. Teenage memories of this realm as a demon's playground tumble through her brain. *Scarlet eyes in brutal wasteland. Incessant battles for survival. Sleep and you might die.*

"Was that you screaming?" A male voice emanates from the nearby convenience store.

"No," a familiar voice replies.

Leandra!

Her sister's voice shakes Alicia from nightmarish recollection. As she sprints toward the scaly monstrosity, now level with the storefront, Ernie screams again.

Alicia shoots between noxious, radiant eyes. The demon collapses to the asphalt, eyelids dropping, concealing the optical glare. Ernie squirms but his ankles remain gripped and bleeding under massive talons. In the Sunny Bargains convenience store, Nigel yells, "I'm calling the guards!"

Alicia holsters her gun, grabs Ernie under the shoulders and starts pulling him from the supposedly dead monster's grip.

Clink! A bullet dislodged from self-repairing hide tinkles to the ground. Reptilian eyes open with a searing glow.

"Oh shit!" Alicia pulls harder on Ernie's shoulders in one final effort to remove him from that lethal grasp.

The monster roars. It keeps one clawed hand around Ernie's left ankle while raising the other with talons like daggers. The demon slices Ernie across the midriff. Blood splatters across Alicia, the ground, and Sunny Bargains as Leandra's former date is ripped open. His attacker slash failed rescuer flies back, still clutching his upper body.

"I'm in the Sunny Bargains on 18 Cenmangerie Lane, north Summerton..." Nigel blabbers behind the blood-soaked window.

Alicia drops Ernie and reaches for her flamethrower. The monster bounds into the night, leaving Alicia and dying Ernie on the asphalt in a pool of entrails.

"...And there's blood splattered across the front window."

The dude's calling the guards! Shit! Serena's having issues with Sheriff Grey veering off script, over-riding digital control. Best not get caught with half a body...

Alicia is about to run.

Leandra! Ernie assaulted her. If this links back to her...

Sudden gritty wind heralds an approaching sandstorm. Alicia winces as she grabs Ernie's gore-splattered wrists and begins dragging him away. "Half my body's gone... I'm dying...." he gurgles through a bubble of blood.

"Try reframing your predicament using positive language," Alicia suggests, checking to ensure drifting sand is covering the trail of blood. "Instead of 'Half my body's gone', try saying 'Half my body is present'."

She presses a button on her goggles. "Body of water." Luminous green arrows point the way to Summerton Oasis.

Alicia stomps across Summerton, dragging dying Ernie behind her.

"If you don't get me to a hospital, I'm finished!" the dying man whimpers.

"You don't need a hospital, you need to practice gratitude," Alicia retorts. The last words Ernie hears before he dies are "Have you tried vitamin B supplements?" Alicia drags his upper body through Summerton park, his entrails snagging on low-lying branches.

After dumping Ernie in the foetid pond, Alicia crawls under a park bench to wait out the storm. She drifts into bemused slumber, stalked by monsters from her youth.

She wakes to her com screen beeping as the sun rises.

"Status report," Serena requests. "I hope Cal and Leandra are relatively well, and you've managed not to kill anyone."

Alicia glances at the blood caked across her body.

"Haha! Yeah. Erm... About that..."

3.08

(065)

Serena stands before a bio printer the size of an upright coffin. This cuboid machine will soon contain a newly created body, with design specifications set to Random rather than Reality Show Clone. As the machine zaps bones, organs and soft tissues into place, R314 steps up beside Serena, fresh off the delivery train that recently materialised in the castle's adjoining rail yard. "Ah, the miracle of life!"

Serena watches rapid lasers print tanned skin over her latest creation. "Alicia played a part in the death of Ernie Trenta outside Sunny Bargains convenience store in Summerton last night."

R314 would laugh if it contained the relevant circuitry. "Are you surprised?"

"I would be less surprised if she had outright murdered him. What happened instead is somewhat unnerving. A Reckish demon was attempting to drag Ernie, alive, out of Summerton toward the deadland outpost."

"Ah yes," R314 responds. "About that..."

Serena whips around to face her favourite silver helper.

R314 presses a button on his side, prompting a panel to slide up his metal torso, revealing an inbuilt screen. "This is what you missed after coms went down."

His chest lights up with Night Shot footage from the deadlands outpost. Pixelated, green-tinted SilverMen with guns are herding a group of nervous NPCs off a passenger train, toward a customs office. A metal door flies open, torn from its hinges. A grey, scaly body resembling a tiger slash lizard slash occult nightmare crawls out of the doorway.

The ambushed humans scream, dashing back onto the train. SilverMen open fire but their bullets embed in the demon's skin without stopping its advance. The demon prowls toward R314, its crimson glance fixed on the robot's inbuilt camera whose shot remains steady and unmoving. Luminous pixels show the demon stopping, gazing directly at the lens as it speaks in a guttural voice laced with slime and malice. "Three above. Three below. Eat the heart. Kill the soul." The creature leers, revealing ivory fangs, and the image drowns in static haze.

Serena's face holds no expression. "It's happening. A second Reckish infestation has begun, and our weaponry is ineffective against the new breed. I should have 'ported you back the minute coms went down."

"Coms cut out frequently due to damaged cables," says R314, pressing a button to cover its screen. "You weren't to know a demon had crawled up the elevator shaft from the underground city."

"Deragon Hex..." Serena regards the blank screens filling the south-east wall. "Subterranean feed has been down for weeks. I never requested explanatory reports. Too busy researching Chroma and spoon-feeding Cal space data to notice what's happening under my feet..."

R314's indigo eyes glow a flickering reflection on the bio printer's door as lasers finalise the constructed character with a bland outfit. "Technically, the dystopian underworld has not been 'under your feet' since you 'rebuilt your home in a more stable location' thirteen years ago."

"No matter," Serena says. "I've invested too much brainpower in that city to let it become Reckish territory. I must reclaim it... 'Three above. Three below...' That suggests six demons. What have you heard from underground?"

"No other reported sightings," replies R314. "The beast emerged in a camera blind spot at fourteen twenty-seven, headed straight for the elevator, clawed its way to the surface then sprinted into the deadlands toward Summerton. No crew were in the city. I considered contacting the guards, but remembered the fault in Sheriff Grey's programming. I figured your fiery younger sister could defend the weak ones. We repaired the broken elevator and got the NPCs through customs before sunrise, then I boarded the supply train before its scheduled 'port back."

Serena nods. "Did you swipe any demon DNA or blood from the scene?"

"It did not bleed." R314 opens a storage tray in its abdomen. "But these bullets dislodged from its hide as it regenerated, and I detected alien tissue in the side ridges." He hands the contaminated bullets to Serena.

She fetches a Petri dish. "Great work, R314." She brings the ammunition to a workstation covered in laboratory equipment and begins scientific analysis.

R314's indigo eyes spark further rapid flickering as he processes an incoming report. "One more thing, boss."

Serena peers up from her microscope. "What is it?"

"Remember the malfunctioning NPC I intercepted trying to board a supply train?"

"Nigel," Serena nods. "What has he done now?"

"Well, with most cameras still down and my crew guarding the outpost, we only just noticed. He jumped onto your latest passenger train as it left Summerton and is headed for the outpost! His programming is for the desert, not the underworld. If he speaks to..."

Serena rubs her temples. "I'm aware of the consequences of a Summerton NPC interacting with new arrivals at the outpost. I'll 'port you to the platform immediately. Intercept Nigel before he can communicate with the herd, then commit him to Trilby Asylum while I decide his fate."

"Aff... yes boss!"

R314 disappears.

3.09

(070)
Alicia wakes in Petroglyph Cave wondering who will die today. Braced for midday sun, she covers her lower face with a scarf, her furious eyes gleaming within multi-vision goggles under the hood of her dark military jacket. She grabs her trusty flamethrower. The atmosphere contains an electric crackle that suggests upcoming murder.

Her mountainside vantage point at the cave entrance peers over the prickly dead trees to Summerton's criss-crossing roads and drab concrete buildings. From a tunnel at the mountain base a train shoots onto the desert, headed for Summerton and the outpost beyond, filled with poor sods whose brains are electronically rigged to seek sanctuary underground. Alicia checks the arsenal attached to her belt is secure, her boot knives are in place, and her flamethrower is fixed in its holster diagonally across her back. Satisfied she is adequately armed for defence or massacre, she sets off down the mountain.

She trots through dead forest toward the tracks, ignoring her stolen car at the mountain base. With today's manic-angry energy she could walk forever.

"Cal." Alicia presses the microphone button on her goggles. A glowing green arrow points to Occreta Gate.

"Leandra." It appears the little lady is taking a walk, blissfully unaware that an alien monster kills her enemies after sunset. Alicia has spent the past six nights digging graves before the dawn. Only room for one corpse in the sad murk of Summerton Oasis.

She keeps walking. Stumps of decayed plant matter creep from arid earth like skeleton fingers and Alicia cannot remember when she last saw a living tree. She once lived west of the mountains in a geometric castle amidst lush woodland, but that was aeons ago. Six desert days have warped her thinking.

A snake hisses to her left.

She fixes a calm gaze on the deadly reptile, all smooth scales and hostile, yellow eyes. "Mornin'!" she greets with a polite nod. "Nice day for it!"

The snake pulls back as if to lunge.

Hand at her hip, Alicia tunes her thoughts to her new acquaintance's frequency.

Avoid human language. Use sequential imagery, a lovely slideshow of its potential future.

She transmits an image of it leaping for her neck, immediately followed by the image of it getting shot in the face thanks to her feline reflexes.

The reptile recoils.

"Not today, dude!" Alicia snickers, kicking up dust as she follows the tracks to Summerton's edge.

Leandra limps across her horizon. *There's the bint!* The crippled model swings a metal walking stick by her side, and glows with lifelight. Her radiant smile provides a ray of hope in these barren wastelands. *How bloody foolish! Drawing attention to yourself when you lack self-defence training, or a gun, is a recipe for disaster.*

Alicia follows her daft sister from a distance, crouching behind orange rocks. A man loiters near Western Crossing and she pulls down her goggles for further information. Facial recognition identifies this dude as Seth Starret, a man with so little brainpower, ambition or potential he has nothing better to do than terrify women in the street.

Seth smiles, spotting new prey. "Who *is* this girl?"

Leandra says nothing.

Smack him in the balls with your stick! Alicia tries mentally projecting some wholesome advice, but Leandra's mind is scrambled by panic, her light fading. Her smile disintegrates as she trembles, turning to walk home. Alicia seethes in her hiding place, her grazed knuckles turning white as they clench jagged stone. She attempts a psychic warning to the lecherous scum, but his mind is an unreceptive void.

"I said, who *is* this girl?" Seth follows Leandra to the now-rattling tracks.

Leandra remains silent, limping again, that radiant glow seeping from her pores like unwanted sweat, blood to a piranha. Her path reaches the rail crossing as another train approaches.

Alicia pulls a gun from its holster.

As the abuser lunges for a kiss, Alicia aims at his smug head, but the terrified Leandra is blocking the shot. She curses.

The train finally passes and Leandra hurries across the track. Her soulless fanboy follows her a while, Alicia tracing his path through crosshairs. With Leandra's nervous disposition, witnessing another murder might destroy her at this point, but she will take this risk if the creep molests her again. It is not until a happy couple appear in the distance walking their dog that the asshole finally turns back toward his pickup spot near the tracks.

Alicia holsters her gun and remains low, her murderous gaze fixed upon her loitering prey. He smokes, reads his com screen, chuckles to himself. She waits until the dog-walkers disappear, pulls back her goggles, then steps out from behind flame-coloured rocks.

"I read an article on the com network yesterday. 'How to approach a woman wearing headphones.' Seriously!" Alicia laughs as she saunters toward her clueless victim. The Reckish demon will be hiding, weakened by daylight, and her blood pumps with rising excitement at finally getting her own kill.

Seth grins at her approach. "Hey girl! You dressed up for Halloween? You got sexy underwear under all that?"

Alicia sniggers, walking closer. "What's next? How to approach a woman who appears terrified? How to approach a woman who's running away? How to approach a woman who has changed address and filed a restraining order?"

Seth laughs and slaps his thigh. "Oo, she feisty! Come on baby. I like 'em angry. You into some kinky shit, huh?"

Alicia stops three meters away. "I, Alicia FieryFace of Castle Mindscape, solemnly swear that as long as public harassment is considered socially acceptable, I will continue to carry and utilise this flamethrower." She pulls the stated weapon from over her shoulder.

"Whoa, girl! You ain't gonna use that thing! You having a hard day, darlin'? Huh?" Seth retains his smug grin, but it no longer reaches his eyes. He starts backing away, toward the glinting tracks.

"My day was fine, until you reminded me why I detest humanity." She steps closer.

Seth flails his arms for balance, almost tripping backwards over a rail. "Hey girl, just chill, alright? How about you drop that thing?"

Alicia lowers her flamethrower and drops one hand to her side, her facial expression conveying pleasant greeting.

"There now, no need to get mad. I've got something that could calm you down." Seth winks.

"What, a train?"

"Huh?"

She whips the anti-matter gun from her belt and shoots Seth in the leg. He collapses onto the tracks, bawling as his upper thigh becomes a bleeding stump. The third train of the morning rattles out of the mountain.

Alicia shakes her head and sighs. "You wait all day for a train carrying suburban cattle to an underground city, then three arrive at once... It's always the way!"

Seth screams as the train approaches.

3.10

(072)

The SilverMen crew re-establish video from the deadlands within twelve days, and R314 stands beside Serena as she compares feed from Summerton and the Reality Show. "I am glad Cal and Leandra are replicating the therapy experience," the complicated librarian says. "They're finally copying a non-destructive aspect of our parallel life."

"Reality Show mirroring has been problematic," R314 agrees, the footage reflecting on his face and torso. "Mainly because, as Alicia eloquently says, *life is shit*. But why copy social and physical aspects from the City of Steel and Vodka into Summerton if you wanted Cal and Leandra's path to diverge?"

"Training montage."

"Excuse me?"

"We were supposed to take strength training and martial arts classes in the Reality Show," Serena explains. "Cal and Leandra were never supposed to mirror our domestic life, only our physical training progress. When Kalakai arrived, Leandra's planned character arc was 'insecure fetish model becomes kick ass alien soldier'. But I didn't account for our connected vessel's chronic pain and fatigue. Attempts at upgrading its capabilities trigger three-month flares of near-catatonic agony, so this training montage lies beyond our capabilities. I can't just make stuff up."

"We're stood in a castle created by your mind," R314 argues. "I think you *can* make stuff up."

"You don't understand." Serena frowns. "There is no lie in saying we have a vivid imagination. There is a blatant lie in saying we've become a brawny space fighter. Maybe Estella's path is the only way..."

"Can't you reprogram Leandra to increase her pain tolerance and fighting skills?"

"My siblings are fragments of my psyche, not robots. Even the NPCs, with their inbuilt microchips and scripted behaviour, have some human agency... That reminds me. I'm worried about Nigel."

"Nigel Paul Charlesworth? The escapee I brought to Trilby Asylum."

"Yes," says Serena. "He was never designed to experience excessive emotion or question his reality. Programmed to be a grocery store assistant, I never gave him the mental capacity to be pained by daily drudgery."

"Do grocery store clerks usually lack mental capacity?"

"No." Serena shakes her head, while Cal on screen stares at a windowsill lizard. "That's a deeply classist belief. However, there is a curious phenomenon of certain humans *enjoying* social interaction, making a customer service role bearable. But I had no idea how to script such characteristics."

R314 gestures at his surroundings. "You can imagine a hexagonal castle, a lab that prints humans, a talking robot, a dystopian underground city... You're a telepathic telekinetic who can teleport and converse with aliens. But you can't imagine enjoying human social interaction?"

"That's correct," Serena nods. "I struggle to program neurotypical behaviour because neurotypicals are more alien to me than Kalakai. So instead, I designed the NPCs to follow pre-designated scripts with limited mental capacity."

"That makes sense," says R314.

Serena smiles, watching Cal have a therapy breakthrough. "It meant I could populate Summerton with background characters who would dutifully perform jobs, accept their place in the system, and never try to leave. Same with the underground city. I designed residents to live simple lives, not questioning the oddness of their surroundings. With Nigel though... He is somehow tuned into our collective psyche's rage. His vexations and miseries are painfully familiar... Perhaps Alicia was ranting near the bio-printers during his creation and he absorbed the radiated energy of her righteous fury."

On a south wall screen Cal rises to leave Dr Favishti's office. Near the south-west wall, below screens depicting polychromatic planets, an array of bio printers is constructing a suburban family.

R314 asks, "Could Nigel join your collective?"

"He didn't split from our consciousness," Serena says. "I doubt our flame-brained protector would deliberately share her psychic energy with somebody called Nigel. He cannot join us, but I also can't leave him rotting in Trilby Asylum... His suffering is my responsibility."

"So, what's the plan, boss?"

"I'll 'port him back here, adjust his microchip, upgrade his physical form in the bio printer, then send him underground with the next batch of refugees. I will make him a skullball player! Aggressive sport will help alleviate excess rage, and the astronomical earnings from that asinine game will solve his socio-economic woes."

"Upgrading the lifestyle of one character who previously suffered in poverty will not address the underlying social inequality that caused his suffering," R314 reminds her.

Serena sighs. "I did create these environments to mirror certain negative aspects of our Reality Show existence."

"Carnival mirrors of demon glances?"

"Exactly. The difference is, *here* our collective has the power to fight against this inequality, whereas in the Reality Show we are powerless. These are exercises in catharsis. I cannot in all conscience create a background character who perceives the prison of these systems but lacks the power to fight against oppression."

"You are a benevolent ruler," says R314.

Serena replies, "God shouldn't be a cunt."

3.11

(075)

After Seth Starret's body is found mangled on the rail track with one leg missing, Summerton's citizens concoct various nonsensical explanations. Some mix up Seth's murder with the previous month's grim discovery of disembodied legs outside Sunny Bargains.

"Is this the same guy?"

"How did he reach the rail track with no legs?"

"No, the track guy was only missing one leg!"

"So he started off with three legs?"

Alicia chuckles at grocery store gossip, and a gaggle of women with overloaded shopping carts turn to stare.

What the fuck? Accustomed to being invisible, the unexpected attention from housewives with identical blonde hairstyles makes Alicia jump. She dials Serena. "Why are grocery store NPCs staring at me?"

"Because bodies have been found locally in various states of dismemberment," Serena explains. "And you are dressed like a rogue desert assassin."

"You said you'd instruct them via those implanted microchips to ignore me!"

"Well, you're making it difficult! Killing people, discussing implanted microchips in a public conversation, not wearing denim or beige..."

"Why the fuck would I wear denim or beige? Jesus. I've never seen such tepid fashion. These people are terrifying!"

"Given your attire, I'd say they're more terrified of you."

"And I only killed one guy..."

"Please stop talking." Serena rubs her temples.

An inquisitive shopper leaves her gossip circle to approach Alicia. As the woman in drab suburban clothing steps closer, the fiery one feels self-conscious at being the only customer dressed entirely in black and carrying a flamethrower. She attempts a bland, professional voice. "Can I help you?"

"Good afternoon," says the housewife who is presumably called Karen. "The gals and I were just saying, we've never seen you around. Are you new here?"

"Yes," Alicia replies, the store lights glinting off the military-grade goggles on her forehead. "Yes I am. Only, I can't stop, I've forty-one cupcakes to bake for the charity coffee morning! We're raising money to buy laptops for orphans."

With that, the unnerved assassin strides from the store with her purchases, pausing only to throw cash notes beside the register. Back under the searing sky, she lowers her goggles and raises her com screen. "I'll stick to robbing stores at night."

"Could you not? I've no control over Sheriff Grey, I need you to avoid him." The librarian's weary face fills the scratched screen on Alicia's wrist. "I'll designate you a storage unit and tell the SilverMen to post food and water. Just... Please stop doing crime."

Alicia nods. "Less crime!"

"No crime!"

"Sure thing, boss!" Alicia spots Cal and Leandra up ahead and dodges into an alleyway. Lizards scamper among discarded boxes from a bakery. Her sinewy frame leaning against a filthy wall, Alicia says, "I've spotted our two deserty minor arcana out walking. Any idea where they're headed?"

Serena types while scanning a neighbouring screen. "Ah. Leandra has a date with a Mr Bod Weye, an arrogant Art History student from Ocorropinta nightclub. Cal is escorting her to the restaurant. The audio feed is glitchy, but I believe they are discussing trees."

Alicia slams her black-hooded head against the wall. "Leandra. Shouldn't. Go. On. Dates."

Serena nods. "Cal will probably walk back to Telf Hall alone. Can you follow him? Summerton streets aren't safe."

"That blasted Reckish demon sleeps all day," Alicia muses. "I can't find its lair. It keeps evading me, and none of my weapons do damage... I've never encountered a Reckish so strong. If we get a whole batch of this new breed, we're fucked! Any luck on the weapons front?"

"I'm working on it." Serena views another screen to her left. "Just keep Cal and Leandra safe for now, OK? And please, keep a low profile."

"No worries, boss!" Alicia ducks behind bakery boxes. "Catch ya later." She peeks over the junk pile as her troubled older siblings pass. Leandra is blabbering about a foresty lumberjack. *As opposed to what? An oceanic lumberjack? A sandy lumberjack? This bint is mental...* She trails Cal and Leandra from a distance. After they reach the restaurant and say goodbye, Alicia follows Cal back to Telf Hall.

(079)
As chaotic days pass, the feisty avenger continues stalking her fragile siblings on various misadventures. Cal works an erratic timetable, traipsing between Telf Hall and Occreta Gate like a man approaching his execution. Leandra keeps dating the obnoxious Bod Weye. Alicia creeps behind each outdoor activity at a safe distance, sticking to shadows and alleyways when the NPCs break programming to notice her outlandish appearance.

The Reckish demon returns each night, people keep dying, and surviving residents keep speculating.

"It's that escaped lunatic from Trilby House! The one who broke onto a train!"

"Well, I saw a stranger in the grocery store last week, wearing the strangest costume. Might have been her! You can't trust people who wear all black."

If they only knew... I am their best defence against that blasted demon! Alicia spends gruelling nights tracking the monster, sometimes catching it carrying a bloody corpse over

Summerton's eastern border into the deadlands. The victim is always connected to Cal or Leandra: a spoilt brat who abused them at school, an ableist bully from Cal's previous office job, bitchy partygoers, a com network troll who told Leandra to kill herself... all dead and dragged toward the outpost. Whenever Alicia intercepts the corpse-thief, they battle over a mutilated body. She never wins. Its scaly hide dislodges bullets, the anti-matter gun does nothing, and the flamethrower bizarrely increases its strength, almost getting her slaughtered by poker-hot talons. Then the damned thing scampers back into Summerton and disappears. Left alone with the gory remains of a hateful Reality Show clone, Alicia shrugs and digs another hasty burial. Sunrise reveals sand stuck to her bloody hands.

Between watching Cal and Leandra by day and fighting the demon by night, Alicia barely sleeps. She hides her stolen car behind a rocky outcrop near Eastern Crossing and it provides an occasional safe spot to collapse from exhaustion. Petroglyph Cave is too high a trek for her aching body.

She wakes one annoyingly bright afternoon to a message from Serena. "Data from Leandra's phone shows Bod Weye terminated their relationship. Watch for additional mental instability." This news elicits a mere shattered laugh as Alicia lacks the energy to punch him in the face. She would have dismissed the thoughtless boy from her memory, had she not heard his screams that evening.

After sunset, she locates the demon in Summerton park, dragging a dying socialite past dead branches. They fight until the monster escapes. Alicia tries carrying the discarded victim to the hospital, but her mission fails with the socialite dying on the way. She hastily digs another desert grave, then returns to guarding Summerton, badly.

Towards midnight, she stalks the side streets near Eastern Crossing. Pedestrians are becoming rarer since the city fell into a state of shock, and each footstep echoes with hollow unease. The only night-time wanderers are sellers and buyers of narcotics. "Yeah, women are *high maintenance*, mate," says a voice around the corner. "Yeah, I'll meet ya–"

Streetlamps stutter beneath an electric sky.

"The fuck is that?"

The demon...

"Get this fucking thing off me!"

Alicia dashes to a shaded alleyway in the remains of the dying light. Her goggles switch to Night Mode. The greyscaled death-bringer is dragging Bod Weye along the concrete, one vicious claw dug into his scrawny arm. Alicia almost runs to help. Then she remembers this asshole digitally dumped Leandra, so instead she just laughs.

"Aargh! It's gonna kill me!"

Alicia stops laughing. *I hate this monster more than I hate fuckboys. Damn conscience!* She sprints to Bod's defence.

The thing hisses at her approach, a sound like sandpaper scraping the soul, staring with those blazing eyes. Dry earth tilts and alleyway walls buckle as though melting. Overwhelmed by merciless premonition, Alicia stumbles, clenches her eyes shut and covers her ears. Her mind flickers with bloody visions past and future, erasing who, where and when she is.

Bod's screams retreat into the distance.

When she opens her eyes, the Cashdamn demon is scampering into the deadlands, the still-screaming Bod Weye tucked against its body. She runs after the monster, into the cracked desert where high sandstorms block the moonlight and without high-tech goggles she would be blind. She follows the trail of blood, panic rising in her fatigued mind the further east she staggers.

Breath ragged in her dry throat, Alicia stops. She peers over cursed deadlands and kicks the bloody stones beneath her. "It's heading for the damned outpost! Why bring more enemies underground? Why is the damn thing baiting me?"

3.12

(088)

"Good afternoon, Leandra. I have some questions," says Sheriff Grey while Serena watches from her library. Screens showing the Reality Show, Deragon Hex and Chroma all play myriad dramas ignored by the perplexed librarian. Feed from Summerton Oasis fills the southern wall. She types frantically into the behavioural modification app, "No need to question this citizen." But Sheriff Grey ignores her and continues to regard Leandra with murderous fascination.

The disturbed fetish model clasps her hands near her waist, a slight trembling betraying her rising lunacy. Cal stands immobile beside her. Leandra says, "My brother and I were taking a walk."

Serena keeps typing. "The citizens were taking a walk. No further information required." Her instructions go unheeded. She scans Sheriff Grey's internal processing and barely recognizes the script. Apart from the history of alcoholism, his entire narrative has been replaced by violent daydreams and memories of inflicting domestic brutality. "He wasn't supposed to be this realistic." She shakes her head at the law enforcer's grim inner monologue.

"Like you 'took a walk' outside Sunny Bargains?" Sheriff Grey insinuates with the subtlety of a blood-soaked window.

Leandra shimmers on Serena's screen. She is flinching under his seething glance. She is returning his glare with equal ferocity, an ironic twitch at the corners of her mouth, dead branches breaking behind her. She is a scared girl again, smiling to entice forgiveness and affection. Cal fidgets beside her.

Estella enters the library from the board room. "They are returning!" she declares with her usual pompous, dramatic flair. Her walking stick is forgotten, and she glows like a creature carrying its own strange moonlight.

"Kalakai's crew? Yes, they messaged yesterday," Serena

replies with eyes fixed on the desert tableau. Leandra and Sheriff Grey hold the coiled poses of prospective shooters, although only one of them carries a gun.

"I'm not talking about Chromans," Estella purrs.

Serena pries her gaze from the Summerton stand-off to face her vexing sister. "The Reckish? One tore through the outpost four days ago carrying Leandra's half-dead ex-boyfriend underground. The SilverMen had to repair the elevator, again. And now those Kaldamn demons have corrupted the programming of an influential NPC... He might interfere with Cal and Leandra's escape."

Estella laughs. "Influential NPC? That's an oxymoron!"

"Not in the guard force," argues Serena. "Guards can inflict heavy damage for supposed background characters."

The screen flickers. Leandra asks, "Any closer to catching the *killer?*" A subtle taunt laces her sweet voice.

Standing proud before the desert pixels, Estella slowly nods. "That's my girl!"

Serena shakes her head. "She has literal blood on her hands since touching a branch that dying socialite was dragged past. This does not bode well." The librarian accesses Deputy Green's programming. She types an instruction to convey the urgency of returning to the guard station.

"The medics need to get this body on ice, Sheriff!" the obedient deputy yells across bloody sand.

The stand-off broken, Sheriff Grey storms from the siblings. In his corrupted headspace, dreams of killing his subordinate push aside reveries of killing Leandra.

"Gonna bludgeon that irritating fool with his damned coffeepot," Estella reads over Serena's shoulder. "Gosh, that *is* a slight deviation from his script."

"No need to sound so smug," says Serena. "The Reckish corrupted *your* mind years ago, and unlike the Sheriff, I see no way of fixing you."

3.13

(090)
Midnight in Petroglyph Cave, Estella's projected spirit lounges in her canvas camp chair of superiority. She pierces Leandra with that unearthly, soul-scathing glance. "Do you remember your dreams?"

Leandra stands in a pastel blue pyjama top with matching shorts, hands on hips, meeting her mentor's eerie half-smile with defiance. "I look back over reams of dream adventure after waking. Epic quests and battles... desert-based, sea-bound, even intergalactic missions! I wake exhausted but excited. Throughout the day these nocturnal memories fade, reduced to fragments of an idea, until an innocuous phrase or casual glimpse triggers an avalanche of recollection. It's intense, but bloody interesting!"

A snake with red, black and white stripes slithers from shadows onto a patch of moonlight. Estella watches its path, eyes twinkling wry amusement. "Do you remember my last visit, twenty-nine nights ago?"

Leandra cracks a grin, starlight glistening on her lip-gloss. "I do now! Last week, I passed another cat on the sidewalk and its eyes reminded me of you... Our cave-based conversation... 'Rescue is not coming.' Then I reached my awareness toward the energy fields of passing sentient beings and took a trickle of lifelight from everyone except the cat. I never steal from children or animals. Adult humans though... If I visit Sunny Bargains at rush hour, the human herd are so happily free from stuffy offices, their energy radiates. They give it away! Sparks of lifelight shoot from them, dissipating into the air. No point wasting it!"

Estella smiles at Leandra. Her canine teeth are almost fangs. "Good girl."

The tri-colour snake coils near her feet.

Leandra chuckles. "Morality and gender are irrelevant. My body runs a constant energy deficit due to a fault in my metabolism. I'm glad you taught me psychic vampirism. Without it, my body is a crippled prison."

The witch nods, a languid movement with narrowed eyes. "I should have trained you sooner. You are more receptive than your siblings."

Leandra gasps. "You visited Cal? He's so dismissive of dreams, yet spends unconscious nights muttering about Chroma... Kalanooka... the Reckish Uprising... Demons underground... While people around us keep dying."

"When you become a light trap, insects die at your feet," says Estella. "This shouldn't concern you. Consume their energy and move on."

Leandra studies her dream visitor. "Are you from Chroma, like Kalakai?"

Estella turns to face the moon, shining umber through distant sandstorms. The snake watches Leandra as Estella says, "We are all from Chroma."

"Chroma's real!" Leandra punches the air.

Estella returns her gaze to her enthusiastic pupil, and the snake lowers its head onto its stripy coil. The strange sorceress takes a deep breath of dry mountain air. Exhales. "There is just under ninety-seven percent chance that none of this is real. This cave, Summerton, the hexagonal hell beneath the deadlands, the geometric castle beyond the mountains, Chroma... All just glorious by-products of hyperphantasia. Electrical impulses across synapses within a mound of grey-pink jelly powered by cake, vodka and vengeance. But then... There is approximately three point one percent chance - providing an exact decimal figure would literally take forever - that it's *all* real."

Leandra's shoulders slump. "Those odds are kinda low. So, it's over thirty times more likely that my progression is a meaningless delusion."

Estella shakes her head, cascading ringlets that gleam in the silvery half-light. "Never assume delusions are meaningless." A massive spider climbs the dark wall behind her. It reaches the ceiling and begins weaving as Estella's unnerving gaze remains fixed on Leandra. "Delusions give millions a reason to live. Conversely, the cruel dreams spawned from Reckish infestations make countless believers commit murder or suicide. Choose your delusions well! They deliver life or death."

While the witch utters her surreal sermon, Leandra struggles to maintain eye contact, distracted by the giant spider whose growing web is an intricate honeycomb. "Right... So, what you're saying is... Choose life. Choose Chroma. Choose joining Captain Kalakai when she returns to recruit us into her intergalactic army-"

"Choose not being a series of outdated cultural references while we're trying to create something original!" Estella snaps. The snake raises its head to fix Leandra with knowing, beady eyes. The spider turns amidst gossamer hexagons.

Leandra attempts to ignore these unfamiliar familiars. "Could anything be original? I feel like a fragment of an archetype of a teenage daydream made from magazine cuttings and spite. You strike me as an amalgamation of various femme fatales, pantomime villains and bad memories bound by pseudo-spiritual psychobabble and fuelled by contempt. I cannot decide whether this cave is an obscure literary reference or Freudian metaphor. Nothing is new."

Estella cracks that vampire smile again. "Your independence and lack of self-pity is new."

Leandra snorts. "Eternal Victim Meets Morally Ambiguous Mentor and Unlocks Latent Powers is far from an original tagline."

The spider scuttles from its hexagonal creation as the snake uncoils. These creepy creatures wait poised between Estella and Leandra, who stands tall while twelve infernal eyes regard her soul. Estella tuts, shaking her ebony curls. "I could make things more original by *killing* you at this crucial point in your narrative to create an unexpected plot twist."

Leandra returns Estella's imperious gaze with unnerving calm. The sun will soon rise over Summerton, and purgatory is almost over. "You won't though. You wouldn't waste your precious time and energy making me less shit, for nothing. You want to know if I can make it, elevate above the mire, transform from failed artist, semi-professional custard model and badly treated girlfriend into a kick-ass space warrior."

The animals creep away.

Estella casts a final, predatory smile as Leandra wakes.

3.14

(089)

Alicia is well-rested since the demon never returned from carrying Bod underground. While Leandra stays home to exercise, high on new-found rage and oblivious to impending demonic uprising, the feisty sibling follows Cal. He trudges to Occreta Gate on his day off. His fierce protector is a shadow in the corner of his eye, hiding whenever he turns. Alicia uses her goggles' zoom function to spy on his surprise disciplinary meeting, and her knuckles go white around the scabs as she clenches her fists ever tighter. "Ableist bitches need to fucking die." The sandstorms return as she follows weeping Cal home, and she zips her jacket while mentally preparing his tormentors' demise. *I need to confront those harpies before the demon returns, and Cal should help me.*

Cal arrives at Telf Hall and shares his humiliating ordeal with Leandra. Alicia cackles as baked beans splatter against the cracked parlour window. *The spooky bint did it! She got the miserable, needy wench to level up!*

Alicia follows Cal and Leandra on their Oasis Park meander. *Must that dog bark at the pond? Shit!*

The guards dredge the murky water and find the missing half of Ernie Trenta. *Another death linked to our collective! And Serena can't restrain that corrupted sheriff. Maybe time to write off this desert disaster and bring Cal and Leandra back to the castle. What a waste though...*

The guard speaks to Leandra while Cal stares into space. "Any closer to catching the *killer?*" Leandra flashes the guard a winning smile. From behind a tree, Alicia views Sheriff Grey through crosshairs while he glowers at Leandra. His weather-beaten hand hovers near his gun until his deputy calls him away.

The troubled twosome spends the next six days in the apartment, only leaving occasionally to buy baked goods.

(092)
Two days after the Fun Psychological Abuse Hour that Cal's former boss euphemistically called a "meeting", the traumatised boy attends a therapy appointment under Alicia's gaze. While Dr Peter Favishti tells Cal he has dissociative identity disorder, Alicia crouches on a nearby fire escape, eating an apple. *Part of him already knew... He's a sad fragment of a dissociative system. Given a fantasy sandbox to develop in, he relives hellish reality instead of embracing the dream. Time for a major nudge to his development!*

Cal's session ends. Alicia is about to descend the fire escape when her com screen starts buzzing. *Shit! I don't need a voice of reason at this point!* "What is it? I'm kinda busy!"

Serena's worried face peers from the screen. "Report from R314: Three Reckish demons have torn through the outpost and bolted into the deadlands toward Summerton. Plus, I caught snippets of Cal's last therapy session. The Reality Show clone of his therapist told him about DID. This delusion contains too much reality... The Summerton experiment has failed. I'll tell the SilverMen to start bringing the townspeople underground and reprogram their microchips to believe they are escaping a barren war zone. I will 'port you, Cal and Leandra back to Castle Mindscape."

Shit! I'm not bringing the fucker back like this!

Alicia thinks fast. "Wait, boss! Won't 'porting them back to the hexagonal castle right now just fuck them up further? How about I catch Cal, we nick a car, grab Leandra and drive back along the rail track? A car journey with plenty of time to explain their situation might be less jarring than a sudden 'port. They've reached a crucial point in their development. Don't wanna undo their progress!"

"OK," Serena nods. "Watch out for trains. This afternoon they will pass through Summerton at quarter past every hour. And hurry! Reckish could reach the city-"

Alicia's screen goes blank as all coms go down.
Best get to work!
She jumps to the ground and stomps after Cal.
"Productive therapy session?"

Cal does not remember his angriest sister. He fidgets, hyperventilates. "It's not safe to go with strangers."

Of course. The fragile boy memorises reams of data but forgets familiar faces. Gun-toting Alicia gives him no choice and marches him toward the nearest car. She smashes the window, rummages beneath the dashboard to hot-wire the vehicle, then shuffles to the passenger side and tells Cal to drive. "To Occreta Gate!"

As Cal cowers behind the wheel, the eager murderess spends the drive across Summerton explaining her narrative and motivation. "I'll bring you and Leandra back to Castle Mindscape when we're done. But first... I came to Summerton to protect you! But you got destroyed... My job would've been easier if you'd quit working for a heartless bitch."

"But then Leandra would have been forced into prostitution." Cal winces as the car jolts, careening over a pothole.

"What the fuck is wrong with prostitution? Sex work is work!" snaps Alicia, her gun still aimed at Cal's chest.

Cal starts surreptitiously glancing around, probably hoping for a passer-by to spot his predicament and call the guards. *Good luck with that!* Residents are walking from their homes with vacant eyes, undertaking an autopilot march toward the station.

"It *is* work." Cal turns a corner, and the next street is eerily quiet. "But nobody should be forced into it."

"Nobody should be forced into anything!" Alicia obliviously tells her gun-point hostage. "You were forced into cleaning up actual faeces for considerably less money than prostitutes earn. Don't kid yourself that you haven't sold your body and your dignity."

Cal taps the wheel with the palm of his right hand. "Leandra is vulnerable... Or at least she *was* before she developed magical brain powers... But what if said powers fail and she ends up alone with a customer who beats or kills her?"

Alicia nods. "Sex work is woefully under-protected in our hypocritical society. It's enough for a person in the unsupported disability middle ground to decide, 'Fuck it! Let's do CRIME!'" At this she giggles maniacally.

She is still laughing when Cal parks in the late afternoon shadow of his former workplace. He tells her, "If all disenfranchised disabled people resorted to violent, criminal activity, this world would be terrifying and unsafe."

His sister regains composure and coolly regards him. "You're already terrified and living in constant danger. Come, I'll teach you how to stop being a victim!"

They exit the vehicle.

A rock slams into the back of Alicia's head.

"Get away from my brother!"

Alicia spins to see Leandra stood beneath a halo of jagged stones. She holsters her weapon as blood drips through the matted curls down the back of her neck. *This is the best endgame I could have hoped for!* She grins and steps forwards with her hands raised. "Leandra, honey! I'm taking Cal to murder his ex-boss. Wanna join?"

Leandra shifts her wary gaze to her brother. "You OK, Cal? Did Alicia hurt you?"

Alicia... Cal remembers his angriest sister, her taunting in the castle library, her everlasting bloodlust. The split skin of her scalp has stopped bleeding and is knitting itself back together. He looks at Leandra. Stones circle above her, like a concussed cartoon character who has no time for stars. He pinches his arm and flinches. He tells Leandra, "Dr Favishti said we are the same person with a dissociative condition experiencing a psychotic episode. Alicia says she is taking me to kill my former boss before we return home to a hexagonal castle beyond the mountains. You are stood near my former workplace beneath a circle of flying rocks... I... I am very confused."

Leandra looks from Cal to Alicia. "I was gonna kill Ms Lessabeth Ross myself. Didn't think Cal would do it."

Alicia does a jolly dance. "We can kill her together! Fun family activity! Yay!"

Cal clutches his temples, rocking between his toes and heels. "Why is this happening?"

Leandra shrugs, dislodging the circling stones to fall at her feet. Alicia throws her a gun. The fiery one then offers Cal a weapon, but he rapidly shakes his head. Leandra says, "Your delusions were right all along, Cal. This is a mindscape! It's the best explanation for my crazy mind powers. Murdering here will help us heal."

Cal stares at Leandra in wide-eyed horror. "But Dr Favishti said-"

Alicia stamps her foot. "Never mind what bloody truths that semi-autobiographical therapist came out with! It's time to become a cold-blooded killing machine!"

"Machines don't have blood."

Alicia laughs. "Well, a cold-blooded *killer* then! You'll never be hot-tempered like me, but you could be the methodical, calculated killing type. It would suit you. You're already disconnected from humanity."

"Just because I can't fathom human motivations doesn't make me a murderer!" Cal argues. "Dr Favishti said, 'The hackneyed stereotype of the split personality killer was created by the mainstream media for cheap entertainment'. Also, I cannot be cold-blooded because core body temperatures below twenty-one centigrade generally result in death."

"Good idea!" Leandra says, marching toward Occreta Gate's front door. "We could trap the malicious wench in a giant freezer, she's already fucking cold!"

"I'm more of a fire gal, myself!" Alicia pulls the flamethrower from her back holster. "Your 'Dr Favishti' forgot to mention that in addition to dissociative identity disorder and autism, we're also borderline as fuck! But yeah, judgement toward these conditions can get in the bin..."

Cal asks, "But aren't you proving those judgements correct if you commit murder?"

Alicia snorts. "We don't murder in the Reality Show, we're not evil. We murder *here!* Human society would be far pleasanter if every anti-social twat contained their destructive urges within their mindscape. Come on, Cal. This is our killing ground!" She motions toward the door with her flamethrower.

Cal trudges toward his former workplace, wringing his hands. "This delusion is not real. This delusion is not real."

Leandra swipes at the front door. It flies open, its lock breaking in splinters of wrenching metal.

The three siblings stomp into the previously comfortable residence, two of them unaware of the Reckish demons already halfway to Summerton.

3.15

(093)

"*Daaamn* girl! You got 'nesis for days!" Alicia is impressed as she follows Cal into the hallway.

Ron's music in the dining room is loud enough to shake the floor, which explains his lack of response to the noisy arrival. Sam Rettie occupies his favourite spot in the hallway. Upon seeing Cal flanked by two furious, armed ladies he shouts, "TEA!"

Cal says, "Go make yourself a cup of tea, Sam."

Leandra is already heading upstairs and Alicia motions for Cal to follow. He whispers numbers and taps his arm, grudgingly ascending between his wrathful sisters. Leandra reaches the top and kicks open the office door.

"It wasn't locked," Cal mutters.

"It's called a *dramatic entrance*, Cal!" Alicia follows her older siblings into the site of Cal's recent psychological evisceration.

Ms Ross sits at her desk holding next week's rota, with Leandra pointing a gun at her head.

Alicia aims her trusty flamethrower at the heartless woman's unimpressed face.

"What's all this?" Ms Ross glares at the intruders.

Alicia tells her, "Cal has something to say."

Cal gulps. "I don't. Really. I'm just having difficulties with my mental health. I'd like to go home now."

"Who are these women, Cal?" Ms Ross demands.

Cal gasps. "Wait... You can *see* them?"

Ms Ross lowers the rota. "I'm not blind, Cal!"

"We are Team Vengeance!" Leandra declares. "We eat sandwiches and murder abusers, and we're all out of bread."

Ms Ross tuts. "You shouldn't be bringing aggressive strangers here, Cal! You said you weren't dangerous."

"He wasn't." Alicia grins. "But he *will* be."

"What do you want?" Ms Ross snaps. "I can't let Cal return to work now, you just *admitted* she's *dangerous!* I suspected this from my staff's complaints."

"Your staff are a bunch of back-stabbing assholes," Leandra snarls. "Cal's not here for his job, he's here to kill you."

Cal raises his palms. "I'm not! Really. I don't kill people."

"She's not real!" Leandra kicks Ms Ross' chair. "This is a constructed entity playing the role of a person who abused you in a parallel universe."

"Ha!" Alicia responds. "Whatever universe we're in, 'person' is debatable. With enough Reckish influence, no soul or humanity remains."

"Some humans are just mean," Cal argues.

"Erm, excuse me!" Ms Ross glowers. "My first priority is the welfare of Occreta Gate residents. Mentally ill employees are dangerous. We have vulnerable adults here!"

"*Cal* is a vulnerable adult, you soulless piece of shit!" Leandra snaps. "But I guess you only care about the vulnerable adults you're *paid* to keep alive."

"She chose not to engage with the Employee Support Program!" Ms Ross sneers. "Her *mental illness* is not my responsibility."

"Well..." Leandra muses. "You denied a regular routine to an anxious, autistic employee. Knowing *he* was suicidal, you told *him* nobody here would miss him. You went around your two-faced employees, systematically compiling a list of Cal's flaws - most of which were frankly ableist complaints - then used them to break him. He's barely stopped shaking since you and your lackey-"

Babs Trabeck picks this glorious moment to arrive. "Hey Lessabeth, I've got those files..." She pauses in the doorway.

"YAY!" Alicia points her flamethrower at the assistant manager. "Another abusive bitch for the bonfire! Well, don't just stand there! Come on in! The vengeance is lovely."

"What's happening?" Ms Trabeck asks.

Cal stops trembling as his glance turns to steel. "My sister asked you to join us."

Alicia nods. "That's the spirit!"

"I just realised..." Cal slaps his forehead. "You accused me of ignoring a non-present resident."

Ms Trabeck stands motionless, clutching a stack of files. "What do you mean?"

Cal clears his throat. "You said, 'Two days ago, you arrived, Sam Rettie answered the door, and you didn't say hello to him'. This formed part of your testimony to my appalling character. It seemed incorrect, but I was too bombarded with multiple accusations to process why. I just remembered... Thirty minutes into that day's shift, you sent me to collect Sam Rettie from pottery class."

Alicia bursts into hysterical laughter. "That's amazing! You're in trouble for ignoring someone... who wasn't there! Brilliant! Imagine if you *had* said hello to him... Smiled at his usual standing spot, said, 'Hello Sam! How are you today?' to the empty air. That would have gone down well!"

Ms Trabeck shakes her head. "I said you didn't speak when you arrived. I said nothing about Sam Rettie."

Cal tells her, "I was there!"

"You make false accusations because you're mentally disturbed, Cal," Ms Ross surmises.

"I WAS THERE!" Cal insists. "And so was my com screen!" He pulls a cheap device from his pocket, opens an audio file and searches for the quote... "Then it happened AGAIN..." "Well, this is *interesting*..." "You're a poor communicator..." and finally arriving at... "You arrived, Sam Rettie answered the door, and you didn't say hello to him"

Cal presses Stop.

Ms Trabeck gulps, eyes darting between Cal and Ms Ross. "I forgot Sam wasn't there. But..."

"You forgot!" Cal is incredulous. "You looked me in the eye - the way neurotypicals insist on doing when they want to create an impression of honesty - and told me I ignored him. I doubted my sanity!"

"Well moving on, Cal..." Ms Ross begins.

"NO!" Alicia yells. "Let's not 'move on, Cal'. Giving false information that contradicts somebody's genuine memory of events is called *gaslighting*... a form of emotional abuse used by narcissists and psychopaths. Is gaslighting a suitable method of communication when dealing with disabled employees, or well... anybody?"

"But Cal didn't talk when she arrived!" Ms Trabeck argues. "She just cleaned for fifteen minutes!"

"He was an autistic man trying to show initiative in an unwelcoming environment!" Leandra snaps.

"She should engage socially," Ms Ross insists. "She should join staff in the parlour for handover. And I think you should stop calling her 'he' and 'a man', because she's clearly a woman!"

Alicia leans toward Ms Ross, and with an eerily quiet voice says, "I think you should stop breathing, because you're clearly already dead."

"They ignored my greeting, which gave me anxiety" Cal remembers. "Plus, the so-called 'handover' involves mindless small talk, which is difficult for autistic people. Colleagues should have some understanding of autism. And the ability to spot potential safety hazards in a dining room should be more important than caring whether Sharon's had her baby, whether a suburban couple are pleased with their renovation, or whether there's another damn sandstorm approaching."

Crash! A heavy object falls in the distance.

The office's five occupants turn towards the sound. Babs Trabeck wonders, "*Is* another sandstorm approaching?"

"There's always a Kaldamn sandstorm!" Leandra snaps. "And guess who walked through brutal weather every day for two and a half hours, getting the skin scraped off his face, trudging with broken shoes so you wouldn't be short-staffed? *This* guy!"

"We're not discussing that," Ms Ross huffs. "We're talking about whether mentally ill people are safe around vulnerable adults."

"That's like asking... Are wheelchair-bound people safe around cripples?" Alicia jokes. "Is somebody who's five foot two safe around short people? Are vapid clowns who read teleprompter scripts safe around gameshow hosts?"

Ms Ross folds her arms. "You're talking nonsense!"

Leandra laughs. "*You* are literally berating a man for cleaning up potential hazards instead of making small talk with rude bitches who ignore his greeting."

"Well, I never heard her say hello!" Ms Trabeck sniffs.

"Riiight," Leandra says. "But you did, absolutely, have a strong enough grasp of the vocal situation in the hallway to say with utter conviction that Cal ignored Sam Rettie."

CRASH! The sound of falling objects gets closer.

"Ah, the cavalry's arrived!" Alicia beams. "And sooner than expected. How convenient!"

"Who's the cavalry?" Cal presses his palms against his ears.

Alicia orders, "Cal, go downstairs! Get all residents, and whatever staff member is hosting their own private rave in the dining room, into the parlour."

Happy to leave the two psychopathic women, and his heavily armed sisters, Cal races from the office and down the stairs. He locates Ron Buce beside an obscenely loud radio.

Ron stops scrolling his media feed on Cal's arrival. "What you doin' here Cal? Thought you were off sick."

"No time to explain," Cal replies. "We must get all residents into the parlour!"

CRASH! The tumble of violent breakage comes from directly outside. Somebody upstairs screams.

Ron dashes to the window and peers behind the curtains. "Fucking hell! Somebody's tipped the car!"

"Help me find the residents, Ron!"

Cal runs to the kitchen, finds Sam Rettie by the kettle. "Go into the parlour please, Sam!"

"TEA!"

"Yes, bring your tea!"

Cal finds Susie Miscorp on the toilet, staring at a potted plant. A searing scream from upstairs chills his spine. "Come with me please, Susie." She stands, pulls up her pastel pink pyjama pants, and follows Cal without speaking.

They meet Ron in the hallway, herding the remaining three residents. "You know what's happening, Cal?"

Cal shakes his head. "No, but my sister does."

"Who's your sister?"

They lead the residents into the parlour, where they join Sam Rettie on the couches. Before Cal can answer, a cabinet in the hallway crashes to the ground. He peers out the white-painted doorway through which he previously failed to adequately communicate. Two demons with grey reptilian bodies and glowing red eyes crouch atop the broken furniture. Alicia and Leandra are sauntering down the stairs, covered in blood. Leandra still holds her gun, but Alicia has holstered her flamethrower and wields a messy knife. "We need to stop meeting like this," Alicia greets the demons. She and Leandra reach the hallway and stand blocking the parlour doorway. "There's two for you upstairs. There's nobody for you in here."

Cal trembles behind his angry sisters as the monsters crawl closer. An internal voice tells him to grab a gun from Alicia's waist and shoot his sisters then himself.

"Get out of my brother's head!" Alicia snaps at the beasts, their eyes basking her limber form in the sickly red glow of sunset nightmares. "We can't kill you, but we can fucking hurt you!" She holds her bloody knife in an unwavering grasp. "I've seen your kills. You're collecting my enemies underground. I don't care why, that's tomorrow's problem. Today, you're taking those two bitches from upstairs, then off you fuck!"

The demons turn from her and crawl up the stairway, sniffing the air, talons gouging the concrete. They disappear into the office.

"What *was* that?" Cal gasps.

Ron asks, "Who are your friends? And why are they talking to nobody and smashing cupboards?"

Leandra punches Ron in the mouth. "That's for being a spineless snitch and betraying my brother."

Ron wipes blood from his split lip. "What the hell? Who's your brother?"

Cal's hyper-sensitive ears detect the slippery scraping of objects being dragged over thick carpet. Alicia guards the doorway as the demons reappear in the landing. They each clutch a bleeding woman, held by a cruel claw against a scaly chest. The front of Lessabeth Ross' head is a slab of bleeding meat. Her dismembered face has been crudely stitched onto the back of Ms Trabeck's head, and both their ankles bleed from severed tendons.

Cal sighs. "So much for getting a reference."

The demons crawl downstairs, each moving on three legs while carrying their quarry.

"Where are they taking my former bosses?" asks Cal.

Alicia laughs. "TO HELL!"

Cal rubs his head. "So, hell is real? Under the earth?"

The demons exit through the broken door, leaving a trail of blood as Alicia smiles at her baffled brother. "There is no greater hell than the one we create. And ours is fucking brutal!"

"Sounds like delusions of grandeur," Cal remarks.

Ron peers into the hallway, his lip still bleeding. "Whose is all that *blood?*"

"Some can be yours, if you want?" offers Leandra.

"Delusions of grandeur?" Alicia laughs. "Some power-trip managers mentally destroy disabled employees for daring to complain about a haphazard rota... How fucking trite! If you must create hell, at least do it with class and imagination!"

Cal stares at the blood-drenched hallway. "Did that heavy-handed metaphor with the dismembered face show class and imagination?"

"No," Alicia admits. "But it was funny."

Before Cal can reply, the overhead blast of an airborne engine is accompanied by the rattle of distant gunfire.

Cal and Leandra turn to each other. "Kalakai!"

The three siblings dash to the front door, almost slipping in puddles of scarlet disaster. The view that greets them knocks a crushing blow to any hope of salvation.

"She's been shot down!" Leandra groans as Kalakai's shuttle careens towards Summerton's edge from the northern sky, trailing smoke and fire.

Vivica IV

(067)
Imagine having enough strength you could punch an enemy through a wall, leaving a comedy cartoon shape in the bricks, but being so uncoordinated you miss their sneering face and fall over the coffee table. Strength without coordination is useless. The same applies to intelligence without mental focus. You could solve complex mathematical equations but cannot focus on the page long enough to read them. You could write amazing stories, but you accidentally set fire to your laptop and lost all your pens. Reams of excessive information relay endlessly through countless synapses, and all this impressive processing power produces is a mute creature who stares at the wall. It is enough to make a person suicidal.

Vivica wishes adults would cease grading intelligence in children. She once channelled her hectic brain's potential into academic achievement, and the world has never forgiven her. You cannot attain high test scores on one occasion then return to the safety of daydreaming. They stamp "Capable of Perfection" on your forehead and anything less than perfect results in parental beating. The perfection mark enrages your peers, who also beat you, devolved into feral brats while your every move is scrutinised, eternally labelled as somebody who should know better. High grades are a gateway to a lifetime of wasted potential and self-loathing.

Straight A's.
Not even once.

Vivica sits with eyes clouded over, existing simultaneously in dream and reality. She cuts herself for a searing moment of clarity. In blissful seconds of escapism, only the blade exists, and nobody expects her to do anything but bleed.

"Vivica's a lesbian!" A braying moron interrupts her fragile serenity. "She's stuck in the closet!" Dodger hunkers on an ebony tile, slamming open the cupboard door. "Hey Vivica! You ever get spooked in there and start thinking you're a ghost?"

She drops the kitchen knife, holding a pale hand over bleeding wounds. "I *am* a ghost. I haunt lonely school corridors and this stupid mansion."

Dodger tries to pass his hand through his sister, but karate-chops her arm instead.

The forlorn girl winces as his filthy digits strike her broken flesh. "Ow! Leave me alone!"

Dodger views her crystalline teardrops and the scarlet stripes of her externalised self-loathing. "Well... A, I thought you liked pain. And B... Ghosts aren't solid."

Vivica blinks back further tears. "A, I only tolerate the pain I can control. B, I'm only metaphorically dead, much to my eternal disappointment. And C..." She reaches a delicate hand. "Give me back my knife !"

"What knife?" Dodger laughs, throwing the kitchen blade into the air. "This knife?" He catches the handle behind his back. "Tell ya what, leave that damned cupboard, come join the family meeting, and I'll give it back. Socialise for a bit! Then ya can come back to cutting yourself in the dark."

Vivica hates group conversations. People speak, fidget, tap their feet, breathe... every noise amalgamates into a wall of sound, and within this cacophony she is expected to formulate sentences that pass for communication. Thanks to her test scores, nobody assigns a reason to her speechlessness other than sullen rudeness. Group activities are a crushing reminder of how awful she is. Vivica turns from the light. Dodger rises and kicks her cupboard door closed. "Whatever, lesbian!"

Vivica listens to her obnoxious brother's stomp into the meeting hall. "Lady Vivica has declined to grace us with her presence this afternoon!"

Sorsha sits at the head of the table. Vivica hears her older sister's reply from her cramped hiding place.

"Leave her alone, Dodger."

Vivica hears paper crinkling.

Dodger kicks a dirty trainer against the table. "She's gonna be a great help if the monsters return, isn't she?"

Paper slides against Doc's rough fingers. "I'll read it again, but my opinion has not changed." The elderly scientist folds the letter as Vivica reaches her visual awareness toward the boardroom, observing her assembled family unit.

"Neither has mine." Nell cleans a smear off a butter knife with her napkin.

A silent presence of projected energy near the ceiling, Vivica regards her mansion family with numb detachment. Brave Sorsha holding court... wise old Doc to her left, wholesome Nell to her right... even studious Lisa has left her attic desk to join the proceedings. Dodger, Jessie and Sunny flick a rolled-up scrap of paper across the table, giggling. For an instant, Sorsha's brown eyes look upwards and Vivica flinches as the collective's fierce leader peers into her soul. Then Sorsha looks away and Vivica's mind is consumed by static fog.

Prophetic vision is useless with no linear grasp of time, you merely hallucinate a shimmering maelstrom of hopeless scenarios. You may as well take drugs. In every future, the alien monsters return. Vivica sees herself as a sacrificial offering, bound and bleeding before their slavering fangs. Their distant hellscape haunts her nightmares. Peblash Reck, the shadow beyond the complicated rainbow. In tortured dreams, the Reckish whisper... *Kill yourself. Kill everyone, then kill yourself. Kill...* She cannot ignore them forever. She might mutate beyond human form, become demonic.

Doc turns to whisper in Sorsha's ear. Despite the space between them, Vivica feels the weight of his words, and their impact sends her reeling.

"Next time, let them take her."

Nigel IV

(094)

"If you redesign somebody's physical body and reprogram their memories, are they still the same person?" Serena stands before a bioprinter where Nigel Paul Charlesworth has undergone adjustments to make him taller and stronger.

Her trusty R314 stands beside her. "Does a conscious entity contain more than physical form, lived experiences and learned behaviour...? Are you asking if I believe in souls?"

"I suppose that is a strange question to ask a robot."

"There is no empirical evidence that souls exist."

"There is no empirical evidence that *you* exist."

R314's indigo eyes flicker, but he emits no response.

Serena checks the matter cartridges to make sure they contain enough synthetic textile, then prints Nigel's skullball player's uniform. Within seconds he wears black shorts and an emerald T-shirt with "Summerton Sharks" on the front and "N-Dog" on the back.

"He has been offline for twenty-eight days, sufficient time for Summerton memories to fade. His new past should take. He was an award-winning defender for his local team before the war. This hopeful refugee believes his sporting skills will bring fame and fortune in humanity's last surviving city."

The bioprinter adds more rubber to the sole of Nigel's sneakers. His eyes remain closed. R314 remarks, "A massive improvement on renting his grandmother's spare room and working in a convenience store."

"Yes," agrees Serena. "And if his scripted personality is still contaminated by our collective's residual anger, he can work off his rage in the arena."

"Only if we contain the Reckish outbreak," R314 warns.

Serena nods. "The outbreak does complicate matters. How long until the elevator is repaired?"

"My crew should have the customs office functional within the hour," R314 replies. "Unless there is a repeat of what happened ten days ago."

"Ah yes, Bod Weye carried underground, still alive…" Serena recalls. "Any sign of him?"

"He disappeared, along with the demon carrying him."

"Well, keep me updated. I am still awaiting response from Chroma regarding effective weaponry against the new generation of Reckish. Meanwhile, I will continue to analyse the tissue samples."

Nigel's outfit is completed with designer sneakers. Serena presses a green button, opening the transparent front panel, then types into the neighbouring computer. Eyes still closed, the upgraded man sleepwalks from the printer, across the library and out into the rail yard.

(095)
Nigel Paul Charlesworth wakes to the sound of gunfire. Peering out the train window to his right, he spies smoke trails across the sky. He holds his face to the shiny surface and observes the receding landscape where a small aircraft is hurtling through the sky toward Summerton's southern edge, its engine on fire.

"The overground is a barren war zone," he mutters, glad to be fleeing the violence.

"Forget about it. A new future awaits!" says a breezy, feminine voice beside him.

Nigel turns from the glass to greet his new travelling companion. His recollection of boarding the train is hazy. All memories since leaving his hometown to escape the approaching soldiers flicker like glimpses through thick fog. *Probably trauma-triggered amnesia. War is brutal. Since curfew started, the skullball field has been closed for months.*

"Hey, not sure if I introduced myself, I'm N-Dog." He holds out a hand to the pretty lady.

As she turns, her suit jacket opens slightly to reveal the cleavage above her low-cut, crimson blouse. "I know who you are," she replies, ignoring his hand. In the distance an almighty crash marks the falling aircraft hitting the ground.

Nigel drops his hand and attempts recollection. *Must have introduced myself before... Don't recall her name... Have I been drinking? No, hey! She recognises me from skullball matches!*

He grins. "Always nice to meet a fan."

The woman rolls her eyes and turns back to her travel screen. Nigel blinks as his own screen - embedded into the chair before him - flickers into life. A voluptuous babe in a green dress stands in a bustling shopping mall. "Welcome to your new life!" She graces the camera with a flirtatious smile, pleased to have found a residence that gives her life meaning. "Welcome to a city with no war, no famine, and ample opportunities for a fabulous career!"

Nigel chuckles, casting a sideways glance at his neighbour's cleavage. "Fabulous career! That'll be me once I reach their famous arena!"

"Yup." His new travel buddy yawns. "Where we're going, everything is *wonderful*!"

Bonus gunfire echoes from the retreating deadlands. "No burning aircraft falling from the sky, anyway!" declares Nigel. His screen now displays a map of his future subterranean home, with hexagonal city blocks forming a six-sided honeycomb. The orientation video lists the city's top features: penthouse apartments, shopping malls, synthetic parks, and Nigel's favourite, the recently refurbished skullball arena. He grins. "That's where I'll make my fortune!"

Around the carriage, passengers whisper eager plans for their imminent new life. Ahead of him, in the upcoming outpost, the SilverMen are hurriedly patching up the elevator for the next batch of immigrants. Behind him, Summerton reels under demonic invasion.

Perspective Four
Kalakai

4.01

(052)
"Your blouse pockets need more custard!" insisted a saccharine voice emanating from Axis' com screen.

Still in his bunk! He should be training those hapless new frags. What the reck is he watching? Kalakai stood furious in the dormitory doorway. "What's this?"

"Erm... Nothing boss!" Axis moved his thumb to close the video. Kalakai was faster, telekinetically snatching the device from his grasp, flying it toward her outstretched hand.

"These pockets hold a whole carton!" the sickly voice continued, as the com device snapped into Kalakai's palm as though pulled by invisible magnets.

"What the reck?" Kalakai responded to the bizarre sight of two custard drenched, Chromanesque models. "Bitches complain about insufficient pockets... Then they fill pockets with yellow pudding? No wonder we are losing teleskill supremacy in multiple sectors. Kaldamn!"

"This is porn from 314-Thera. Thought I'd research the... psychology of... y'know... the local culture," Axis explained, his right hand still under the covers.

"Axis! Are you...?"

The private raised both hands in surrender. "It's research, boss! I wasn't-"

"Just... don't." Kalakai closed the video and threw her subordinate's screen back at him. "Get yourself to the training room. Break's over! Those fragile new frags aren't gonna teach themselves."

"Yes boss!" Axis replied as Kalakai stomped from the dormitory.

The irritated captain marched along blue and silver corridors toward her ship's starboard port as nervous new recruits hurried past on their way to training. "Hey Laz," Kalakai buzzed her Lieutenant through her com screen. "I'm taking Shuttle Two. Not bringing the whole Kalship into headfuck mindscape atmosphere for a simple frag collection. Can you send the next mindscaper's file to read as I land? I can't keep track of recruits with all these CRIBs activating."

"Sure thing, boss!" her helpful lieutenant replied.

Kalakai reached Shuttle Two's chrome hatch and typed the six-digit security code. The thick metal sheet slid up to reveal a four-Chroman seating area, with two drivers' chairs and two for passengers. Kalakai hopped into the first driving seat, entered the flight sequence, and re-closed the hatch. With a sound that would remind her of thunder if she were a melodramatic bint who compared everything to weather, Shuttle Two detached from Kalship VI and began its descent toward the target mindscape. Kalakai tapped a secondary screen on the dashboard to view the mindscaper's official case notes.

"Another damn Oprish..." Kalakai grimaced as she scanned the content. Serena Solas was an impoverished researcher who had mostly completed feline missions, hence her request for Chroman army training being designated low priority. Kalakai kept reading. "Another supposedly self-aware multi-trip researcher who believes they're special. What fun!"

The shuttle's main info screen displayed a map of the medium-sized mindscape's upcoming surface. *First generation Reckish activity everywhere... A relatively safe area within a perimeter fence... A dormant, buried CRIB, due for re-activation in... Kaldamn! This place is recked!* Most frags, including the original were gathered in a hexagonal castle beside a mountain range. Kalakai programmed a course toward the ridiculous building then re-read the collective's case notes.

Mindscape #31451380139198202261405

[006] Serena Solas took the mindscaper aptitude tests in the village of [redacted] on Opree Shengra in GE year 1880, day 63. Her promising scores led to a researcher recruitment offer from Godshi Enpire. Due to her extreme shyness, she was assigned a mission with a non-verbal, non-Chromanesque vessel, from which she returned six years later with a feline fragment, known as Snuffle.

Serena and Snuffle undertook twelve further research missions, always opting for a non-dominant species with limited communication skills. Serena preferred to let her Snuffle fragment socially front while she remained on her mindscape, collating information about the dominant species.

[008] On GE year 2255, day 213, impressed with her research and emerging teleskills, the Godish council selected her for a privileged life in a Chromanesque vessel. She was to inhabit the necessary social and financial position to be a great scholar. This was thwarted by the Reckish attack on Godshi Enpire that precipitated the GWAKZ war. Serena and her feline companion were among the upcoming researchers who were rushed through random portal doors for safety from the Reckish onslaught. Serena's portal jump created the above-named mindscape in the outer Mindfields, connected to a Chromanesque vessel named Claire Katherine on the planet 314-Thera.

[009] On GE year 2260, day 163, rebuilt Godshi Enpire communication networks received the following message from Serena Solas:

Greetings Chroma! Due to either local environmental trauma or a portal door glitch, the amnesia regarding my previous Chroman existence has faded, and I find myself in the bizarre position of being a self-aware mindscape researcher. I hope you are receiving this and Godshi Enpire has recovered from Reckish invasion. I fear this telepathic connection is temporary, but I will take this opportunity to provide an early mission report.

Shortly after gaining self-awareness, my psyche fragmented for the second time, creating a Chromanesque, infant entity I have named Baby Zero. This fragment was initially the social front for my connected life on 314-Thera, but soon became incurably brain damaged, retaining an age of approximately nine months old.

[011] Three years into my mission, I underwent a third fragmentation. I tried to control the process by creating a happy, smiling child called Clairey who could serve as an acceptable social front. However, I also inadvertently created a disturbed twin fragment, named Katie.

Now four years since its creation, our mindscape has grown exponentially, perhaps due to chemical interference in our connected vessel's environment. I have developed teleportation ability sufficient to explore approximately one eighth of the surface. The landscape is a combination of mountains and woodland. I have also regained my previous telekinetic powers and built a small library in which to gather my research.

I rarely front in my connected 314-Thera life, preferring to delegate this task to my Clairey and Katie alters. I monitor their experiences on a small audio-visual display unit in my library. I call our parallel life the Reality Show, due to sentient beings on 314-Thera insisting that their planet inhabits the one true reality, and anything I experience on the mindscape is a delusion.

My feline alter, Snuffle, also developed teleportation ability and now disappears for long periods. I keep Baby Zero in a box under my library desk.

Yesterday a large Chamber of Reckish Intergalactic Botherment materialized in a nearby valley. I used my developing telekinetic powers to bury this cursed structure by collapsing mountains over it, creating an area of flattened wasteland to the east of my present home.

Communication ends.

[012] In GE year 2263 the GWAKZ recruitment drive reached Mindfield sector 314. GWAKZ leaders were still teleporting to mindscapes to personally greet researchers before induction. This was Kalanooka's report from their visit to Serena:

GE day 272, time 15:92. Giyakai scanned the mindscape's surface before teleportation and detected Reckish activity emerging from a buried CRIB. She estimated we had approximately four hours before the demons reached Serena and her fragmented alters. Serena was studying in a small, wooden hut in a forest. We teleported into the space between three large bookshelves and her desk. We found her watching life through the eyes of her connected vessel on an analogue audio-visual device, taking handwritten notes. Her parallel life was being directly experienced by a subordinate alter, named Clairey, who was simultaneously playing in a nearby clearing.

We learned from previous correspondence that Serena was a self-aware researcher, so we skipped our usual recap of Chroman history and cut straight to our recruitment drive.

Serena declined our invitation, citing a duty to protect her vulnerable frags from the upcoming Reckish attack. She suggested we recruit Clairey instead, due to the infant's strong lifelight connection.

Serena's teleskills would have been an asset to our army, but we cannot unwillingly remove a researcher from a living mindscape.

We teleported to the clearing.

I told Clairey, "We've come to take you away. Soon, it will not be safe for you here."

Clairey asked me, "Why won't it be safe?"

I told her, "It's better you don't know why." We then teleported the infant frag to the nearest CHAOS warship.

Report ends.

[013] Clairey joined the pseudo-ironically named Chroman Home Army Obliteration Squad, where child frags were fed a simplified tale of Chroma, or "the Rainbow Galaxy", and taught how to create lifelight forcefields and shoot Reckish-attacking lifelight rays.

This medical report was written three months into her training:

Clairey collapsed on deck at 14:15, convulsing in a seizure. She was brought to medical, where her seizure ended abruptly. Upon regaining consciousness, she told the doctor, "Someone broke from me. She's lost in the haunted forest." Clairey later had no memory of this.

We have witnessed these fits before in kids whose systems are experiencing further fragmentation on their mindscapes. Clairey has shown no other signs of ill health and is making considerable progress with lifelight manipulation.

Report ends.

[015] Following the resolution of the GWAKZ war in GE year 2267, all child recruits returned to their mindscapes. The Beshper passenger ship from which Clairey's shuttle departed wrote this report:

We received a distress call from Clairey during her landing. "I see monsters in the forest. My ship is breaking. I don't like it." We requested further details, but our messages were blocked, possibly by deadlight interference from surface Reckish activity. The route into her mindscape's atmosphere was now obstructed by deadlight storms. We fear this mindscape may be lost to the Reckish. This issue has been reported to the new research base on Godshi Enpire.

Report ends.

The next several pages contained details of attempted communication with Clairey and Serena, all thwarted by deadlight interference.

On the final page, Kalakai learned how this unlikely mindscape made her recruitment list.

(030)
After twenty-five years with no communication, Godshi Enpire received this message from Serena Solas:

I have created technology to boost my telepathic ability, and hope this message reaches you uncorrupted. So much has happened. Two of my newest alters would make excellent Chroman Army material, and I hope you can collect them for recruitment. I have been monitoring Reckish activity and fear our buried CRIB will soon reactivate.

4.02

(054)

GE year 2298, day 59, thirteen-ninety-one, Kalakai's shuttle enters mindscape atmosphere and time acquires that wonderful, surreal quality which makes everything that ever happened seem like now. She hates it.

She heads straight for the hexagonal castle, where the occupants have thoughtfully placed a landing pad on the roof's northern segment. After landing she kills the engine, but her arrival has already drawn attention.

Two figures emerge through a sliding hatch in the flat rooftop, dressed in black and carrying machine guns.

Well, she wasn't lying about the two frags!

Kalakai steps from her shuttle, palms raised. With the barest hint of a smirk, she instructs her heavily armed hosts, "Take me to your leader."

The captain and her welcoming party disappear from the rooftop, then reappear in a hexagonal boardroom. Her mind reels with the dizzying jolt of an unrequested teleport.

When the white mist clears, Kalakai finds herself stood before a rag-tag bunch of frags assembled round a rectangular table. She recognizes Serena from her file's photo. The spooky woman to Serena's right could be her clone, except she is dressed like a fantasy villain, her face contorted with arrogant fury, and lousy with deadlight.

Kalakai tunes her mental output to a frequency she hopes only Serena can detect. *Your 'port skills are impressive. How's your 'pathy?*

Ms Villainy Deadlight slowly smiles by Serena's side. *Our telepathy is excellent. Thank you for asking.*

Serena glances at her corrupted doppelgänger then back to Kalakai. *Meet my most troublesome sister, Estella.*

Kalakai sighs.

A non-pathic alter with a spectacularly unoriginal name then introduces themself, but Kalakai brushes them aside. "*Please* tell me I'm taking these two." Eyes fixed on Serena, Kalakai inclines her head toward the two meet-n-greeters, who still hold their guns raised.

"I'm afraid Ash and Alicia are needed here," Serena replies. "Your new recruits are Cal and Leandra, who presently reside in the desert city east of the mountains." She blinks and the screen behind her shows an effeminate guy hunched over a laptop in a room full of weird artwork. He is accompanied by a horribly familiar woman in a peach nightdress.

"Is this a joke?" Kalakai folds her arms and glares at the screen, where Axis' favourite custard model is babbling some nonsense about breadcrumbs.

"I'm serious," Serena insists. "I have been feeding Cal useful information via our com network. Blessed with autistic hyper-memory, he has memorized every stellar coordinate between here and Chroma, and would make an excellent ROM."

"What about Ms Puddin' Pockets? What's she gonna do, surprise the Reckish demons with her bizarre use of sticky food substances?"

"She has potential to be a fighter pilot," replies Serena.

Kalakai shakes her head. "You request Chroman training after twenty-five years of radio silence, then pass us your rejects? We're no longer running a Kaldamn kindergarten! The days of making lifelight forcefields to save the 'Rainbow Galaxy' are over. This is Chroma, lady! We need fighters!"

Serena's gaze is unreadable. "Leandra is a fighter."

Estella casts a derisive glance at Kalakai's outfit. "Not all fighters stomp around in... *generic blue military uniforms* to prove a point."

Kalakai attempts to telekinetically throw a pen off the table at the upstart witch, but it snaps in two. Estella sneers. "You think you can use 'nesis against *me*? *Here*? That's cute."

Kalakai regards Estella with no emotion. "If you return to Chroma without evolving, I will destroy you." She then turns to address Serena. "Watch out for *that* one. Now, where can I find these Reject Frags?"

The unimpressed captain takes a moment to commit Serena's directions to memory, then storms up the winding staircase. Her hyper-sensitive ears detect a clueless underling demanding, "Was that blue alien bint real?" as she reaches the rooftop.

Kalakai laughs.

Alien bint... I fucking hate mindscapes!

Her next stop is Summerton, an unremarkable desert city constructed by telekinesis and robots.

4.03

(057)

"I recking HATE mindscapes!" yelled Kalakai after leaving mindscape atmosphere, seething as she re-entered Mindfield space. "Deluded researchers think they're some hyper-special main event." Her shuttle hurtled toward Kalship VI. "And it's so Kaldamn confusing how everything is *now*!"

Once the static cleared, her lieutenant's grim countenance appeared on the coms panel. "The Hespers say *all* time is now," Lazarus reminded her. "Mortals only perceive linear time to establish cause and effect. And prevent insanity."

Kalakai uttered a bitter laugh. "The stuck-up rulers of Hew Espireth talk reckshit. If that gibberish is true, why can't mindscapers experience linear time to preserve their sanity? Seriously. Those magic rocks are crazy! I was visiting their host's base in some dumbass hexagonal castle, flying over mountains to a weird desert city, meeting a potential ROM frag and his bimbo sister, taking your call, flying the hell off that rock... all at once! Stepping off my normal timeline into some eternal present... Who lives like that? With your future already happening, how can you have free will?"

"The Hespers say we-" Lazarus took a panicked glance at a neighbouring monitor. "Can we discuss philosophy later-"

"There is no later," Kalakai quipped. "Only the present."

"OK, then at present we have fourteen re-activated CRIBs in this sector alone, including the one underground in the mindscape you just departed. But firstly, a Level One mindscaper three sectors from here cannot hold much longer against Reckish invasion. They have his base surrounded."

"Prepare to fly the second I dock," Kalakai ordered.

"Engines already prepped, Captain," Lieutenant Lazarus replied, typing into a nearby control panel. "I assume the two frags weren't suitable?"

The two frags! Was there ever a sorrier pair of losers? And that insubordinate host! This always happens when they get creator skills and start thinking they're a Kaldamn deity.

Kalakai had wished for army backup, anything to intimidate that stubborn host. "Not from that backward dump!" she spat. "The primary frag chose to keep the two best fighters. Probably to serve as bodyguards against her impending personal apocalypse. Or to protect her from the demented deadlighter by her side... She sent me on some idiot's errand to collect two weaker frags from a desert city and save them from a failed psychological experiment. The male was a potential ROM, but the female... Recking hell! I'd just seen her on Axis' com screen, after having the misfortune to interrupt his *private nap*. You know he enjoys videos of Oprish-looking femmes getting humiliated? Well, the wench I just visited was his favourite 'model'. She was a deluded mess!"

"You're kidding!" Lazarus snorted as he forwarded information about the latest emergency missions for Kalakai's perusal. "I've sent you the latest coms... Axis showed me those weird Thera-314 vids yesterday, which model was it?"

"The peachy skinned broad with the long, black curly hair that gets messed up because she doesn't understand how food works." Kalakai scanned the new files. "I mean, you're supposed to *eat* food, right? Not wear it as clothing. Bitch is a Kaldamn creamy disaster."

(063)
Kalakai exited her shuttle as her ship sped towards the high-priority mindscape. She found her crew gathered on the main deck.

"No new frags, Captain?"

"Don't ask! Never speak of that ridiculous mindscape again." Kalakai took a deep breath of filtered air. "Now, listen up!" She glowered until her crew stopped fidgeting. "We are heading to rescue a mindscaper with influential family on Pyro Eshwelle. We cannot reck this up! For some of you, this is your first rescue mission. So, here's a brief recap on mindscapes and the CRIBs."

[002] "Mindscapes exist due to portal doors. These were initially invented by Godish researchers for the purpose of visiting other galaxies. Instead, they created new asteroids in the Chroman galaxy, called mindscapes. Reaching from Godshi Enpire across dimensions, the portal door connects with the lifelight energy of a faraway birth. The resulting mindscape rock is linked to a sentient being in another universe who happens to be born the exact moment the researcher steps through. After crossing through a portal doorway onto a new mindscape, the researcher becomes totally immersed in a parallel life. They forget Chroma, forget everything... Their appearance alters to resemble some distant creature. This is better than travel!

"The scientists of Godshi Enpire soon realised they could use mindscapes to research other lifeforms through immersive experience. They created countless more portal doors. Today, clusters of mindscapes known as 'the Mindfields' are found throughout the Chroman galaxy.

[005] "As for the CRIBs... After the Reckish stole Godish portal tech during the Second Fall, they attempted to create their own mindscapes, but failed due to lack of lifelight. Next, they tried constructing portal doors to access Chroman mindscapes. But all prospective invaders disintegrated on arrival because mindscapes have a lifelight core, like Hew Espireth. Reckish deadlight poses environmental incompatibility. They solved this by creating Chambers of Reckish Intergalactic Botherment. These structures house Reckish infants and contain enough neutral material to be teleported directly to a mindscape's surface without disintegration. Young Reckish grow inside the CRIB, acclimatising to mindscape atmosphere, while their sinister, invasive home corrupts the surrounding land.

"Now, some of you joined as technical or teleskills backup, but you've all trained for battle!" Kalakai continued. "We have a crucial mission to rescue a mindscaper from Reckish invasion. Who's with me?"

The assembled crew yelled an obedient affirmation.

Kalakai gave a curt nod and headed to the bridge.

"Are the mindscapes as weird as they say?" a nervous mechanic wondered.

"Weirder," replied Private Bexit, who was a general's son and a general nobhead.

Once Kalakai was in the captain's chair, Kalship VI hit Priad Speed and traversed three sectors in eighty-nine GE minutes, reaching Mindscape #32311959092164201989380 at sixteen-zero-seven. What happened between then and sixteen-eighty-six was pandemonium.

The Kalship VI emerged from mindscape atmosphere and crew members who had just made their first mindscape trip were stunned and shaken.

"What the reck just happened?"

"How does anyone live like that?"

"Kaldamn! We were flying down to land, fighting our way to the host's mansion, dragging Reckish demons off the guy while he just sat there with clouded eyes, killing all Reckish in the mansion, bombing the fuck out of that CRIB, barricading his massive home and adding decent security in case of remaining Reckish, then flying the hell out of there... all at recking once!"

"Yup!" Axis cracked a sarcastic smile. "Welcome to the mindscapes, kid!"

"That was awesome!" exclaimed Smokey, the formerly nervous mechanic. "I wanna be a mindscaper! I'm gonna apply to Godshi Enpire the minute we return to Chroma. Gonna convince those boffins to allocate me a shit-hot portal door."

"Ha!" Private Bexit laughed. "You think they'll give *you* some high-priority research assignment? You'll be a pointless dweeb on some backwater rock. If the Reckish drop a CRIB on your 'scape, *I'm* not saving you!"

"I won't need your help," Smokey bragged. "I'll frag. I'll become my own army! We'll be so deadly, you'll be visiting *us* for training."

"You don't frag on purpose, idiot!" Axis snapped. "It's an unconscious defensive response to trauma in the connected universe. A way of dividing shit memories between multiple points of awareness to reduce their impact. Frags are recking insane!"

"Hey, we have ears you know!" yelled Fizzy, the latest frag recruit.

"Whatever, frag!"

"Mindscaper fragmentation happens when the poor little researcher's crappy life is too much to survive." Bexit wiped a pretend tear from his eye. "If you fragged, Smokey, every frag would still be *you*. You'd transform from one dweeb into an *army* of dweebs."

4.04

(082)

"Listen up!" Thirty-three GE days later Kalakai stood before the remains of her beleaguered crew. Smokey's arm lay limp in a sling. Fizzy sat with his broken leg in white SetFix covered in unreadable scrawling. Everyone's face was a tired bruise. "Just one more Reckish outbreak to contain before we return to Chroma!"

The crew groaned.

"This was supposed to be a frag collection dispatch!"

"We're in no state to fight!"

"We're down to our last ROM since the sector 358 disaster, and you're the only 'netic strong enough to steer. How the reck do we return to Chroma if anything happens to you or Shertrid? Do we just float through the Mindfields awaiting rescue like the universe's shonkiest space damsel?"

"QUIET!" Kalakai placed her hands on her hips and glared around the loading bay. "You heard of the chain of command? Well, it's hanging round my neck when I report to the recking Hesper elite. If I disregard an order just to deliver some bruised low-ranks and frags to the Kaldamn hospital, whatever punishment I get from Hesper, I will heap tenfold on you!"

Kalakai diverted her furious gaze to a nearby empty chair. The chair rose. Her subordinates flinched, unsure who she intended to smack with furniture.

The captain glanced at the nearest escape hatch. Its inner door opened. "This chair represents the next damned reck who argues with me." She glowered at her wary crew. "Here is the door." Kalakai flicked her hand and the chair flew over the anxious crowd, smashing against the escape hatch's outer door. The inner door slid closed. "This is where anyone who won't follow my orders is welcome to go." The outer door opened, and pieces of broken chair dispersed into the void.

The outer door closed as her crew sat silent.

"Any questions?" asked Kalakai.

Lieutenant Lazarus raised a hand. "What weapons we using? Not complaining, but most of our guns are recked."

Kalakai nodded. "There's still guns for you, Axis and Bexit. I'll stick with 'nesis. Alfie and Snowi, you're 'netic too. This mindscape's terrain is mud and boulders, plenty of heavy materials to raise a brutal storm. We got this! The rest of you, stay on board Kal six. Guard our last ROM, he can't fight for shit. Polyexa, you'll have temporary command. Stay in range of the host's MS base. We're down to our last four-Chroman shuttle, so you'll have to land us then wait for my signal. Smokey, I want all shields functional before we meet another Reckship. Now, suit up!"

The non-crippled members of Kalakai's crew leapt to obey orders. The less agile members shuffled in a vaguely order-obeying direction. The captain's five chosen fighting buddies donned battle gear, with the designated shooters grabbing the last functional guns. Shertrid, the crew's only remaining ROM, hid in a corner, hunched over his com device memorising navigational information. Polyexa took the pilot seat and lowered Kalship VI into Lessabeth Ross' rancid mindscape atmosphere.

4.05

(083)

The upcoming battleground looms across the Kalship's windshield. Polyexa reaches for the intercom. "Uh, Captain... Not complaining, but you might wanna see this."

Kalakai strides onto the flight deck. "There a problem?"

"Uh... This mindscaper we're rescuing... She lives *here*."

A twee cottage occupies a white picket fenced enclosure on scorched ground beneath charcoal clouds. An ivory flagstone path leads from the broken front gate to the missing front door. Kalakai notices two alarming things about this incongruous residence. Not only is it surrounded by Reckish demons, it is also on fire. Amber flames creep up frilly lace curtains over a smashed bay window. Three monsters crouch on the roof, their talons cracking fissures into the brittle, sloping tiles.

Kalakai asks, "When was her last distress signal?"

Polyexa checks the coms log. "Three hours ago. It says, 'The medication is not working. The demons are here.'"

Kalakai nods. "So, she could still be uncorrupted."

"Yeah but..." Polyexa gestures to the ruined residence. "There's demons on the roof. And it's on fire."

"I've seen mindscapers survive worse! Bring us down."

Polyexa mutters, "This is a suicide mission."

"I've survived twenty-six supposed suicide missions. Bring us down. That's an order!"

Polyexa takes a deep breath. Exhales. "Well, nobody lives forever!" She heads for a viable landing spot within suicidal marching distance of the burning demon cottage.

"Have fun guys!" Polyexa quips through the intercom as Kalakai and her select fighting team exit via the lowered ramp.

The six Chroman soldiers commence their reckless stomp toward the burning building while Kalship VI departs. Polyexa guides the ship beyond projectile range. Five wary crew members and their fearless leader approach the looming wreckage of a pleasant, middle-class residence.

The demons cease prowling the garden and leap over the picket fence in the team's direction.

Lazarus, Axis and Bexit shoot anti-Reckish bullets at the monsters, while Alfie and Snowi use their emerging teleskills to smash rocks on the beasts' scaly heads. Kalakai telekinetically reaches toward the biggest one, slams its head down with a downward swipe of her left hand, then uses her right to smash a jagged stone over its head. The first wave of Reckish defeated, the soldiers keep marching.

Three demons leap from rooftop to flowerbeds. One crushes a wishing well under a giant claw, another's tail destroys a swing set. While the gun-toting soldiers aim at the monster on the left, whose bloated body just crushed a colourful selection of garden gnomes, Alfie and Snowi use telekinesis against the monster on the right. Kalakai takes the middle bastard.

After a round of Chroman gunfire, the bullet-riddled demon collapses, gushing oily blood.

When rocks fail to break their demon's skull, Alfie mentally grabs its left side while Snowi takes its right. They swipe in opposite directions and rip the monster's skull apart, its brains spilling over jaunty paving slabs around the broken swing. Kalakai nods. She stops remotely slamming her demon's head into the ground, telekinetic-grabs one side of its skull with each hand, pulls her palms apart and rips the monster's head open.

The soldiers recommence their stomp toward the burning cottage, trying not to slip in bloody puddles. They reach the battered door expecting more opponents to emerge, but the dwelling is silent apart from crackling flames. Nothing moves behind sooty windows except a shadow on the first floor.

Kalakai marches through the smouldering doorway and her team nervously follow. A cackle echoes from above. The only conscious presence Kalakai can detect is in a first-floor bedroom. The stairs are only partially on fire. Kalakai turns to her anxious crew, huddled in the smoke-filled hallway. "You guys wait outside. This building is unstable."

As the soldiers pile out, Bexit mutters, "It's not the only thing that's unstable."

Kalakai uses teleskills to levitate off the ground, up the scorching stairway, toward the bedroom where strange laughter emanates.

"I'll make an example of her! Staff will see what happens when an insubordinate opposes me!" The shrill voice sounds like it belongs to a menopausal woman who has been denied another glass of wine and wishes to speak to the manager. Kalakai lowers herself onto the creaky landing, then steps into the bedroom of her nightmares.

Pastels. Everywhere. Floral wallpaper. Little dollies with lacy dresses. Ceramic cottages. The only parts of the room not hideous are the bits on fire. A woman in blue denim jeans and a beige polyester blouse sits on a rocking chair by the window overlooking a bloody wasteland.

Kalakai clears her throat to dislodge sooty catarrh. "Your demons are dead. We'll destroy their portal before we leave. You're safe. Well, apart from your house being on fire..."

The manic trollish nightmare woman turns a leering face toward her military guest. "I am a manager! I do what I want. After I destroy her, nobody will dare complain about the rota again!"

Kalakai's gut sinks. There is a teensy-weensy chance this rescue mission came too late. In the corner of her eye, she sees the room's only doorway catch fire. *Well, shit.* "I said, your demons are dead, lady. The Reckish uprising has been contained. How about you chill the reck out while my crew extinguish the fire?"

The suburban harpy raises a bejewelled, bony hand. Flame flickers in her palm as her eyes glow red.

Kalakai sighs. *Yup. Just ever so slightly too late...*

The harpy throws a fireball at Kalakai. The captain leaps sideways as a cabinet of tiny cottages bursts into flame behind her.

Another flame materialises in the crazy bitch's palm.

Kalakai telepathically throws a *Freeze!* command to slow the woman's movements, sprints past her rocking chair and jumps out the window. Gasping in fresh air, Kalakai tumbles within a cloud of shattered glass. She telekinetically slows her fall enough to not break her legs, then lands in the bloody garden beside her crew, who duck from shiny, falling shards.

"We're too late!" Kalakai states the painfully obvious. "She's fully Reckish! Her soul is dead. Run!"

Demented laughter echoing from the ruined dwelling behind them, the Chroman soldiers leap the picket fence just before it bursts into flames. Smoke fills their lungs as cackling rattles the broken windows. Kalakai yells into her com device, "Bring my ship down, now!"

She receives no response.

The six soldiers keep sprinting, reach a ridge of crumbling earth and scramble down, beyond range of the crazy cottage. Kalakai scans the open sky: blankets of smoke twirling through electric storm clouds, but no Kalship VI in sight. "Where's my recking ship?"

Her com device finally flickers a hazy image of Polyexa's green face, emerald blood dripping from a gash below her olive hairline. "Uh, Kal... We've had some trouble."

"What's happened to my ship?"

"Uh... We were spotted by a Reckship. It opened fire before Smokey could patch the shields. We found a canyon near the CRIB with partial cover and faced off in laser fight. Our new frag can really shoot! We brought the Reckship crashing down over the CRIB, destroying both cursed constructions. We're heading back your way now."

"Great work!" Kalakai cheers. "Pick us up and we'll head straight back to Chroma."

"There's uh... A problem though..."

"What Kaldamn problem?"

"Um..." Polyexa coughs. "We got a hull breach near Shertrid's favourite study nook. Smokey's patched it now. But... well... Shertrid is dead."

"Kaldamn!" Kalakai kicks a rock with her bloody boot. "Our last ROM is dead? Literally his only task this mission was to stay alive. He had one job!"

Her long-suffering battle crew groan.

Lazarus sits heavily on rocky earth and holds his head in his hands. "We are recked!"

Polyexa's weary image flickers on the captain's wrist. "There are paths avoiding the electromagnetic fields..."

"Take the long route home?" asks an incredulous Kalakai, grimly eyeing the approaching vessel. "With my ship in that state? Now *that's* a suicide mission!"

"No choice, Captain," Polyexa sighs. "The Chroman army's too overwhelmed with Reckish uprisings to launch a rescue mission. And even if Hesper signs off another frag collection, where will we get a ROM who already knows all nav co-ordinates between here and Chroma?"

4.06

(096)
Captain Kalakai is back on a mindscape she swore she would never return to. She is not happy. She crosses the desert city of Summerton from the north, and of course, gets shot down by an NPC guard with an anti-aircraft missile. Her shuttle is presently careening into the deadlands, and within seconds she will crash near Summerton's south-eastern edge.

Worst. Frag collection. Ever!

Kalakai presses a button on her wrist to activate her anti-impact bubble. Her shuttle's shield is fucked, but hopefully this last defence will ensure she survives the crash without being broken into burning pieces. *Everything happens at once on these damned rocks!* The shuttle smashes into craggy earth, but her bubble holds. Her only injury is a scratch on her left arm where a chunk of broken windshield bounces off.

"We have you surrounded, alien scum! Come out with your hands in the air! Your kidnapping days are over!"

Well, shit. Kalakai regards the NPC law enforcers surrounding her broken shuttle. *Why must over-imaginative mindscapers create fictional people? Weren't her crazy frags enough company? Why create police, give them functional guns and script them to shoot suspects on sight? Such realism is unnecessary. There should be a law against mindscapers creating anything that would assault a Chroman officer.*

Still wearing her invisible bubble, Kalakai steps through fire, over strips of torn metal onto desert dust. The sun shines blood orange through distant sandclouds as a snake with red, black and white stripes slithers into the shadow of the wreckage. *This could be Opree Shengra... If the orange sphere was governed by backward hicks instead of wise, ancient mystics.*

An intermittent breeze hits her skin as the temporary defence bubble wavers.

"I'm here for Cal and Leandra." Kalakai squints into the sun, wondering if she will die, as the gun-toting guards step closer.

Sheriff Grey startles at this second name. "Would that be the Leandra connected with every murder and disappearance in Summerton these past months?"

Kalakai peers at the sheriff, the apricot sun still dazzling. "You know any other Leandras?"

The sheriff opens his mouth to respond when a flying rock smacks the back of his head. He collapses unconscious, and his colleagues turn to aim at the empty space behind him, then back at Kalakai. "She's a witch! Shoot her!" They try to open fire, but their fingers freeze.

"She's not a witch!" an imperious voice booms from the shadowed hillside.

Kalakai turns toward the speaker, expecting to see what passes for management in this shonky backwater.

Leandra?

The formerly crippled bint stands tall on a rocky hillside, wearing a blue dress and surrounded by hovering rocks. She waves a skinny arm toward the frozen Summerton guards, dispatching the airborne stones like her personal army of flying monkeys, smacking each law enforcer's lab-grown skull. "But maybe *I* am!" She emits deranged laughter.

Kalakai shakes her head. "You were hobbling round that shitty apartment waiting for a prince! I never would've pegged you for proficiency in teleskills."

"Evidently." Leandra smiles as Alicia and Cal walk down the slope to join her.

"What happened?" Kalakai wonders. "Training montage with an edgy soundtrack?"

"Not exactly. I had some *interesting* dreams."

"How goes the custard modelling?"

Leandra laughs. "Why be viscous when I can be vicious?"

Alicia reaches Leandra's side, staring at the smouldering wreckage. "Shit! Your shuttle's fucked!"

"Yup," Kalakai agrees. "That's our last functional shuttle. I made poor choices on this dispatch. If I'm stuck here now, I might actually kill myself."

"No need for melodrama," says Cal. "I've memorised the repair manual for this model of Beshper shuttle. With my encyclopaedic knowledge of its construction and Leandra's telekinetic skills, we can easily fix this vessel to a flyable standard before nightfall."

Kalakai turns to Cal. "I might actually love you. It doesn't even need to be flyable, I can levitate it using 'nesis. It just needs to be intact, with adequate oxygen and... Not on fire."

Leandra raises her arms, scoops a mound of amber sand in a smooth telekinetic lift then dumps it on the wreckage. Once the fire stops smouldering, she mentally brushes off the sand, lifts a piece of bent metal, straightens it out and asks, "Where does this go?"

(097)
Kalakai and Alicia stand guard while Cal and Leandra fix the shuttle. As the sun sinks toward restless horizon, Kalakai becomes overwhelmed by hopelessness. The barely functional Kalship VI is a glinting speck in the darkening sky, like a sad insect clinging to a cracked windscreen. A series of judgement errors have brought death to all her ROMs and the necessity of returning to this backwater mindscape where her survival is dependent on lunatic frags. She starts turning her gun toward her head, drawn toward the ultimate escape of suicide.

"I wish I was dead," Leandra moans, pausing in the act of mentally manoeuvring a piece of metal.

Kalakai takes a moment to recognise this as external dialogue rather than inner monologue. "Shit!" She ceases gazing forlornly at her weapon and wields it before her, scanning the shadows for glimpses of the enemy. "There's Reckish here!"

"Those blasted demons?" Alicia draws a second gun. "We saw two earlier! Ran off with enemy clones in their scaly grasp, just before your shuttle came down."

"The damn things are madness and despondency incarnate!" Kalakai growls. "You got the latest anti-Reckish bullets in those things?"

"Nah, this shit just bounces off the latest gen, only slows the fuckers down. The boss is working on new weaponry... Why? What *you* shooting?"

Kalakai pulls out a second gun. "Freeze bullets."

Alicia holsters her guns and catches Kalakai's thrown weapon. "What the-" She drops it, clutching a sore hand and cursing.

"Sorry, you need special gloves." Kalakai removes her left glove with her teeth and throws it to Alicia.

Alicia forces the glove onto her right hand and picks Kalakai's second gun from the sand. "This fucker's cold!"

"Yep. The bullets release a cooling liquid to extinguish that blasted red light in their eyes. Cracking their skulls apart also works. I have no idea why you brought a flamethrower."

Alicia shrugs. "I like fire."

Cal and Leandra stand staring sadly into space.

"Get back to work, you two!" Kalakai commands.

Leandra's shoulders are slumped, the broken shuttle pieces she was magically lifting now discarded on the sand. "Why is everything so awful?"

"Reckish influence," Kalakai explains. "They latch onto a mindscape, corrupt the host. Or hosts, in fragmented systems. They erase positive memories, shift your focus to the worst aspects of your existence, make you suicidal and or downright evil. Some hosts are more sensitive to their influence than others. The worst bit is, they don't kill you... they make you kill yourself."

"I'm not suicidal," Alicia remarks. "Am I immune to their influence? Also... the Reckish kill *some* people. I've seen it!" As if to prove her point, Deputy Green's unconscious body is dragged behind a bloody boulder in a blur of shadow and malice. "See! That was almost definitely a killing."

Kalakai steps forward with her gun raised. "The Reckish are dragging your enemy clones back to their CRIB because they want you to follow. Their end game is to turn you against each other, corrupt you, drag you to hell... If you're swaggering round with a flamethrower, if you've ever attacked your frag-siblings or sabotaged your parallel life with impulsive, destructive behaviour, I doubt you're as immune to Reckish influence as you think."

Alicia sighs. "Well, that's me owned."

A scaly head rises from behind the bloody boulder, scarlet eyes glowing in the twilight. A catlike reptilian body begins creeping over the rock. Alicia shoots the left eye while Kalakai shoots the right. The demon screams. A metal bar careens through the air and smashes its head open.

"That's teamwork!" Alicia cheers, punching the air.

"Was that part of my shuttle?" Kalakai demands.

Leandra shrugs. "You said something about cracking open the skull."

"Also, that was part of the steering mechanism, which is broken beyond repair," Cal adds. "But you said you can steer using 'nesis."

Cal and Leandra return to fixing the shuttle as the sun becomes a scarlet sliver.

(098)
Leandra pushes the final piece of metal into place.

"The shuttle is ready!"

"Good!" Kalakai says. "I've wasted too much time with petty drama on backwater rocks. With all these recent CRIB activations, an intergalactic war must be imminent. No more time for frivolous side plots!"

"Can I bring this gun back to the castle?" Alicia asks. "Serena should see this."

"Sorry kid, my crew's down to our last three. But you could remove a bullet outta that dead demon." Kalakai catches the weapon from Alicia then steps toward her patched-up shuttle.

Cal stares at the ruined monsters head. "What happens to those we leave behind if the Reckish take over?"

"Not gonna happen!" Alicia insists.

Kalakai returns her guns to her belt. "Everyone not real will die. Everyone real will suffer worse than death."

Cal gasps. "They'll be forced into jobs where they have to answer the telephone?"

"No," says Kalakai. "They'll endure lives wracked with twisted, violent misery before being dragged to Peblash Reck for an eternity of torment."

"Are there telephone headsets in Peblash Reck?"

"Yes, but they're made from barbed wire dipped in battery acid."

"Well, at least with a melted face, you'd have an excuse for not meeting your sales targets."

The captain glares at Cal. "You'll struggle to retain that mocking, detached view of your surroundings once the agony makes you start screaming."

A gunshot shatters the still desert night.

Kalakai looks down to see her stomach covered in purple blood. "What the-"

Sheriff Grey has regained consciousness and stands tall, raising his aim towards Kalakai's head. Alicia shoots him in the face before he can take the second shot. He collapses dead onto bloody sand as Kalakai falls between Alicia, Leandra and Cal, clutching her abdomen.

4.07

(099)

"It's over!" Kalakai clutches her stomach and bleeds violet onto poisoned earth.

"Fucking dickhead!" Alicia grabs the flamethrower from over her shoulder and sets the sheriff's corpse on fire.

Cal crouches by the fallen captain. "Could Geren Eshper's doctors save you? I've memorised all required coordinates for the journey to Chroma."

Kalakai represses a scream. "The crew need my 'nesis skills to steer Kalship VI home. It's sustained-" She whips her head round to view Leandra, who is mentally lifting a rock and bashing it into the head of every unconscious guard who is not on fire. "You! Custard model bint! Save your energy for the ride home, my crew's gonna need your help steering."

Done making human bonfire, Alicia holsters her flame thrower. "You sure you'll make it back? We could get you to the castle, see if the boss can-"

"I'm not some Kaldamn frag who's gonna regenerate on this soil! Or some machine-printed bio puppet. Does your librarian leader even have medical training? No, I need a Geren Eshper hospital. Get me to the Kalship so our medic can patch a temporary fix, then get me straight to Chroma."

Cal, Leandra and Alicia lift Kalakai's bleeding body into the shuttle's back seat.

"I hope you guys reach Chroma," Alicia says. "I gotta stay. I'm needed here."

"Will we see you again?" wonders Leandra.

Alicia smiles. "Probably. When this rock falls to nothing."

Cal and Leandra hug their fiery sister goodbye as Kalakai yells from the shuttle, "Anytime now, guys!"

Leandra rolls her eyes and climbs into the main driver's seat. Cal sits beside her and reels off memorised information from the shuttle's instruction manual while Kalakai silently screams in the back. Under Leandra's mental guidance, the aircraft rises. Behind them, Alicia salutes the shuttle as it disappears into the night sky.

Cal flinches at Leandra's eyes, wide with manic glory. He gets a hunch their combined madness has reached a tipping point. They are finally leaving sanity behind. "You stopped taking your medication, didn't you?"

Leandra laughs, power flowing between her brain and the flying machine. "The whole time I was medicated, I perceived reality through a dusty, cracked window." The ship responds to her words by spraying cleaning fluid across its windscreen. Leandra cackles. "The hazy, obscured vision became my normal." The engines roar louder as arid ground recedes.

"It was dangerous outside, too many overwhelming tasks and vicious people, so I hid in my cocoon of soft fabrics and numbing prescriptions. Coming off the tablets would always resuscitate toxic memories. But those nightmares fuel me now." She smiles. "The neglectful caregivers, abusive partners, supposed friends who stabbed me in the back at bitchy parties, trolls who mocked my fetish modelling when I had no other income and needed to fucking eat… they all resemble ants from here. I am destined for something greater, somewhere over the complicated rainbow. I am rising beyond their futile grasp."

"What about your depression?" asks Cal. "What if your problems follow you? What if the Chromans mock and ostracise you, creating the same social difficulties, just on a different coloured rock?"

"I don't care," insists Leandra. "If we hate Chroma, we keep moving. Our life will not remain stagnant. We won't return to what we were."

"But it was never a choice!" Cal argues. "You fought to survive before, but ended up collapsing into semi-coma. You've always had energetic phases. During this phase, you're unmedicated and flying a Chroman shuttle. But what about your next relapse? We could be stranded miles from the familiar, at the mercy of strangers who owe us nothing."

Leandra laughs. "Most humans were strangers who owed us nothing. We survived among *them*, didn't we?"

"No," Cal replies. "You ended up crippled by physical disability caused by emotional trauma. I was subjected to verbal abuse during every disastrous attempt at employment. This was hardly survival."

"Well, we're not dead!" declares Leandra. "You have your wizard memory, with Mindfield coordinates at your disposal. I have telekinesis, guiding a half-broken shuttle to its mothership. We have bloody improved!"

4.08

(100)

Cal and Leandra exited mindscape atmosphere and guided the shuttle toward Kalship VI, which was waiting in nearby orbit. Kalakai clutched her wounded stomach, purple liquid dripping through her blue fingers. "Dock... starboard..." she groaned, a rivulet of blood exiting her grimacing mouth.

"Who's Doc Starboard?" Leandra asked, her skin glowing with wholesome lifelight, each movement of the shuttle mirrored by a slight tilt of her head.

"Urgh! This shuttle's docking bay is the other side! Kaldamn frags..." Kalakai's eyelids fell with the slowing of her pulse.

"This is a Beshper 592!" Cal exclaimed. "My com network contact shared these blueprints. Docking should be straightforward."

Leandra inclined her custard-free head an inch to the right, guiding the shuttle toward its bay.

"I am glad the dairy bint can fly, and her brother makes a useful navigator slash recking encyclopaedia," Kalakai muttered before losing consciousness.

The docking mechanisms clicked into place and Cal opened the door to Kalship VI. Leandra followed him on deck and found herself facing a line of Kalakai's crew. One wore an expression of shocked recognition, and another wielded the ship's last remaining gun.

Cal raised his palms. "We come in peace!"

"You've come in a stolen shuttle, covered in Chroman blood!" Lieutenant Lazarus snapped. "Where's our captain?"

Leandra regarded the state of her outfit, covered in a purple slime that was neither blackcurrant jam nor beetroot sauce. She then raised her wary glance to Bexit's gun as he aimed at Cal.

"We brought Kalakai to you!" Cal hurriedly explained. "She requires urgent medical attention."

Bexit's eyes bulged in his bald head as he released the safety. "I'm done with you psycho frags!"

Leandra cleared her throat. "One, 'psycho' is a sanist slur. Two, my brother does not lie, he his pathologically honest. Three..." Eyes fixed on the gun, she nodded. "Don't shoot yourself in the foot."

"Kaldamn!" Bexit swore as the gun barrel was telekinetically wrenched toward his feet.

Lazarus barged past the intruder siblings to the shuttle door. "Kalakai's been shot!" He grabbed the gun from Kalakai's left holster.

Leandra whirled, 'nesis pulled Kalakai's second gun to her right hand, grabbed Cal's arm with her left, then teleported them both three meters behind the enraged crew. Lazarus aimed over Alfie's shoulder. The crew spun round to see Leandra clutching Cal for support as her legs buckled.

Bexit raised his gun.

Cal took Leandra's weapon, swaying his aim between Bexit and Lazarus.

The Lieutenant screamed, "What the recking hell have you frags done??"

Vivica V

(101)

Vivica remains in her cupboard, coiled in the unlit, warm space like a sad serpent. She has cigarettes. She presses orange embers against her arm, the searing pain providing fleeting relief from the turmoil of existence, crystallising thought into single focus, burning away insecurity and failure in pure moments of destructive escapism. The scar tissue forms pink constellations against her skin's battered sky.

Light falls across the mess of her limb as the cupboard door flies open.

"Your lungs aren't in your wrist, dickhead!" Dodger snipes. His uncombed hair frames a mocking countenance as he peers into her wretched darkness.

"Leave me alone!" Vivica pleads, reaching with her ruined arm to pull the door back, wincing as skin stretches around an unhealed wound.

Dodger chuckles. "Sorsha wants you to answer the door." He pockets Vivica's silver lighter while she stares over his shoulder, out into the hallway, slack jawed and wide eyed.

Now the cigarette is removed from her skin, Vivica can hear the knocking. Since when did anybody pounding their fist unexpectedly against a wooden rectangle lead to anything but trouble? "Please leave me alone!" Vivica frets, reaching for the cupboard door.

With the reflexes of a wildcat on steroids, Dodger grabs the door and slams it back, making the cabinet shake and a plate smash onto the nearest white tile, breaking into sharp pieces. Vivica shrieks and curls tighter into a ball.

"Out!" Dodger tells his fragile sister.

Vivica clutches her matted hair, hearing strange voices from the porch. Visitors bring nothing but change and chaos. "I don't trust strangers! I want to be left alone!"

Dodger reaches to grab the terrified girl.

An assertive voice rings across the entrance hall, freezing the younger siblings. "Vivica, get out of that cupboard and answer the door, now!" Sorsha commands from the stairway, still dressed in battle gear from her latest venture, monster's blood dripping from her blade.

Dodger grins.

Her frail body shaking like a sapling in an earthquake, Vivica steps from her shadowed nest, stands on legs half numb from crouching. The bangs repeat themselves. Vivica shuffles toward the mansion's entrance as though walking towards her execution.

Cal and Leandra stand before the heavy oak door of a stately home. Their skin has a faint blue sheen as though caught by faraway sapphire lights. The com device on Leandra's wrist beeps. "Hey, it's Serena!" The siblings forget the closed doorway and peer instead at a tired, pixelated face so far away.

"Kalakai said you passed your evaluation. Well done!" Serena stands in her library slash laboratory slash master control room in a hexagonal castle on a distant mindscape. Silver R314 stands behind her, indigo eyes flashing.

Leandra grins. "Thanks! Yeah, that wounded bint was barking orders soon as the medic brought her round. While she *recuperated* on Geren Eshper, her crew dragged us to Godshi Enpire for endless questions and skills tests. I haven't 'ported since. And it's near impossible to use 'nesis in Chroma, more powerful twats keep blocking my brain... But the Chromans were impressed with Cal's memory and my aircraft control. Anyway, Kalakai's taking early retirement... and we got her old job! We're on a frag collection now."

"I'm surprised Cal didn't stay on Godshi Enpire as a researcher," remarks Serena, typing while checking a neighbouring screen.

Cal nods. "That's my long-term ambition. But during the psych evaluation, the doctors flagged our mental instability and depressive tendencies. They thought it best we stay together for at least one Godshi Enpire year while we adjust to no longer being mindscape bound."

Leandra laughs. "Yup! They reckon collecting troubled frags from other 'scapes will be good for us. After all, we understand their pain, everything they went through as a child, how *brave* they've been, blah blah... How's things back home anyway?"

"So much has happened since you left, it's a whole other story," Serena tells her. "But I'm glad yours reached an acceptable ending – or beginning – with this new employment. I'll keep Cal's site running. You can keep us updated with your intergalactic adventures."

The door handle turns.

"Door's opening!" Leandra beams. "Gotta go!"

Vivica opens the front door and gasps. Two pale blue figures in army uniform stand on the mansion steps: one with long hair and a walking stick, the other with short hair, sunglasses and a clipboard.

"Vivica," the azure-tinted woman greets her, smiling at the anxious girl.

As the unsmiling man peers over his clipboard, Vivica spies her quivering face reflected in his dark lenses. He asks, "Can you spare a moment to talk about our lord and saviour, Kalanocka?"

Vivica squints into painful daylight. She trembles and clings onto the door's iron handle, scared she might faint. "I don't understand."

The blue woman elbows her clipboard-wielding companion. "Don't scare our promising new recruit, Cal!" She hands Vivica a pair of blue-rimmed sunglasses. "Hi! I'm Private Leandra-"

"You're the least private person I know," her companion mutters into his clipboard.

"Shut up, Cal!" She elbows her colleague again. "And this delightful chap is Private Cal. We have been sent by Chroman authorities-"

"What are Chroman authorities?" Vivica is trying not to hyperventilate. All futures have lain behind fog for days, nothing but static haze...

"That'll be the electrical fields between here and Chroma blocking your prescience," Cal explains.

"What..." Vivica peers over the visitors' shoulders, sees the shuttle gleaming beyond the mansion grounds. Its sleek, metal surfaces shine incongruous against the ancient landscape. "I... I don't understand," she repeats. "Who is Kalanooka?"

The woman called Leandra places a gentle hand on Vivica's shoulder. "It's OK. The ancient ones can teach you Chroman history, and help you control that wonderful brain! Just come with us."

Vivica shivers in the hallway, scared to part from her beloved cupboard. "Must I leave now?"

"Yes. Hurry!" Leandra commands, winking at Vivica's confusion. "Before lizards eat your breadcrumbs."

ABOUT THE AUTHOR(S)

The Carlie Nooka Martece collective is an autistic, gender-fluid, dissociative system working as a visual artist, "model" and independently published writer. They reside in a violent but hilarious dreamworld. They are eternally grateful to everybody who has helped repel Reckish invaders with acts of kindness, particularly the people involved with beta reading this novel.

Martece wrote their first book, the semi-autobiographical Toxic Nursery, to provide insight into the often-misunderstood diagnosis of dissociative identity disorder. Three years later, Deragon Hex: The Vipdile Key was their first work of science fiction. Along with Chroma: Calanooka, these books form the Constructed Sanity Sequence, an ongoing series of autobiographies and novels that will increasingly entangle as the overall story progresses.

If you enjoy their work, please leave reviews online. This is a great way to help independent authors.

The collective is presently living Toxic Nursery's sequel, and continue to share their artistic creations with the world via their website at www.carliemartece.com

www.ingramcontent.com/pod-product-compliance
Lightning Source LLC
Chambersburg PA
CBHW020417010526
44118CB00010B/286